Praise for *YumUniverse*

I've admired Heather Crosby, founder of YumUniverse.com, since she started out years ago. Through her wildly popular website, she has truly changed the way hundreds of thousands of people transition into, and maintain, a plant-powerful lifestyle and now she brings her energy, dedication, and approachability to *YumUniverse,* the long-awaited book. Heather takes an often intimidating topic, and shows us that this lifestyle is absolutely possible. And her recipes are some of the most creative and delicious out there. The idea here isn't deprivation or drastic measures. It's about cumulative change — making incremental, deliberate health-boosting decisions until they stick, because true wellness is a life-long journey.

— Brendan Brazier
Former professional Ironman triathlete and author of the Thrive book series

Heather's enthusiasm for healthy living will inspire you to get busy in the kitchen! It's hard not to fall in love with her fresh, vibrant, and accessible plant-based recipes.

— Angela Liddon
Author of *New York Times* best seller, *The Oh She Glows Cookbook* and creator of OhSheGlows.com

If you are looking to improve your health, eating a plant-based diet is the best thing you can do. In *YumUniverse,* Heather shares recipes that will give you the very best of health without sacrificing any flavor or fun, proving just how delicious plants can be. More than a cookbook, this is also a guidebook — her helpful tips for the transition period make this an invaluable resource for anyone who is new to this way of eating. If you're interested in test-driving a plant-based diet, let Heather be your guide, and enjoy the journey!

— Neal Barnard, MD
Author, and founder of the Physicians Committee for Responsible Medicine

YumUniverse is a gorgeous cookbook filled with tasty, creative recipes that is perfect to kickstart a plant-powerful diet. It's also a comprehensive guidebook filled with the must-have tools and know-how to help transition and maintain an inspiring wellness adventure for a lifetime. Heather Crosby's spirited and encouraging approach to "simply eating more plant-powerful foods" leaves you feeling confident that you can make healthful changes, and keeps you excited about every step ahead.

— Julieanna Hever, MS, RD, CPT
Author of *The Complete Idiot's Guide to Plant-Based Nutrition* and host of Veria's wellness talk show, *What Would Julieanna Do?*

I believe you become a plant-based eater by having fun and experimenting with new recipes. Heather is a creative recipe goddess...her recipes provide that "yum factor" to inspire you to skip right into the kitchen and get cooking more whole, plant foods. Her step-by-step tips help you feel confident and supported. I appreciate that her approach is nonjudgmental and embraces all types of plant eaters — even those who eat some meat.

— Dawn Jackson Blatner, RD
Author of *The Flexitarian Diet*

 Heather Crosby is as glowing, beautiful, and health-inspired as the plantiful, UnDiet-friendly decadence she creates in the kitchen. Her creativity using fresh, real-food ingredients makes this way of living effortless. I love having her join me as a crusader for the great life — and this book makes the great life so easy and delicious!

— Meghan Telpner
Director of the Academy of Culinary Nutrition, author of *UnDiet*

 Heather Crosby's *YumUniverse* is a bold and beautiful tribute to plant-based, whole foods. These recipes will prove to you that there is no need to choose between food that will nourish your body, and food that will delight your taste buds. Heather is a passionate and knowledgeable guide, and her culinary talent is only rivaled by the intelligence and common sense that she brings to healthy living.

— Gena Hamshaw
CCN and author of *Choosing Raw*

Think plant-based, gluten-free food can't be exciting? Think again — with her inspired recipes, beautiful photography, and infectious enthusiasm for healthy living and cooking, Heather Crosby shows that fueling your body with whole, high-energy foods can be anything but boring.

— Matt Frazier
Creator of NoMeatAthlete.com and author of *No Meat Athlete: Run on Plants and Discover Your Fittest, Fastest, Happiest Self*

Finally, the comprehensive, plant-powerful book you've been waiting for! So much more than just a cookbook, *YumUniverse* provides all the tools you need to thrive, beginning with "why" you'll benefit from eating more plant-based foods, to "how" to implement baby steps toward change, and ending in a drool worthy collection of what to "eat." If you've ever thought about moving toward a plant-inspired diet — or even if you're already a long-term vegan — you'll find something to love in this enticing, engaging, and educational culinary universe. Heather's extensive knowledge and experience as an online plant-powerful pioneer and foodie is evident throughout this lavish, stunningly photographed book. *YumUniverse* goes beyond recipes to prove you can take control of your health and achieve vibrant, plant-inspired wellness — all without gluten or refined sugars!

— Ricki Heller, RHN, PhD
   Author of *Naturally Sweet & Gluten-Free* and *Living Candida-Free*

*Yum*Universe

—

Infinite possibilities *for a*
**gluten-free, plant-powerful,
whole-food** lifestyle.

—

Heather Crosby

Founder *of* YumUniverse.com

FOREWORD BY

Brendan Brazier

Former professional Ironman triathlete and author
of the Thrive book series

BenBella Books, Inc.
Dallas, Texas

BenBella Books, Inc.
10300 N. Central Expressway, Suite 530
Dallas, TX 75231
BenBellaBooks.com
Send feedback to feedback@benbellabooks.com

Printed in the United States of America
10 9 8 7 6 5 4 3 2

Library of Congress Cataloging-in-Publication Data is available for this title.
ISBN: 978-1-940363-24-0

Editing by Maria Hart
Copyediting by Stacia Seaman
Proofreading by Chris Gage and Amy Zarkos
Cover design by Heather Crosby
Interior design, text design and composition by Heather Crosby
Photographs, illustrations and styling by Heather Crosby unless otherwise indicated on page 302.
Index by Clive Pyne Book Indexing Services
Printed by Versa Press
YumUniverse.com

Distributed by Perseus Distribution
perseusdistribution.com

To place orders through Perseus Distribution:
Tel: 800.343.4499
Fax: 800.351.5073
email: order entry@perseusbooks.com

This book is for YU
(yes, you).

CONTENTS

Why 1

How 2

Let's Eat 3

Foreword

In high school, I made the decision to become a professional endurance athlete, and I knew early on that if I wanted to achieve my dream of becoming successful at the highest level, I would have to really focus on the fuel I was putting into my body. I tried many diets, but eventually found that I recovered from my workouts more quickly, was able to sustain energy longer, and built strength more efficiently when I consumed nutrient-rich, plant-based foods. Even as coaches and fellow athletes questioned my approach, I continued to experience superior performance results — that eventually even they couldn't deny. I had discovered the competitive advantage I was looking for. By adopting a plant-based diet, I was able to train harder, longer, and at a higher level, which inevitably separated me from my competition — both in high school and later as a professional Ironman triathlete and two-time winner of the Canadian 50K Ultramarathon championship.

The sustainability of my athletic achievements was, without a doubt, a direct result of the food I was eating, but it's important to know that these benefits go beyond athletic performance and well into everyday life. The standard American diet has resulted in a nation facing one of the gravest health crises in recorded history. Millions of people in this country sustain themselves daily with a diet consisting mostly of chemically enhanced, processed, nutrient-devoid "foods." The result is a population with soaring obesity rates across all age groups and steady increases in heart disease and cancer. Cases of depression, insomnia, chronic stress, and anxiety also continue to rise in this country. But there's a simple solution that, while rarely talked about as an option in mainstream culture, is finally gaining some well-deserved traction.

A diet rich in whole, plant-based foods has been shown to consistently, and almost immediately, help people lose excess weight, boost mood, decrease stress levels, improve sleep, and prevent and improve numerous physical and emotional conditions. And long-term studies about the effects of a plant-based diet have also revealed dramatic reductions in cases of heart disease and certain cancers.

From an environmental perspective, eating plants over meat makes sense, too. Simply put, producing plants requires less water, less land, and less fossil fuels than producing meat. Drastically fewer CO_2 emissions are released as well, and the ripple effect of production-related damage to the environment pales in comparison to that of the meat and processed-food industries — with many of

its members concerned about only one thing: profits. It's not exactly a secret anymore — a healthy diet makes for a healthy life, any way you look at it.

While the benefits of this lifestyle are clear, many people assume that it's too difficult to make the transition, which is why this book is so important. I've admired Heather Crosby, founder of YumUniverse.com, since she started out years ago. Through her wildly popular website, she has truly changed the way hundreds of thousands of people transition into, and maintain, a plant-powerful lifestyle, and now she brings her energy, dedication and approachability to *YumUniverse,* the long-awaited book. Heather has translated an award-winning design career into an inspired approach to a "wellness adventure." The artistry she puts into her recipes, and the support and comprehensive resources she develops for the plant-powered community, are on a level all their own.

YumUniverse.com has always remained one of my personal favorite online food resources — excellent design, packed with plant-based, whole food recipes and beautiful photography. What ultimately distinguishes *YumUniverse,* however, is how Heather takes an often intimidating topic and shows us that this lifestyle is absolutely possible. Her real-talk approach to transitioning helps us realize that we're more than capable of incorporating plant-based foods into our busy lives. And her recipes are some of the most creative and delicious out there. The idea here isn't deprivation or drastic measures. It's about cumulative change — making incremental, deliberate health-boosting decisions until they stick, because true wellness is a lifelong journey.

YumUniverse stands as a beacon in the plant-based diet movement. Heather passes no judgments, and instead invites folks of all kinds into her own inspiring experience so that they can better understand their potential. She has an incredible loyalty to her community, and it shines through in her ability to encourage people on any level that they can do this, one delicious step at a time.

You're about to start making a lasting impact on your quality of life and those you share the planet with. Congratulations, and enjoy the ride.

Brendan Brazier
Former professional Ironman triathlete and author of the Thrive book series

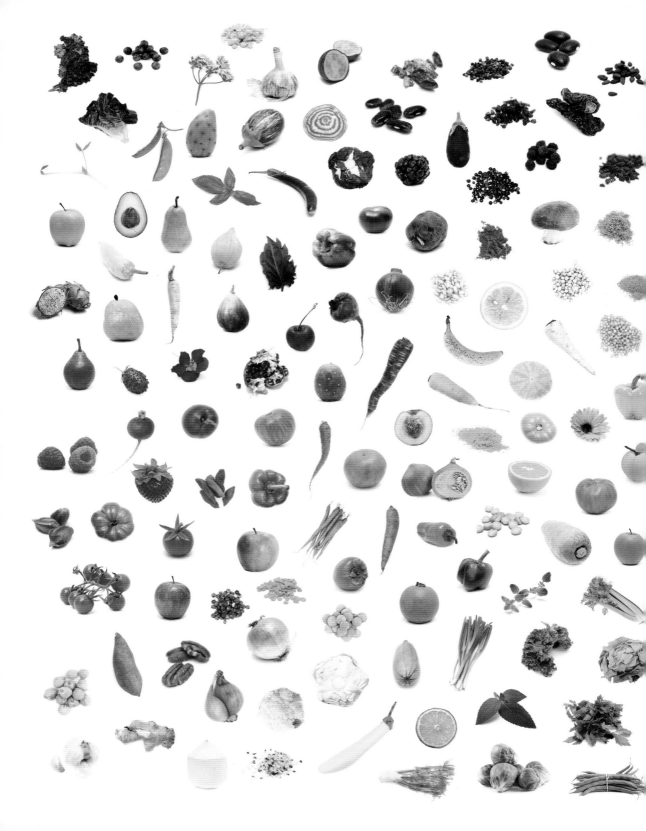

Plant-Powerful &
Plant-Inspired

It's all about bringing more freshness,
brightness, and flavor to the diet (and life)
by simply eating *more* plants.

THE POSSIBILITIES ARE INFINITE.

This is an exciting moment, because you're about to kick off a remarkable adventure, loaded with countless rewards and powerful lessons. I know, because I'm on this wellness journey, too.

It begins with a simple truth: Eating more plants is the best thing we can do to bring more "life" to our life.

Whether you're here to turn around your health; to prevent disease; to improve animal welfare, the environment, your spirituality, and the health of your family; or if you're simply interested in adding more creative veggie dishes to your menu rotation, I applaud your curiosity. See, that desire to discover is the golden ticket to health and happiness.

It Takes Guts to Venture Outside of Societal Norms

Making a plant-powerful lifestyle change — in a world designed to support and enable the opposite—is a courageous thing to do. I personally know how exciting and overwhelming this transformation can be, so I'm officially giving you permission to start breaking some "rules." So, instead of always doing what the mainstream or a supposed "authority" tells you to do, maybe ask questions first. Turn down the opinions of others and turn up the volume on your instincts. Let them catalyze some good old-fashioned sleuthing. You're going to clear your own path and have fun doing it, and I've got your back if the going gets tough.

Thanks to the increasing awareness of the benefits of a plant-powerful diet, more and more folks like you are motivated to give it a try, but after a few weeks or months, many people fall off track. Old habits, emotional food associations, and straight-up food addictions can, and will, return with brute force. Then the guilt and resentment usually follow, right? This is not a sustainable approach to health, and instead, I'm going to provide you with the tools you need for a lifetime of success.

There's a Japanese term I like to think of when it comes to many aspects of life — *kaizen.* It means "change for the better" and consciously finessing, learning, and applying new ideas and experiences to shape a stronger, more successful daily process. Wellness is all about this type of continuous improvement. It's like a practice of any kind — chess, yoga, parkour, knitting — things we have to keep working at on a consistent basis. And when we do, we get better at that thing. We'll have moments of bliss and mastery, and we'll have moments where we feel frustrated or unmotivated, yet we can learn from all of these experiences if we just keep moving forward, with all lessons neatly filed under "Now I Know."

So be nice to yourself on this journey. Be proud of every step you take. Even if you fall off track, it means you're trying. Missteps and victories will walk hand in hand — it's how we learn, and it gives us a basis for comparison. Let's measure success by how quickly we get back on course toward our goals every time we derail. Mistakes are great teachers.

YumUniverse Is More Than a Cookbook

It's the ultimate guidebook — filled with the know-how and recipes you need to take the journey from S.A.D. (Standard American Diet) to plant-inspired. And it's written from my perspective as a former veggie-phobe who ate her first salad at 19 years old. Yep, that's no typo. I truly understand the challenge of shifting to a plant-powerful life. YumUniverse is the WHY, the HOW, and the EAT. The whole enchilada, so to speak.

I'm here to be honest with you, support you, and give you the tools to build a comprehensive foundation so you can discover how creative, comforting, and fun the journey can be. I've helped thousands of people transition and it all started because of my own experiences (including those mistakes).

My Journey to YumUniverse

I never touched vegetables as a child. Even as a baby, if it was puréed and green, I'd seal my mouth shut. I was that dinner-table-all-night-standoff kid who would create the illusion of eating my broccoli by stealthily spitting it into my opaque whole milk and then offer to do the dishes so no one was the wiser. I would hold my breath and swallow lumps of cooked spinach whole so I wouldn't have to chew it. Lima beans were my absolute nemesis. But bread, sugar, potatoes, chips, soda, candy, juice, tater tots, doughnuts, and pancakes? Now, *they* were my besties. And like any troublemaking friends, they got me into bad situations, like coming home from the dentist with at least one cavity per visit. It's really no surprise that I also suffered from chronic strep throat and colds most of my childhood. This ill health turned out to be a profound catalyst and the very thing that helped change the way I looked at food.

Creative expression is in my bones and luckily, I grew up on a farm surrounded by inspiration. I always had a project going on — building multilevel hayloft forts (with trapdoors to the hay chute for my little brother to find); designing clothes, jewelry, and shoes (thanks, Mom, for actually wearing the notebook paper and hay-bale twine flip-flops); baking, sculpting, building death-defying dirt-bike ramps — you name it.

When I went to college, like many other arty-farties with a few opinionated family members, I chose to major in graphic design because I was convinced that it was the "only way" to make a living while still being "artistic."

THE C&O CANAL TOWPATH

This path is a stone's throw from my West Virginia home and runs 185 miles along the Potomac River, from Washington D.C. to Cumberland, Maryland. While I enjoy walking, running, and biking along it as much as possible, some of the most fun I have is when I leave the trail, pave my own way, and explore.

After graduation, I moved to Chicago — 800 miles away — for a three-day-a-week freelance gig at a respected design firm. I've always been brave — I had a chance and I wasn't going to miss it, even if there was only one month's rent rolling around with the tumbleweeds in my bank account. That job kicked off my "dream" design career. But how did I feel when I first won an award for my work? Shockingly unfulfilled.

So I started to create side businesses to satisfy a corporate-free calling — painting, fashion design, jewelry design, fire performance (yes, even that). But wherever I found myself — whatever passion I was pursuing at the time — there it was: "This isn't *it,* Heather." For years, I dismissed that voice, instead focusing on continued distractions.

During this time, my body was also sending me a message. Shortly after I moved to Chicago, I would wake up in the middle of the night with intense stomach pain and nausea. One night I ended up on the floor involuntarily, passing out and hitting my ol' noggin on my way down. I was scared. After countless visits to my doctor asking her why this was happening to me, I finally scheduled a bunch of invasive, embarrassing tests to gain some insight.

Let the disappointments begin. After slipping on the gown, drinking the gallon jug full of gelatinous liquid, getting radiated, and experiencing other unpleasantries, I was told, "Sorry, we don't really see anything. You might have IBS." *Might?*

How could they not see anything after those tests? Why didn't they know why this was happening to me? IBS? I needed something more specific that I could act on. But with no answers, I kept living the same lifestyle because I didn't yet understand the powerful connection between food and health.

And then one summer, while jogging along a sidewalk in Chicago, I was run over by a fella trying to score a prize parking spot. My left foot was crushed when he hit the brakes — it was under the back tire —

and my knees were blackened from impact. All in all, it could have been a lot worse, but after six months with a persistent limp and no sign of healing, I somehow ended up in an acupuncture office for some help.

I heard something life-changing there that toppled the first domino in my happy, tumbling journey toward cleaning up my diet:

"We are not cows."

We. Are. Not. Cows. That's exactly what my acupuncturist, Diane, told me when I asked her why on earth she wanted me to stop consuming dairy in an effort to heal my squished foot. *How does one affect the other?* I remember my brain swirling with questions: "But what about calcium? How will I ever live without cheese…?" and the desperate "What on earth will I eat for breakfast?" Yet her simple statement stood secure against my status quo questions.

On the bus home, it started to sink in. *Why do humans consume dairy?* It's a liquid, designed by nature, to help a baby calf (not a human) grow from birth to 1,000 pounds in its first year of life. And we're the only animals on the planet to regularly drink the secretion of another animal — into adulthood, no less. A door had opened. A domino had fallen.

Despite a fear of needles, I became an acupuncture pincushion. (I say that lovingly.) And to my surprise, I experienced some powerful truths about how incredibly interconnected the body and spirit are, and how it takes both to heal. Within a few months, by following Diane's entire diet and acupuncture protocol, I was back to my old self. Dancing (in heels!). Running (not in heels). There's no greater motivation than results, so I was fully on board. It was quite a victory, but I still had a long way to go.

I had switched to almond milk, and quit beef and pork, and only ate chicken sometimes, but despite these changes, I continued having serious health issues. Once again, I found myself in a specialist's office looking desperately for answers. After some more humbling and uncomfortable tests, here were my "options": I could come into the office once a week — for an indeterminate amount of time — and be injected via catheter with synthetic goo (shiver), and I could also try taking a particular antidepressant (even though I wasn't suffering from depression) because the side effects of said medication were known to help a whopping 8 percent of folks in my position. I could do one, or the other, or both.

I looked right at the doc, took a long deep breath, said, "No thanks — to any of it," and walked out the door. It was officially time to take matters into my own hands. There had to be another way.

Dear Internet, I've never officially said this, but thank you. Thank you. Thank. You.

A Tireless Search for Answers Finally Led Me to Some Solid Ground

To start, it looked like I was suffering from something called acidosis, which was manifesting in all sorts of inflammation-based illnesses that could be reversed if I simply ate the right stuff. If I could reduce my intake of acid-forming foods, like animal products, gluten, sugar, and processed foodstuffs, and increase my intake of alkaline-forming goodness, like green vegetables, I could balance the pH in my cells, quiet the cry-for-help symptoms of inflammation, support my body's attempts to properly assimilate the nutrients in my food, and then heal.

I finally had an action plan, but how was I going to start eating vegetables? The closest I got to vegetables was maybe tomato sauce in a jar, and even then I'd locate all the tiny onions and shove them to the side of my plate.

Pea by pea. Step by step. That was, and still is, the name of the game. It can take years for us to end up at the poor health point where we need to make changes, and it can take just as long to kick the unhealthful habits that brought us there. But remember this — sometimes the wrong choices lead us to the right places, and progress is determined by how we choose to look at a particular situation.

> *We can come upon an obstacle and see it either as an opportunity or a dead end.*

We can let uncomfortable moments in life empower us or disempower us. I chose the former because *it is a choice.*

LOVE FOR COOKING

Even though veggies weren't my thing as a kid, give me a spoon and a bowl, and I could play for hours. Or gimme some mud, my sidekick cousin Greg, and a cinderblock wall, and it was mud pie time! Childhood games always seemed to revolve around "cooking" up something tasty.

ANIMAL FRIENDS

My mother has always loved animals and she got me started off early with a love for them, too.

I began by trying a couple of new recipes every week — mostly the desserts, but hey, it's a start. Eventually, I became courageous enough to try ingredients and techniques that I was completely unfamiliar with, like pitting dates, massaging kale, and blending hemp seeds.

I'd process vegetables into soups. Green smoothies were my hero too — I could blend everything I wasn't quite ready to chew and drink it on down. It was nature's medicine, after all. I started to notice, even after a week, that I was sleeping better. My belly wasn't swollen. I had more energy. My symptoms were less severe. My palate was even changing. I was more sensitive to sugar — desserts at restaurants were intensely sweet. I began to *want* broccoli and even onions. Unbelievable. My body was asking for more plants because plants were healing my body.

But the creative gal in me wasn't satisfied with the recipes available in cookbooks and online at the time. (This was years ago.) The stereotypes about plant-based food were sadly being perpetuated left and right. *Cardboard?* Check. *Tree bark?* Yep. *Carob chips to replace chocolate chips?* Oh, the humanity. There were more flavorless, boring, downright ugly recipes than there were the kinds of foods that made me excited to eat them. Then it clicked.

After a lot of practice in the kitchen, confidence developed.

And with that, I started to experiment with ingredients and flavors that reminded me of the rich, comforting foods that I grew up with. I started to curate a pretty solid library of original recipes that vegans and omnivores loved. I kept a binder loaded with these spilled, splattered, scribbled-on recipes in my kitchen for years, and then I went on a big summer road trip out West.

HOMEGROWN GOODIES
Dill, cherry tomato, and carro[t]
from my happy garden.

I Had Two Significant Realizations on This Trip

One: On the road for three weeks without a single stop at a gas station or fast-food restaurant for grub, I knew I finally had this plant-inspired lifestyle mastered. I had prepared, packed, and made it work without compromising my goals. I traveled a long way — and instead of feeling overwhelmed, I was energized and inspired imagining the miles ahead.

The second realization was more of an admission. It's the kind that you can either sit still, hear, and accept as the honest truth, or ignore its brightness with distractions and busyness. With the windows down, Neil Young on the stereo, and my hair blowing around into a proper road-trip nest, I had nowhere to escape. So I faced it in all its floodlight glory: I needed to share what I'd learned with others and letting go of my corporate design career would lead to a much richer life experience.

It was a milestone domino. And aren't dominoes beautiful when they zig and zag and knock each other down?

Like many life-changing realizations, though, it made me sad, scared, excited, and hopeful all at once. When I returned to Chicago, I popped my dusty clothes into the washer and sat down to create YumUniverse.com. Over 500 recipes later, an important tidbit mentioned in my very first "hello" post still rings true — a journey is always better shared with friends.

Helping folks find more health and happiness in their lives by sharing what I've learned along the way fills up my heart and speaks to my spirit in a way that designing a branding campaign never could.

I love whole food. Its power to heal. Its freshness, brightness, and flavor. Its connection to the earth. So, after 16 years of adventure in Chicago, I completely changed my life again. I moved from the big city to the country (where I wrote this book for you) — it was another important step as I walk along the path of a healthy lifestyle. I had been living plant-powerful for almost a decade, but removed from the garden, my journey felt incomplete. Now I live within that full circle of food, because I have nature, too.

Getting sick was an opportunity, and discovering the healing power of plants changed my life in more surprising ways than I can count. I've compiled information, recipes, experience, and tools to help you feel encouraged and less isolated on your journey. And this book is an extension of my dedication to YU (yes, you). Write in it. Spill tasty creations on it. Dog-ear your favorite pages for easy reference — make it your own version of my well-loved recipe binder. *YumUniverse* is your road map for this challenging, rewarding, extraordinary, delightful, and, no doubt, delicious journey we're on together.

So, hop in, pal. Let's go.

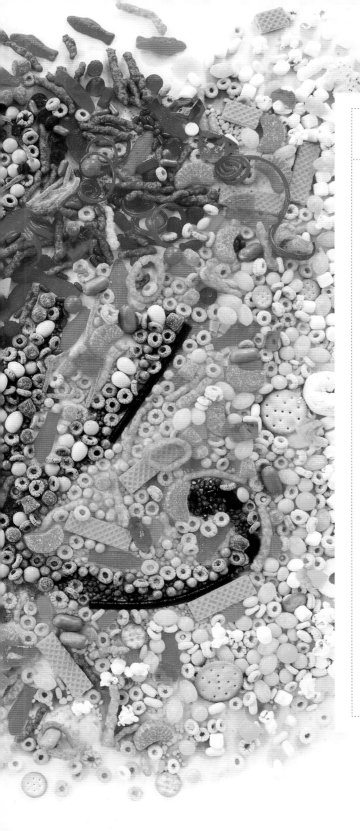

Why

I'm all about new perspectives. Questions. The truth. And here comes a bunch of it. So curl up in a comfy chair and let's talk honestly about food. And life. And YU.

There are many wonderful, world-wise reasons to consider a plant-inspired diet and super-smart rationales that go well beyond the basic and incredible health benefits. Books, scientific studies, and anecdotal evidence have raised awareness about the power of plants these days. Once we venture down one "reason" road, it often forks into three others, then four more: animal welfare, personal health, chemicals and GMOs in our food, environmental concerns — and that's just a few forks in our food. It can be overwhelming. Disorienting. Even a bit of a bummer.

My favorite reason of all to go plant-powerful? It's an opportunity to build a healthy and informed relationship with food. That's where the wellness and happiness we all want in this life begins. But whatever catalyst put this book in your hands, it's enough — because now you're here — and we can get started bringing more "life" to your life. Let's begin responsibly, with an understanding of the big picture.

Why Plant-Powerful?

I'm a foot-stomping fan of being accountable for the choices we make in our lives, but if you're confused about what it takes to be healthy, it's not entirely your fault. There are countless reasons why we're unclear about how to take good care of ourselves, and the noise and contradiction out there is borderline deafening.

All you have to do is turn on a television set, compare family photos from the 1940s to the 2010s, or just look around in a public place to see that we're a nation of overfed (yet undernourished) folks who tend to be more preoccupied with quick weight loss than long-term health gain.

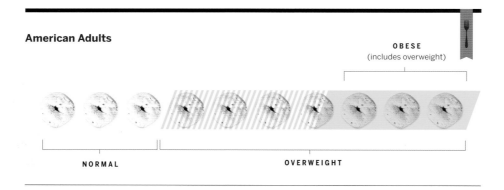

American Adults

OBESE
(includes overweight)

NORMAL   OVERWEIGHT

More than one-third of adults in the United States are obese. Not just overweight (that's almost 70 percent of the population), but obese. Now, I know that stats don't always have the emotional impact that we really need to understand the gravity of a situation, but think about that one for a minute. "One-third" means that when we find ourselves in line at the grocery store, odds are that one out of every three adults in the same store will end up suffering from some form of preventable obesity-related condition like heart disease, stroke, diabetes, and even certain types of cancer. And each diagnosis is much more than devastating words presented from a doctor to a patient. Every single one of these people has a family, friends, and loved ones who will have to suffer along with them (think about who these people would be for you). And since almost one out of every four children and adolescents aged 2 – 19 are also obese, the future health of Americans looks pretty grim. These obese kiddos are simply more likely to become obese adults.[1] Friends, we're experiencing an unprecedented health crisis and it affects us all.

American Adolescents

OBESE
(includes overweight)

NORMAL

OVERWEIGHT

Would you believe that the health risks associated with obesity now rival those from smoking?[2] It's true. What we're eating is killing us, and as with smoking, many of us are actually addicted — to convenience and to the chemicals and ingredients in processed foods. If Americans continue on this path, it's going to cost the United States about $344 billion in medical-related expenses by the year 2018.[3] (Hello, taxpayer!) And if we bring it on home, the average cost of a family healthcare policy has jumped from $6,000 a year in 2000 to $16,351 in 2013 — an almost $800-a-year increase![4,5] The saddest of sad ironies is, the United States spends more money per capita than any other country on healthcare, but we rank near the bottom of the list of the world's healthiest.[6,7]

How Did We Get Here?

Well, it's a lot like headphones. You wrap them up as neatly as possible, put them in your purse or backpack, and within a few minutes, they're a tangled mess. They're tentacles that have somehow knotted over a few times and grabbed onto your lip balm (opening it, no doubt), a pen, and car keys in the process. Well, the state of our food system is kinda similar: it's a mess of flawed systems, wrapping around each other and tangling into what seems like a point of no return.

See, billion-dollar industries depend on sickness and confusion to make a profit. And marketing efforts tap into our fears and hopes to sell products that make us sick. Hamster wheel, anyone? It's a time in history where profit and lobbying power win out over the health of the public almost every single time. And simply, we've become disconnected from ourselves and our instincts, and distracted in too many ways — gadgets, social media (with kids easily falling prey to these distractions). However, if we put this jumble through the strainer, turn down the relentless marketing noise, and take off our blinders, we'll begin to see a through-line: that despite the aggressive efforts of food engineers, agricultural biotechnology, and countless pharmaceutical developments, our health as a nation continues to rapidly decline. We don't need more diets, more pills, more gadgets, more processed foods, or even more time. What we need is to start being honest with ourselves. We need to find the courage to look behind the curtain and finally become accountable for our health. (And a green smoothie can help, too. ➡)

Where Do We Begin?

Let's look through a new lens as we venture forward. There's a canal towpath along the river by my West Virginia home, and it's a beautiful trail. I'm not the only one who knows how lovely it is; on any day, year-round, you'll see families, folks with their pups jogging, and loads of cyclists.

One morning while taking a run, I noticed a large tree had fallen down across the path up ahead and a bunch of colored dots were scattered all around it. The closer I got, the more the shapes of people came into view — a park ranger and a fit group of about 15 with bicycles. They were all buzzing around and I overheard the ranger say, "It's safe to continue on, we'll be cutting it apart in an hour or so." Now, there was walkable ground around the path; it just wasn't manicured into a proper, "official" trail. There were also low, wide spots in the tree (a mere step over) that the group could easily lift their bikes to overcome. But no one was moving. They all stood around perplexed, disappointed, waiting for someone to stand up and make a decision about what to do next. So I smiled, gently patted some shoulders, said, "Excuse me," and weaved my way through the stagnation of indecision, hopped over the tree, and kept on running. The other side of the trail was clear and open and quiet — fresh and ready to be explored. To my surprise, on my way back a good thirty minutes later, the tree and the group were still there. Waiting for someone else to tell them what to do. And because of it, they'd missed the new blankets of emerald and lime moss growing on the cliffs, Mr. and Mrs. Duck and their fuzzy babies toddling across the trail, the crackle and sparkle of the river flowing by, the blue jays, cardinals, woodpeckers, and life beyond the fallen tree.

That new lens I mention: when we're confronted with unpleasant decisions, news or circumstances, we can let them slow us down, even intimidate us, or we can use them to empower us. We have the choice to assume the role of victim or adventurer. Ready to be adventurers?

Start by turning obstacles into opportunities.

The "Training Wheels" Green Smoothie

2+ SERVINGS

GREAT FOR BEGINNERS

If you're afraid of greens or you're new to veggies in general, there's no better way to get beneficial phytonutrients into the bod than drinking them down in a snap. This creamy, naturally sweet smoothie is a great one to start with because the first sip will surprise, delight, and turn skeptics into believers.

INGREDIENTS:

1 – 2 packed cups of mixed salad greens

2 teaspoons almond butter

½ ripe banana

2 cups water

1 – 2 teaspoons raw, wild-harvested honey or maple syrup (optional)

1 tablespoon hemp seeds (optional)

psst! Try adding strawberries, a drop of vanilla extract, or swap kale for mixed greens.

STEPS:

Put everything in a blender and mix until smooth. Add 1 cup of ice cubes if you want it cold.

Fire up curiosity. If we make an effort to ask questions instead of doing what we're told, the unobvious becomes obvious, and we'll forge ahead in informed fashion (and everyone looks stunning in "informed fashion"). So let's connect some dots here: the Standard American Diet (S.A.D.) — was there ever a more accurate acronym than S.A.D.? — is composed of 25 percent animal products, 62 percent processed foods, and only 5 percent of calories from fruits and vegetables.[8]

Now, it's widely accepted that more fiber, less cholesterol, and less saturated fat prevents disease. But did you know that whole plant foods have no health-diminishing saturated fat or cholesterol, and tons of health-promoting fiber, antioxidants, and phytonutrients? While on the other hand, animal foods all contain saturated fat and cholesterol, and they possess zero disease-fighting fiber, antioxidants, or phytonutrients? Also, when you cruise the aisles at a traditional grocery store, almost three-quarters of the foods that line those shelves contain genetically modified ingredients, and many of them contain dyes and chemicals that are banned outright in other countries. Since only a teeny fraction of the S.A.D. comes from plant-based foods and the vast majority comes from animal-based and processed foods, it's pretty plain to see why we're overweight and sick — it's simple cause and effect.

Consumers are catching on, though. We're learning every day about the changes that need to be made, and WHY. It's the HOW that can be the biggest hurdle for us. We have rich family traditions, busy lives, emotional attachments to food, actual food addictions (that manufacturers insidiously exploit), and decades' worth of habits that could use some adjustment. As a former processed-foods junkie, I know it can be done. We need to find the courage to

Eating More Plant-Powerful Foods Can

Reduce excess body fat

Build more lean muscle

Strengthen the immune system

Improve digestion (regular #2s)

Clear skin and make it glow

Balance blood sugar

Clear eyes

Build healthy nails and shiny hair

Clear sinuses

Improve circulation

Provide more sustained energy

Build strong bones

Relieve joint pain

Lower bad cholesterol and raise good cholesterol

Regulate blood pressure

Boost happiness

Make you feel free and empowered

Spur creativity

Improve athletic performance

Kick dieting to the curb

trust our instincts, especially when they take us away from the comfort and perceived safety of mainstream beliefs and approval.

Starting at this very moment, we have the power to prevent and heal from disease without meds. We have the potential for incredible energy, strength, and resilience as we age. And whether you know that outright or a little voice inside has been whispering it to you, the fact that you're reading this book tells me that you have the curiosity to open doors and the bravery to go after what you want. That's a magical combination, and if you nurture it, you can create healthy habits that last a lifetime.

When it comes to what we're "supposed" to eat for maximum health gains, there couldn't be more approaches to try out. Should we go Paleo, Vegan, Fruitarian, Raw Foodist, Pescetarian, or Vegetarian-Who-Eats-Bacon-on-the-Weekends? While labels like these help locate other like-minded folks and create a sense of community in the beginning of a wellness journey, they can establish boundaries that inhibit exploration and stifle growth. We can't discover what's best for us if we can't venture outside of our "label" to investigate and experiment. So for now, skip hemming yourself into a label. Instead, let's look at the common denominator for most of these dietary approaches and begin there. The simpler we keep things, the easier it will be to navigate through the mess of information and find what works for our special selves. Author, journalist, and activist Michael Pollan sums it up most succinctly:

Eat food. Not too much. Mostly plants.

— **Michael Pollan,** author of *The Omnivore's Dilemma* and *Food Rules*

That's how we begin—by eating more whole, plant-based foods as often as possible; by learning to identify and keep processed foodstuffs out of our bodies; by educating ourselves and becoming responsible for our choices; and by committing to our intentions and our actions, rather than our excuses.

This beginning will involve learning about how and when we're being played by food marketers and industries with deep pockets and substantial lobbying power. And it will provide us with the chance to vote for the kind of food system and world we want through our wallet.

And while we're at it, let's forget about dieting altogether.

That's Right, Never Diet Again

You probably don't need me to tell you this, but diets don't work. They're a regimen designed to achieve a temporary goal in a short amount of time — not a sustainable plan for a healthful lifestyle. "Diets" also bog us down with guilt and resentment, and those feelings never motivate.

Understand that when I use the word "diet" in this book, I'm referring to what we're biologically designed to eat for the long haul — meals either entirely or primarily composed of nuts, seeds, legumes, fruits, and vegetables that come from nature (not a lab or factory). It's important to know that what we eat for health and what we eat for enjoyment don't have to be mutually exclusive. This book will prove it. Once we learn how delicious a plant-powerful diet can be and we have the tools and know-how we need to start changing bad habits into health-promoting new routines, we'll look forward to each new week, new recipe, new discovery, and guess what? The extra weight will fall away. No need to assign points to food, or weigh it, or measure it, or feel like we're missing out. If we can simply say "goodbye" to the health-diminishing junk that congests our food system and bodies, if we can turn away from contradictory marketing noise and return to our biological diet, our bodies will find their healthy, happy weight.

Plant-Powerful Is Freedom

This book focuses on a particular approach to food that has helped me, and thousands of others, heal from disease. Even though these recipes don't include meat, eggs, dairy, fish, gluten, or highly processed foods, it's not about deprivation. Quite the opposite, really. (See, there are even chocolate chip cookies! ➡)

Once we have the know-how to realistically incorporate a variety of whole foods into our routines — step by step — we'll realize that there's tremendous freedom with this new lifestyle. We'll get in sync with our bodily needs, knowing what to give it so it won't hold us back with ailments. We'll be stronger and more pain-free than ever. We'll feel happier. And we'll have more energy to exercise, to play with our families, or to dive into a new project that we've wanted to get to for years. We'll not only see things differently, but we'll feel and taste things differently. And the new experiences are ones we won't want to give back. This is an approach to eating that empowers.

My mission is to help us all incorporate more good stuff into our diets, because some plants in the mix is better than no plants in the mix. I'm not here to judge. I'm here to share tools and ideas that can help us all build our happiest, healthiest lives sooner than later. I'm a guide. A copilot. A head cheerleader for Team Plant-Inspired.

Walnut Chocolate Chip Cookies

INGREDIENTS:

Dry Ingredients:

1 cup oat flour

1¼ cups almond flour

2 tablespoons arrowroot powder

1 teaspoon baking powder (aluminum-free)

¾ cup Sucanat

1 teaspoon fine-ground sea salt

¼ teaspoon ground cinnamon

Wet Ingredients:

½ cup red apple, cored and diced

½ cup + 2 tablespoons water

7 tablespoons unrefined, virgin coconut oil (gently warmed to liquid on the stove top if solid)

1 teaspoon vanilla extract

Mix-ins:

¾ cup vegan, gluten-free chocolate chips, or vegan, gluten-free chocolate bar chopped into chunks

1 cup walnuts, roughly chopped

A CLASSIC TREAT

STEPS:

1. Preheat oven to 350°F and line a baking sheet or two with unbleached parchment paper. (If you don't have two baking sheets, bake in batches.)

2. In a large bowl, sift together dry ingredients and dump in any Sucanat that didn't make it through the sifter.

3. In a separate bowl, stir together wet ingredients and then transfer into the dry ingredients bowl and fold the mixture in. Add mix-ins.

4. Scoop or roll out 1" balls and place about 3" apart on baking sheet.

5. Bake for 10 – 15 minutes and cool on a baking rack.

psst! Using unbleached parchment paper, roll the dough into a log and freeze in an airtight glass container. Thaw, slice, and bake a cookie or two as you need them.

—

Try equal amounts of pecans or almonds instead of walnuts. Fold in ¼ cup dried cherries or ¼ cup toasted coconut for extra yum-factor.

—

Want to skip the oil? Use 1 whole apple instead of ½ and omit the coconut oil. The texture will be drier, but the cookies will still be very yummy.

Plant-Powerful Benefits

The catalyst for a plant-inspired diet is different for everyone. You may have picked up this book because you're frustrated with digestive issues and the lack of answers coming from your doctor. Maybe you have a respected friend who shared a powerful article, nutritional study, or documentary with you.

Perhaps you've been a vegan for years now, but you're ready to say goodbye to gluten and processed vegan foods. Or maybe someone lovely served you my Almond Crunch Kale Chips recipe ➡ . No matter how you arrive at this door, you've no doubt heard about a plant-powerful benefit or three. And the best reason is the one that brought you here and put this book in your hands.

Let's Start with Being Disease-Free

A long, vibrant life free of ailments, pain, and disease is the kind we all want. And there's a growing body of evidence based on more than 40 years of scientific research that demonstrates a plant-powerful diet's effectiveness in reversing and preventing chronic diseases. But it's not just diabetes and heart disease that respond to a whole-foods, plant-rich diet. It may also help protect us from autoimmune diseases, depression, colds and flu, high cholesterol, hypertension, Alzheimer's, and bone, kidney, liver, eye, and brain diseases. That's a mouthful of badness you can avoid with the goodness of plant-inspired eating.

For several decades, genetics have been blamed for the likelihood that we'll contract a particular disease, but it's actually our diet and lifestyle that determines whether those genes are switched on.[1] I have a pal who's father died of heart disease in his 40s, and his father's father also died of heart disease young — in his 40s. Naturally, this friend was concerned about his genes. Both Dad and Grandpa were meat-and-potatoes kind of men, so my buddy did some research and decided to lead a different lifestyle. He found an exercise routine that he enjoyed (not resented) and diet-wise, well, you may know where I'm going here: more plants, less processed. His family doctor is in a constant state of disbelief at how good his medical tests look compared to the other men in his family.

Just because we have a family history of illness doesn't mean that we have to go there, too. A change-up in the family eating patterns may just do the trick. There are foods that promote health and there are foods that diminish health— every bite you take is either going to add to your quality of life or diminish it. Keep that in mind when shopping, eating out, and planning meals. It's a simple guideline that can help tremendously.

Almond Crunch Kale Chips

I know we're starting with a lot of kale here, but as moisture dries, you'll be surprised by how much the leaves shrink up. Use 2 baking sheets lined with parchment, and bake in batches if you need to. (And if you have a dehydrator, by all means, use it for this recipe.)

GREAT FOR BEGINNERS

INGREDIENTS:

2 heads of organic kale

1 teaspoon unrefined, virgin coconut oil

½ cup of almond flour

1 pinch of fine-ground sea salt

STEPS:

1. Preheat oven to 170°F.

2. Wash and remove stems from kale (save them for the veggie stock recipe on page 122).

3. In a large bowl, massage together leaves, oil, flour, and salt.

4. Spread coated leaves on parchment-lined cookie sheet. Don't overcrowd the pan(s); leave ½" of space around each leaf so it can dry out properly.

5. Bake for 30 minutes. Then flip chips on the tray. Continue baking until completely dry — check them every 10 minutes until they have a dry, brittle look (but don't let them burn).

psst! Don't over salt the kale before baking — flavor intensifies once baked and you can always add more later if needed.

—

Add ¼ – ½ teaspoon dry chipotle powder for some kick. Or 1 teaspoon lime zest, 1 teaspoon dry onion, and ½ teaspoon dry garlic powder for a ranch-style flavor. Or make them sweet! Massage in 2 tablespoons Sucanat, ¼ teaspoon ground cinnamon, and ½ teaspoon vanilla extract.

—

If you use a dehydrator, lay out prepared kale on a dehydrator screen(s). Dehydrate at 95°F for 4 – 6 hours until dry and crispy.

—

Skip the oil if you like. Massage kale with 2 – 3 teaspoons of water or veggie stock instead.

Inspiring Leaders & Important Research

Founder of the Physician's Committee for Responsible Medicine (PCRM), **Dr. Neal Barnard** has been reversing type 2 diabetes in his patients for years using a whole-foods, plant-based diet. Learn more at **NealBarnard.org.**

Cornell professor and author of *The China Study* **T. Colin Campbell, PhD,** advocates that a whole-foods, plant-based diet is the most effective way to prevent, and even reverse, many cancers, as well as heart disease and other chronic illnesses. His decades of research identify animal protein as a powerful cancer-causing agent. Learn more at **TheChinaStudy.com.**

Dr. Caldwell Esselstyn reversed atherosclerosis in end-stage heart disease patients using a low-fat, whole-foods, plant-based diet — and all his compliant patients are thriving 20 years later. Learn more at **DrEsselstyn.com.**

Dr. Joel Fuhrman specializes in preventing and reversing disease through plant-powerful nutritional methods. His "nutritarian" diet-style recommends eating more nutrient-dense calories, therapeutically, for longevity, and to maximize healthy life expectancy. Simply stated, nutrient-dense foods give us the most nutrients per calorie. Rather than calorie counting, he strives for nutritional excellence in the overweight to remove cravings and food addiction and to maintain favorable weight. Learn more at **DrFuhrman.com.**

For more than 30 years, **Dr. Dean Ornish,** founder of the Preventive Medicine Research Institute (PMRI), has conducted scientific research studies demonstrating that even the progression of severe coronary heart disease can be reversed with plant-powered diet and lifestyle changes. Learn more at **OrnishSpectrum.com.**

As I mentioned before, plant foods contain disease-fighting fiber, antioxidants, and phytonutrients, which you just won't find in animal-derived products. Fiber is famous for keeping our systems moving (aka pooping — go ahead and get your giggles out — it's an important part of your health), but foods containing fiber provide other health benefits as well, like lowering your risk of diabetes and heart disease and preventing certain cancers.

Plant foods also contain incredible amounts of disease-fighting phytonutrients. Also known as phytochemicals, these battle-ready compounds are part of a plant's immune system. They help the plant world stand their ground against environmental challenges like disease, injury, insects, drought, climate variations, UV rays, and environmental poisons and pollutants. They're what make blueberries blue,

> Disease is not something we catch. It is something that we build over time: piece by piece, habit by habit. We may have an inherent weakness or genetic predisposition to certain conditions, but they are not life sentences, and they are also not inevitable.

— **Meghan Telpner,** director of the Academy of Culinary Nutrition, author of *UnDiet*

carrots orange, kale green, and raspberries red, and they can protect our bodies the same incredible way they do themselves. Even the American Cancer Society supports the idea that consuming more phytonutrients means less disease.[2]

Antioxidants are a familiar plant nutrient. You hear about them all the time. But do you really know what an antioxidant is or why you want them? This is where that curiosity I mentioned comes in handy. If we start asking questions, instead of purchasing a product simply because it's labeled as "loaded with antioxidants," we'll start finding the answers. And those answers will lay an informed foundation for wellness that lasts well beyond the latest diet fad.

Here's the simple definition: an antioxidant is a nutrient that protects and repairs cells in the body against free-radical damage. So, let's reach back in our mental files to Chemistry 101 for a minute. It's there we first heard that our bodies are made up of different types of cells, which are made up of different types of molecules, which are made up of one or more atoms joined by chemical bonds. A nucleus, neutrons, protons, and electrons make up atoms. Electrons (on outer "rings" of atoms) are what bond atoms together to make the molecules. Remember? Now, atoms seek stability by sharing electrons, and they usually don't split if such an action leaves an odd, unpaired electron. But when weak bonds split, this creates a free radical. Free radicals injure cells, can damage DNA, and lay the foundation for disease if they dominate our body.

How are free radicals formed? Well, in plain terms, our bodies are constantly reacting with oxygen. And while these interactions enhance our lives, in true balancing-act fashion, they also create free radicals. Think about when an apple browns after prolonged exposure to air, or when iron rusts — this is the oxidative process in action, and with it comes the formation of free radicals.

Cooking Up Cancer

According to the National Cancer Institute at the National Institutes of Health, heterocyclic amines (HCAs) and polycyclic aromatic hydrocarbons (PAHs) are chemicals formed when muscle meat (beef, pork, fish, and poultry) is cooked using high-temp methods such as open-flame grilling or panfrying. Exposure to high levels of HCAs and PAHs can cause cancer in animals. And currently, no federal guidelines address consumption levels of HCAs and PAHs formed in meat. Ongoing studies are analyzing the associations between meat intake, cooking methods, and cancer risk, but know that PAHs can also be formed during other food preparation processes, such as smoking of meats, too.[3] Yikes.

Mixed Berry Fruit Salad *with* Tangerine Juice & Fresh Mint

ANTIOXIDANT RICH

I came up with this quick and easy fruit salad for a last-minute family sleepover. It was served in the morning as-is, with the option to add it to Chia Pudding (page 164) or Granola (page 168), and either way, it received rave reviews. Try adding it to the Easy Vanilla Bean Ice Cream (page 285) or fill a Pie Crust (page 288), drizzle with ¼ cup honey, and bake at 325°F for about 25 minutes for a delicious tart.

STEPS:

1. Wash berries well and lay out to dry on a dish towel (the non-precious kind I recommend in HOW).

2. Finely cut the mint and set aside.

3. Whisk together juice and honey.

4. Put it all in a bowl and lightly toss.

psst! Try this recipe with peaches, apricots, and plums instead of berries.

—

Add a pinch or two of fresh basil or lavender buds.

INGREDIENTS:

Fruits

1 pint strawberries (1½ – 2 cups)

1 pint blueberries (1½ – 2 cups)

1 pint blackberries (1½ – 2 cups)

1 pint raspberries (1½ – 2 cups)

½ cup pomegranate seeds aka arils (optional)

Mix-ins

½ cup sunflower seeds, toasted

3 tablespoons hemp seeds

3 tablespoons fresh mint leaves, chiffonade

Juice

½ cup fresh tangerine juice

2 teaspoons raw, wild-harvested honey

When we sit in traffic breathing behind a city bus, free radicals are formed. When we eat and digest food, free radicals are formed. When we work out, free radicals are formed. It's impossible to avoid them, but we can calm them down by bringing in specialists who can give them that extra electron they need. Antioxidants are the specialists and they keep free radicals in line by blocking and neutralizing the damage they cause. They're — quite literally — our own personal bodyguards. And we want as many as we can get into our systems to counter the health-destroying effects of oxidative stress. What we eat makes all the difference.

If we want to start feeling great, we have to recognize the diet-disease connection. When our body calls out for help, in the form of symptoms (e.g., headaches, rashes, constipation, cramps, joint pain, irritability, inflammation), let's respect that call instead of quieting it with synthetic medications that ultimately cause more issues.

Think about when an animal falls ill. The first question a vet or owner will ask is, "What did he/she eat?" Now, when a human becomes ill, sadly, that's one of the last questions asked, if it's asked at all. When Americans feel discomfort, rather than making diet and lifestyle changes, we default to meds to mask symptoms of a larger problem. If we have acid reflux, our body is not happy with the acid-forming food we're giving it. If we have acne or a rash, our body is likely trying to rid itself of toxins by pushing them out through the skin (the body's largest eliminative organ). If our bellies are swollen all the time and we can't poop, there's something our body needs that it's not getting — sleep, exercise, fiber, water, or a combination of all of the above. The body is an amazingly powerful machine, designed to function and heal and thrive at optimal levels. If the fuel we give it is bad, it breaks down. It's a straight line, folks, connecting dot A to dot B.

Plant-Powerful Saves Money in the Short- and Long-Term

There's a reason why an entire fast-food meal is the same price as a single bunch of organic kale: the government pays farms (with the taxpayer's dollars) based on their size and production history, not based on their harvest. How does that connect to fast food? Well, according to the Congressional Research Service, 90 percent of government commodity payments (subsidies) go to farmers for the crops used to create factory-farmed animal products and processed junk foods — corn, wheat, rice, and soybeans — not organic produce. This makes boxed and packaged food prices appear cheap, but the long-term costs in health and potential doctor's bills are substantial.

Very simply, we subsidize high fructose corn syrup in this country, but not carrots. While the surgeon general is raising alarms over the epidemic of obesity, the president is signing farm bills designed to keep the river of cheap corn flowing, guaranteeing that the cheapest calories in the supermarket will continue to be the unhealthiest.

— **Michael Pollan,** author of *The Omnivore's Dilemma* and *Food Rules*

These government subsidies (along with current food policies) encourage the overproduction of crops that become ingredients in the vast majority of what most Americans eat. To use up the cheap excess grain, unhealthful by-products, like high fructose corn syrup and soy lecithin (to name just two), replace more expensive ingredients in sugary, fatty, factory-made industrial foods. All this means the wheat in our fast-food bun is cheap to produce; the high fructose corn syrup in our condiments is cheap to produce; the unnatural diet of corn and soy fed to cattle is cheap to produce. But it's not just fast food where this junk turns up. These commodity crop by-products end up in everything from "natural" veggie burgers to "healthy" granolas. (Not that you have to give up burgers or granola. See pages 244 and 168.)

The "Cheap" Price Tag Is an Illusion

And our consumption of these crops absolutely parallels the increase in pollution, the expansion of our waistlines, and the incidence of disease. Think about it.

> *Taking medication for every ailment is not only expensive, but it's a lot like putting a Band-Aid over the "check engine" warning light in our car and continuing to drive.*

These symptoms are evidence of a larger problem — almost always something we can remedy by changing dietary and lifestyle habits. Unfortunately, swallowing a pill takes a lot less effort than creating new habits. And we trust the messages we're given in advertisements — Got a headache? Take this pill — instead of launching our own investigation where we'd discover that we ate or drank something toxic.

Healthy doesn't have to also mean expensive. Think about it: the more a manufacturer has to formulate, preserve, process, bag, bottle, box, distribute, transport, and market their products, the higher the price tag will be for us. Meals prepared from legumes, grains, spices, nuts, seeds, fruits, and veggies can be a significant cost savings if you shop in the produce and bulk sections. Use the cash you save for more organic fruits and vegetables, new kitchen appliances, and other investments in long-term health.

In Section 2, I illustrate HOW to efficiently and cost-effectively shop, and how to properly store and use up every last bit of purchases — stretching hard-earned dollars as far as they'll go.

Creamy Quinoa & Kale Salad

2+ SERVINGS

$3.35 DINNER RECIPE

This easy, comforting recipe has become a YU community favorite over the years. And it costs a little over three bucks to prepare if you hit the bulk section for ingredients. It's great warm or cold. Pricing varies, but these prices are the average for organic ingredients.

INGREDIENTS:

5 large leaves kale, stems removed and chopped ($0.90)

½ cup of cooked quinoa: see page 144 for tips ($0.75)

Sauce

½ cup cashews, soaked ($0.62)

1 tablespoon fresh lemon juice ($0.30)

1 clove garlic ($0.09)

1 cup water

1½ teaspoons unrefined, virgin coconut oil ($0.10)

2 tablespoons nutritional yeast ($0.18)

1 teaspoon fine-ground sea salt, to taste ($0.01)

1 tablespoon tahini (optional) ($0.40)

STEPS:

1. In a blender, blend together sauce ingredients and transfer to a large pot. Place the pot over a burner heated to medium.

2. Fold in cooked quinoa and kale, stir for 3 – 5 minutes — just long enough for kale to soften a tiny bit.

3. Serve and enjoy.

psst! Add a chipotle pepper for heat, or a roasted red pepper for an orange color that kiddos respond well to.

—

Swap out the sauce here and try this recipe with a veggie-based sauce on page 208. Fold in sautéed mushrooms, carrots, or other veggie goodness.

—

Skip the oil if you like.

> **Every time you spend money, you're casting a vote for the kind of world you want.**
>
> —**Anna Lappé,** educator and author of *Diet for a Hot Planet*

Purchases Are Your Voice, So Vote

By reducing our consumption of processed foods (including animals) and increasing our intake of organic, plant-based foods, we'll not only set up simpler, healthier lives, but our purchases can send a much-needed message to the unsustainable systems that our food supply is built upon.

Let's use factory farming as an example. Livestock are meant to consume grasses, but they're fed inexpensive surplus commodity crops like soy and corn instead. Inexorably, just like humans who don't consume their natural diet, the livestock get sick. So, to keep them alive and producing unnatural amounts of milk and meat to satisfy demand, powerful antibiotics and hormones are regularly administered to them (often with each meal). Yes, really.

Think about when a human mother is nursing her infant, and a doctor recommends that she avoid "harmful" foods because they'll go straight to her baby through her breast milk. So, why wouldn't the dioxins (very persistent environmental pollutants produced from herbicide production), antibiotics, blood, pus, feces, bacteria, viruses, herbicides, pesticides, and hormones present in the milk from factory-farmed dairy cows affect us the same way? Especially since most of us drink this secretion into adulthood. If hormones used for livestock are designed to fatten them up quickly, and we are what we eat... well...

Factory farming is not only abusive and cruel (a Google search for "Factory Farming" or "CAFO" can prove that), but it also uses 75 percent of total agricultural land for production.[4] Since the global demand for meat has increased in recent years, more concentrated animal feeding operations (CAFOs) are needed, an ugly practice that consumes enormous amounts of energy, pollutes water supplies, generates

Genetically Modified Organisms (GMOs)

GMOs are plants (or animals) that have had their DNA blueprint changed in a laboratory. This genetic manipulation is practiced with commercial agriculture so crops can withstand large quantities of herbicides and even produce their own pesticides.

GMOs were the biotech industry's proposed solution for world hunger, drought, pests, meeting "demand," and boosting the nutritional value of crops. But in nearly two decades, these promises have proven empty, since none of the GM products on the market deliver in any way demonstrated by long-term study. People all over the world still suffer from chronic malnutrition and hunger.[6, 7] Increased use of pesticides parallels our increase in illness and environmental damage, and has led to a rise in pesticide-resistant "super weeds" and "super bugs," which forcess farmers to use even more powerful pesticides and herbicides more frequently. Seventy percent of the foods in a typical American grocery (health food stores, too) contain GM ingredients (corn, soy, canola oil, and sugar beets are the most prevalent).[8]

What can you do?
Visit nongmoproject.org for more information about how you can take action now.

significant greenhouse gases, and requires ever-increasing quantities of corn, soy, and other grains to feed the animals. The United Nations Food and Agriculture Organization (FAO) estimates that livestock production is one of the biggest contributors to environmental pollution — even more than driving cars.[5] Particular herbicides used in genetically modified crops have been linked to birth defects, reproductive difficulties, miscarriages, infertility, DNA damage, and behavioral disorders in humans, and even cancer in animal tests.[9, 10] Studies also show that GM toxins have been found in human blood samples, even though most manufacturers claim that they break down in the human digestive system.[11] When GMOs are approved by government agencies, they're relying on findings from 30-, 60-, and 90-day studies (funded by the companies who will profit from the sale of the product in question) involving short-lived laboratory animals. These tests simply can't determine the long-term consequences for people who consume genetically engineered foods over a lifetime.[12]

All over the world (in more than 60 countries), the development, distribution, planting, and sale of GMOs are restricted or banned entirely. According to a 2012 Mellman Group poll, an almost unanimous 91 percent of American consumers wanted GMOs labeled. But somebody's not listening.

If you don't have something to hide, what's the harm in giving the people who trust you with their health, and the health of their families, the choice to consume GMOs or not?

We just don't know enough yet about GMOs but the good news is that we don't have to support these practices. By going plant-powerful, local, and organic as much as possible, our dollars will move away from broken systems and toward sustainable ones. By taking good care of ourselves and our families, we're making a significant ripple in the water. It's pretty exciting.

Infuse Your Life with Creativity & Variety

A plant-powerful diet provides the opportunity to tap into creativity, play with new techniques, combine unexpected ingredients, and have fun in the kitchen. Because so much of this lifestyle can be new, we get to use ideas the way that works best for us. That's creativity, my friend. Embrace the abundance of possibilities available.

Eating a variety of plant-based foods keeps weekly food boredom to a minimum while acquiring all of the disease-fighting nutrients we need. For example, we don't have to get protein from one source; we can get it from a variety of cost-effective sources like lentils, chickpeas, amaranth, buckwheat, quinoa, legumes, rice, nuts, even seaweeds. A range of bright, colorful foods really is our best insurance policy against nutritional deficiency.

The Missing Link?

The buzz about gluten is no short-lived craze. It's actually an acknowledgment of a real issue that affects millions of unsuspecting folks — maybe even you.

Gluten (appropriately from the Latin word for "glue") is a protein found in wheat that makes pasta chewy and holds bread together. It can also be naturally found in rye, spelt, barley, faro, kamut, farina, bulgur, durum, triticale, couscous, bran, products packaged in facilities that also process wheat, and even oats that shouldn't contain gluten but are highly susceptible to crop contamination.

Hybridized Dwarf Wheat, quite different from ancient wheat, like einkorn, used generations ago, was developed and enthusiastically released into the food supply without thought for human safety.[13] Modern wheat can cause inflammation in the gut, which in turn causes excess oxidation of stomach cells, and that results in a plethora of free radicals. This damage compromises digestion and absorption of minerals, and it can lead to all sorts of nutritional deficiencies and issues, like leaky gut, a syndrome that's as awful as it sounds: the lining of the intestines becomes so porous that undigested food molecules, yeast, toxins, and other waste flows right into the bloodstream. The liver then has to work in overdrive to clean up the mess (if it can) and the immune system ends up fighting these invaders so hard that it eventually can't tell the difference between good and bad, and it can end up attacking its own tissues—the very definition of autoimmune disease.

Often talked about hand in hand with gluten is the most serious manifestation of this vicious inflammatory cycle, celiac disease — an autoimmune digestive disorder that damages the villi (finger-like projections that absorb nutrients) of the small intestine. Nutrient absorption is compromised when gluten is consumed by someone with celiac disease, which can lead to malnutrition, osteoporosis, and even some cancers. And it's more commonplace today than it was 50 years ago.

> *You probably know someone with celiac disease, since it's estimated that 1 in 133 Americans have this devastating disorder.*

But did you know that 83 percent of Americans who have celiac disease are undiagnosed or walking around misdiagnosed with other conditions, and it can take an average of 6–10 years to even get that diagnosis?[14]

That's a heck of a lot of people suffering from some of the 300+ symptoms of the disease, bummers that include gas, bloating, queasiness, muscle cramps, rashes, abdominal cramping, constipation, diarrhea, or an alternating combination of both (often diagnosed as IBS — irritable bowel syndrome), headaches and/or migraines, joint, bone and overall body pain, leg numbness, fatigue, infertility, inability to gain weight, depression, and sudden, irrational mood shifts.

So, what happens when you get the celiac disease test, it comes back negative, and you're left continuing to suffer from these symptoms? Whether we have a proper diagnosis of celiac or not, research estimates that 18 million Americans have non-celiac gluten sensitivity (with the same symptoms I mentioned)—that's six times the number of Americans who have celiac disease.[15]

Gluten-Sensitive Americans

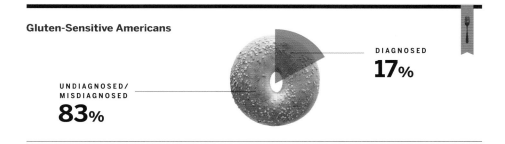

DIAGNOSED
17%

UNDIAGNOSED/
MISDIAGNOSED
83%

Wheat-free advocates (including best-selling authors and physicians) claim that wheat can be just as addicting as hard drugs like cocaine. They also claim that wheat has contributed to the obesity epidemic in America, which leads to diseases like diabetes. Do manufacturers know about these potential addictive qualities? Well, gluten makes its way into the food supply mostly via familiar wheat products like breads, pasta, cereals, and cookies, but it's also hidden in a surprising number of inconspicuous foods like soups, gravies, sauce mixes, ice creams, salad dressings, imitation cheeses, pickles, hot dogs, and even candies.

If you aren't gluten-free but recognize some of the symptoms of sensitivity I list, think: how would you feel going without it for 30 days or more? Trembling at the thought? Already planning the "last hurrah" binge? Hey, I've been there.

Withdrawal is the pits, and that's exactly what you may experience, but it's worth it to kick the gluten. Listen up, skeptics: if you're rolling your eyes right now, I encourage you to give yourself a little test. Go without gluten products for one week and see if you don't experience symptoms that resemble withdrawal — nausea, headaches, and insatiable sugar cravings. For some of you, it may be startling. People are always sharing with me that gluten was the last wellness hurdle for them, and now they feel better than ever.

If you already eat a clean, whole-foods, plant-powerful diet, but still suffer from some of symptoms I mention, going gluten-free will more than likely be your key to a complete health transformation.

Turning Down the Noise

Switch on any TV, and within minutes, you'll see ads and news reports rotate through junk and fast foods, chemical cleaners, and beauty products — "innovations" that perpetuate the sham that fast and easy is better.

And then, by design, we'll hear all about the newest medication that will ease the symptoms unknowingly caused by these foodstuffs and personal or household products. Here's the medication to help your *erectile dysfunction, allergies, wrinkles, depression, obesity, heartburn, acid reflux, excess belly fat, headaches, migraines, arthritis, diabetes, stress, anxiety, digestive disorders, yeast infection, eczema, thyroid problems, high blood pressure, heart disease, constipation, irritable bowel syndrome, high cholesterol, hair loss, insomnia, a cold, the flu, acne, and/or chronic pain.* Ugh.

We hear and see anywhere from 250 to 3,000 advertisements per day, and it's a big reason why we're desensitized to the barrage of preventable ailments (not to mention the mile-long listing of downright horrifying side effects listed on a box of pills or at the end of a commercial). The average drug label lists 70 possible side effects, and some drugs list more than 500![1] Advertisers don't want us to marinate on the very real danger of meds, so they divert our attention with bright, colorful boxes and promises of relief instead. I know this approach well, because as much as it makes me cringe to admit it, in the past, I worked to design this type of nonsense marketing myself.

In a report by the Mayo Clinic, 70 percent of American adults, teens, and even kids are on at least one prescription drug. More than half take two, and 20 percent of these patients are on five or more prescription medications.[2] That's an awful lot of product, totaling $711 billion in net profit for the top 11 drug companies over the last decade.[3] Also at this time, the majority of physicians in America receive very little training for nutrition and diet while in medical school — only an average of 19 hours out of 40,000 hours of their medical career.[4, 5, 6] And there are significant conflicts of interest within the committees that establish our national dietary guidelines. As a result, when it comes to nutrition, we're left to fend for ourselves against deceptive claims from the food and drug industries and the ambiguous dietary guidelines put forth by our government.

We've simply handed our well-being over to industries and companies that care more about profit than our health. (The pharmaceutical industry spends more on product promotion than it does on research and development.[7]) But we can find our way, if we can turn the volume down on the shouting that's vying for our attention.

Not quite as attractive without all of the chemicals is it?

If you removed all the flashy dye and preservatives from the processed foodstuffs that make up this image, you can bet this half is what it would look like.

Does Food Science Know Us Better Than We Know Ourselves?

Getting us hooked on food-like substances that are inexpensive and convenient has been the name of the game for food manufacturers and the food scientists that work with them for over 60 years.

Humans are designed to seek out calories (fuel) because neural circuitry — aka instinct — tells us to eat to survive. Let's go on a field trip back in time, say, tens of thousands of years, and take a peek at our ancestors' day-to-day lives. That was a time when humans ate to live and lived to reproduce. Gathering fruits, vegetables, legumes, tubers, nuts, and seeds, and hunting (or coming across) the occasional animal comprised the day's "to-do list." And when food was discovered, it was eaten quickly before it could be taken away or had the time to perish.

Humans knew what to eat thanks to taste and smell and instinct. If it tasted good and smelled fresh, that meant fuel, so they consumed as much as they could, since it might be their only opportunity to eat for a while. Our ancestors weren't born with instructions directing them to eat at 9 A.M., 12 P.M., and 6 P.M. And they weren't given expiration dates, dietary pyramids, or labels with each meal they came across. They consumed whole foods, and with them, a variety of nutritional benefits that helped them evolve.

Before modern technology, salt, fat, and sugar were only occasionally consumed as components of whole, natural foods — they were survival gold. For example, sweet honeycomb and luscious macadamia nuts were rare finds (that naturally came in small, inconvenient serving sizes).

When we eat high-calorie foods, the hormone dopamine is released in our brains, rewarding fortunate survival discoveries (like honey) with the feeling of happiness and bliss. So naturally we want to repeat them again and again. A high-calorie eating experience has become an emotional one. But in modern times, with excessive repetition of this physiological reward process comes addiction. And present-day agriculture and food science develop foodstuffs that trip the pleasure centers of the brain to a degree that nature never intended, to get consumers hooked.

By formulating profitable combinations of scientifically altered salt, fat, and sugar, they've been able to tap into what's known within the processed food and beverage industry as "bliss point." This is simply another name for our brain's biological reward system for consuming calories that help us survive.[10]

If you make a fist, that's about the size of your stomach. Now open your hand. That's about the size that your stomach can stretch to, which was mighty handy during those times when our ancestors came across a rare feast after a period of famine. "Get it while the gettin' is good" was their motto. But in modern times, the gettin' is always good, thanks to the convenience and availability of processed food.

What was once an occasional event is now an all-day-long festival.

When we consume our biological diet — foods containing fiber and nutrients in their whole form — stretch receptors in our bellies create a sensation of fullness, and we stop eating sooner rather than later. Processed foods, however, dupe our bodies into believing that all of our survival problems are being solved (cue that dopamine bliss). And since these processed options are also stripped of their whole-food context — and are nutrient deficient — our satisfaction alarm doesn't really go off until mass quantities of empty calories, fats, sugars, mineral-depleted salt, and chemicals are consumed. Think about how eating an entire apple filled with fiber satisfies, while eating six gummy fruit chews — the same amount of calories as that apple — does not. Overconsumption is actually the body trying in vain to meet its nutritional needs. But satiety is bad for sales.

Mother Nature is a smart cookie, and she helps us locate food by calling it to our attention in vibrant reds and oranges and greens and yellows. There's no doubt, color is an important part of a pleasurable eating experience. It creates a physiological expectation of taste, and in nature, bright color can tell us that a food is fresh and full of nutrients. When fruits and vegetables begin to perish, vibrancy diminishes, and ultimately that food becomes less attractive because it isn't as beneficial to eat. But processed foods can deceive, covering up that it's nutritionally "less attractive" with artificial colors, scents, and flavors.

Processed foodstuffs are stripped of nutrients, bleached, and rendered lifeless. If the FDA ever outlawed artificial dyes (many are banned in other countries), we'd see these fake foods for what they really are: aisle after aisle of gray, white, and beige lifelessness.

Most of us would equate gray chips with blandness. But dress those same chips up in a combo of Red 40, Blue 1, and Yellow 5 (that will hold color for decades) and we no longer can identify that our snack is as dead as cardboard.

We have to put our new lens on when we shop. Think about it: colored sports drinks aren't even remotely close to natural. In fact, their nuclear hues should be a warning flag, not an attraction. Dig a little deeper and you'll find the chemical that helps blue dye stick to sports drink liquid is the same product used as flame retardant for carpeting (and it's banned in Europe and Japan). Instead of seeing sprinkles as festive must-have additions to a cupcake, recognize them for what they are: chemically colored little pieces of trans fat derived from petroleum. (Why not top a cupcake with a beautiful edible flower instead? It's far more unique and elegant.) Also, deep down, we know that diet soda is too good to be true. It tricks our brain into anticipating calories and fuel that never arrives, and that leads to cravings. Processed foods are designed to dupe us on many levels — with outlandish color, amplified taste, and loud marketing claims to seal the deal.

Don't Believe the Hype

No one wants to be played. Bamboozled. Or tricked. But that's what happens in grocery stores all over this country, every single day.

> *Food is a relationship. And as many of us know, a relationship built on dishonesty will either be painful or short-lived.*

Big Food (the top processed food and beverage companies) sees that consumers want to be healthier. So they position themselves at the forefront of the health movement, while at the very same time, they develop and market products that diminish health. Fast-food chains sell "healthy" breakfast options, like cereal containing more sugar than a candy bar. Milkshakes have been renamed "smoothies," and deep-fried root vegetables are packaged, dyed, and sold as "veggie chips." That simple addition of the word "veggie" helps us feel better about our choice, so we dismiss the fact that these veggies are deep-fried (most likely in inexpensive

Junk Is Junk

Processed food manipulates ingredients to a degree where nutrient quality is compromised, and oftentimes color, texture, vitamins, and minerals are added back in via chemicals and synthetic ingredients. Fake meat, soy corndogs, vegan butter alternatives, dairy-free cheeses, vegan mayonnaise, gluten-free breads, and egg replacers, for the most part, are no different nutritionally than marshmallowy cereals, blue drinks, pizzas, margarines, and other processed foods that line the shelves. There is just as much processed "vegan," "organic," and "all-natural" junk out there as there is unnatural, non-vegan junk.

genetically modified oil like canola). We know better instinctually; we're just giving our power over to addiction and its partner-in-crime excuses instead of honesty and a little tough love with ourselves.

Picture this: you're walking happily down the street, and someone on a corner in a bright outfit shouts from across the way that they "HAVE SOMETHING YOU NEED!" You hesitantly walk over to them and they latch on to you, following up with, "C'mon, you can trust me." That would probably make you suspicious, right?

Well, the grocery store experience isn't all that different, if you really think about it. Next time we pick up a box with that virtuous marketing glow claiming in bold, exciting typography that it's "FORTIFIED with X, Y, and Z," we know that if it could be trusted, it probably wouldn't need to talk us into it with all sorts of loud health claims. The more roaring the call, the more suspicious we should be. Most "fortified" foods are actually stripped of fiber, vitamins, and minerals during processing, and synthetic replacements (most of which are poorly absorbed by the body, if at all) are added back in before they hit the shelves.

Manufacturers respond quickly to increasing desire for healthier options, and this speediness creates the appearance that they're trying to protect us. Sometimes, that's all it takes to trust a product. If a box is green and says "organic" or "natural," someone must be listening to our needs, right? Sometimes, yes. Many times, though, it's a trap that many consumers fall into.

A typical American supermarket carries almost 40,000 products. Most of these, though, even the "organic" ones, are owned and distributed by only a few large companies. Many of us don't realize just how much the top processed food and beverage companies have come to dominate the "organic" and "natural" food market. Fact is, it's a fruitful business for these corporate titans. And with their power, not only are they able to influence the standards by which foods are labeled, but they are also in control of what's considered acceptable under the organic label. The bigger the company, the more clout they have to position products at eye level on the shelves, too. They target adults up high and kiddos down low.

Many trusted natural-food brands are being bought up by the same Big Food companies that bring you blue yogurt in a tube and nitrate-loaded lunch meats. While Big Food has the right to buy up these natural companies, most of us interested in supporting small-scale organic businesses are unaware that our dollars aren't going to the pastoral farms or family businesses pictured on the packaged goods we place in our carts. And most of these organic business acquisitions aren't even listed on the megabrand sites, so how would we know? (I've got you — visit the appendix for helpful resources.)

When a small, organic business is gobbled up by a megabusiness, it's not uncommon for the acquired company's ideals to become watered down in an effort to reduce costs. What were once quality organic ingredients are now substituted with poor-quality, inexpensive, oftentimes genetically altered options. If we've trusted a particular brand for years, we don't always feel a need to be as vigilant in checking their labels. So when the "organic" seal is stealthily removed because ingredients are swapped out, we hardly notice. Gulp...

What can we do? Stop believing claims shouting at us from a box or package.

We don't get the entire story with labels of "low fat," "sugar free," or even "all natural." Do the majority of shopping at the perimeter of the store, where singular ingredients like bulk items (nuts, seeds, legumes, spices) and fruits and vegetables can be found. Keeping our food purchases whole and package-free is our best bet.

And let's focus on the ingredients list versus the nutrition label. That's where we can get more of the story. Make sure you recognize every listed ingredient (should be no more than five or six), and don't be fooled by "natural" flavoring, etc. Those ingredients may have once been natural, but they passed through a lab before ending up in that box. Apple cinnamon granola, for example, should contain apples, oats, nuts, and cinnamon — not "natural" apple or cinnamon flavor. The simplest options are foods without ingredient listings at all — shopping is a much more efficient experience when we don't have to sweat over every ingredient label. Besides, no cereal from a box tastes as yummy as the cereals starting on page 163.

With a little practice and some planning, we can to stock our pantries with whole ingredients and homemade foods. Instead of buying an "organic" frozen quiche, let's make one out of whole, organic ingredients like the one on page 177. Instead of pouring "all-natural" salad dressing on our salads, let's toss a handful of plant-based ingredients into the blender to mix up our own Ranch (page 227) or Ginger Miso Dressing (page 226), or Pomegranate Vinaigrette (page 226). Whip up a big batch of homemade Chickpea Protein Burgers (page 244). Freeze them for last-minute dinners instead of eating the "veggie" burgers manufactured by the same companies that donate millions of dollars to block the labeling of genetically modified foods.

> *If it seems that we can't trust manufacturers to make our food for us, then what better reason do we need to start making it ourselves? And if we say we don't have time, we're simply not making the time.*

I can help you with most aspects of this journey, with the exception of the most important one: you have to care enough about yourself to make the necessary changes. This includes caring enough about loved ones to disappoint them by saying no when they ask for purple sports drinks, blue ice cream, or pink cereal with marshmallows. Make the flavorful and comforting recipes starting on page 157 for them — or better yet, with them — instead. Know that they'll forget all about that junk once their palates have a chance to rebound from the chemically amplified flavors, textures, and smells of processed foods.

Despite the best of intentions, I know it can be difficult to stick with a healthy lifestyle. But we have more power than we realize. If there's no demand for particular products, manufacturers will notice. We can gain attention and begin to shift our food system in a direction better serving our health (and our planet's health) with each choice we make.

> *Don't think it's possible? Look at what happened with the fall of Big Tobacco.*

The YU Approach

Along this journey, there are a handful of important things that I ask: be kind yet honest with yourself; respect your instincts; be curious; make time; be accountable for your decisions.

Growth and change can be uncomfortable, but nothing hurts worse than staying in a place where we don't belong. Don't waste time feeling guilty or frustrated if something doesn't go as planned. Remember, change the view of a "negative" situation simply by changing the lens: instead of beating ourselves up, let's learn how to do it better the next go-round. Notice how you feel; look for an alternative; write it all down. Recycle the empty box of cookies, dust the crumbs off, and get back on track quicker each time.

I want to provide a structure for eating that's simpler, so we can quiet the noise out there and discover the freedom and confidence to bloom in our own lovely ways. Don't be intimidated. You belong here. Don't be overwhelmed. One step at a time is the name of the game.

Whole Is Simple — Parts Are Problematic

Let's un-complicate things a bit, shall we? When it comes to what to eat, we're conditioned to focus only on the scientifically identified parts of what we eat. It's how very different foods like beef, avocados, and nuts can be lumped together into a "high-fat" category. It's also how a corn syrup-covered, synthetically fortified cereal dyed with carcinogenic chemicals can make it into the same category as lentils with the label "high fiber."

Foods from nature are incredibly complex — a universe of identifiable and unidentifiable compounds in one whole form. Hold a navel orange in your hands and you can see that it's a beautiful food. It doesn't need a package making health claims. Instincts tell us that it is good for us, it smells good, it feels good, it looks good. We want to eat it, and that's how we're supposed to feel about it.

Vitamin C is a singular component of said orange that science has identified as beneficial for health. And it is — yet it's invisible to us. There's a lot going on in that orange that we can't see, and not all oranges are the same. Seasons, soil, quality, and storage of the orange can result in varied amounts of particular nutrients. But that's okay because our bodies are wise — using the nutrients it needs when it needs them.

When we take on a reductionist view of food — focusing only on specific components — our instinctual human connection to that food (and nature) is severed. It immediately confuses things. Instead of simply eating the whole orange

Nutritionism

Nutritionism is basically the assumption that the key to understanding food lies within its identified nutrients — leaving it up to scientists to discover healthful particles in food and determine if it will sustain our health. This reductionist approach leaves Americans bewildered and frustrated, but it's been great for business ever since 1977, as Michael Pollan explains in his article "Unhappy Meals" published in the _New York Times_ (January 2007):

> Responding to an alarming increase in chronic diseases linked to diet — including heart disease, cancer and diabetes — a Senate Select Committee on Nutrition, headed by George McGovern, held hearings on the problem and prepared what by all rights should have been an uncontroversial document called "Dietary Goals for the United States." The committee learned that while rates of coronary heart disease had soared in America since World War II, other cultures that consumed traditional diets based largely on plants had strikingly low rates of chronic disease. Epidemiologists also had observed that in America during the war years, when meat and dairy products were strictly rationed, the rate of heart disease temporarily plummeted.
>
> Naively putting two and two together, the committee drafted a straightforward set of dietary guidelines calling on Americans to cut down on red meat and dairy products. Within weeks a firestorm, emanating from the red-meat and dairy industries, engulfed the committee, and Senator McGovern (who had a great many cattle ranchers among his South Dakota constituents) was forced to beat a retreat. The committee's recommendations were hastily rewritten. Plain talk about food — the committee had advised Americans to actually "reduce consumption of meat" — was replaced by artful compromise: "Choose meats, poultry and fish that will reduce saturated-fat intake."

and reaping a variety of nutritional benefits, we wander out in search of this inconspicuous friend C. Which gives food manufacturers a golden opportunity to doctor up their nutritionally void foodstuffs with synthetic versions of this "prized" component of the orange. We'll pass by the quiet, label-less orange, and instead grab a bright bottle of synthetic vitamin C. Or better yet, because we're conditioned to opt for easier, we'll reach for a flashy carton of "100 percent pure" orange juice. Now, we'd never be able to eat the eight to ten whole oranges it takes to fill a large glass of orange juice, and that's by natural design — the fiber from one or two oranges would fill us up. The juice from an orange is supposed to be consumed with all of the fiber in that orange to regulate the release of the sugar into the blood. But since we're so busy, and more is better in our culture, most of us choose to "pour" over "peel."

Also, the oranges in that premium juice are processed and highly pasteurized (which strips the juice of its flavor and nutrients). It can sit in ginormous tanks for months at a time, and before it goes to the store, proprietary blends of volatile

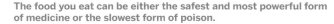

chemical flavorings are added to the "juice" along with synthetic vitamins.[1] In our quest for more vitamin C, faster, we've spun out of control and allowed ourselves to be duped.

Let's eat the orange instead. Keep it simple and focus on eating a colorful variety of foods each week, noshing on peppers, herbs, dark greens, broccoli, and berries. Not only will we get plenty of vitamin C, but we'll benefit from a host of other identified and unidentified nutritional benefits as well.

In his book *Whole: Rethinking the Science of Nutrition,* Dr. T. Colin Campbell discusses a philosophy that turns the current reductionist paradigm on its head:

> There is almost no direct relationship between the amount of a nutrient consumed at a meal and the amount that actually reaches its main site of action in the body — what is called its bioavailability...

> It means that we can never know exactly how much of a nutrient to ingest, because we can't predict how much of it will be utilized... The reason we can't predict how much of a nutrient will be absorbed and utilized by the body is that, within limits, it depends on what the body needs at that moment... In more scientific language, the proportion of a nutrient that is digested, absorbed, and provided to various tissues and the cells in those tissues is mostly dependent on the body's need for that nutrient at that moment in time.

> This need is constantly "sensed" by the body and controlled by a variety of mechanisms that operate at various stages of the "pathway," from nutrient ingestion to nutrient utilization. The body reigns supreme in choosing which nutrients it uses and which it discards unmetabolized. The pathway taken by a nutrient often branches, and branches further, and branches further again, leading the nutrient through a maze of reactions that is far more complex and unpredictable than the simple linear model of reductionism would suggest.

You're unlike anyone else. Your genetics are unique, your lifestyle choices vary, and your body experiences a universe of exclusive cellular interactions every second. The nutrients in food immeasurably influence each other, and when you eat, a complex process begins that's absolutely exclusive to the combination of the food and you. While we have guideposts that we can collectively follow on this wellness journey —variety, whole foods, simplicity —let's realize that our bodies are wise and start giving credit where credit is due.

Reducing Inflammation

Chronic inflammation is the bedrock of practically all disease (not to mention premature aging). Modern medicine would classify osteoporosis, atherosclerosis, Alzheimer's, arthritis, diabetes, allergies and food intolerances, fibromyalgia, digestive disorders, obesity, and even cancer as unrelated, but all have their roots in imbalance, and that causes inflammation.

Now, the inflammatory response is a natural thing. A good thing, really. It helps to protect us from injury and outside irritants. When we fall and cut ourselves, the immune system fires up, the wound swells, and the body goes into healing us right up. But the extremely acid-forming S.A.D. and our stressful, busy lifestyles keep that inflammation on a slow burn 'round the clock, year after year.

Stress comes in many forms — emotional, environmental, and nutritional — and it creates inflammation in the body. Even "good" stress like exercise causes inflammation.

That means that what we eat, think, feel, breathe, and experience every day can either overwhelm and irritate or balance and heal our bodies. "Balance" is the key word here. Too much sun and we burn. Too much exercise and we start to get aches and pains. Too much negativity at home, or too many late nights at work, and we end up with a cold. Too much processed, nutrient-poor foods and we get fat. And sick. The key to finding balance?

Rest. Fight the glorification of busy. And, you guessed it, a variety of whole plant-based foods.

There's convincing scientific evidence that a plant-powerful diet not only reduces inflammation but contributes to lowering the risk for cardiovascular disease and cancer.[2] By decreasing our intake of acid-forming, inflammatory foods and upping our intake of alkaline-forming, healing foods, we are giving our bodies what they need to fight, recover, and renew without burning out. More dark leafy greens, sprouts, green veggies, and certain grains, fruits, legumes, and nuts will bring a healing balance to your body, while animal products, gluten, sugar, and processed foods will fuel up that inflammatory fire.

pH Scale for Testing

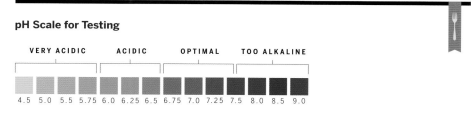

VERY ACIDIC · ACIDIC · OPTIMAL · TOO ALKALINE

4.5 5.0 5.5 5.75 6.0 6.25 6.5 6.75 7.0 7.25 7.5 8.0 8.5 9.0

The pH scale begins at 0 and runs to 14. A score of 7.0 represents a neutral pH. As the numbers go higher than 7, they get more alkaline; as they go lower than 7, more acidic. A decrease from 7 to 6 may not seem significant, but in actuality, it will take ten times the amount of alkalinity to neutralize. 7 to 5 = 100 times. 7 to 4 = 1,000 times. 7 to 3 = 10,000 times.[3]

Pick up a pack of litmus testing paper. Test using saliva or urine first thing in the morning. If testing with urine, make sure you test the second pee for more accuracy — the first is more acidic due to the metabolic process of preparing for elimination.

To further assist my body to find balance, I use a few simple tricks. Stir ½ teaspoon of baking soda into a gallon of purified water. Baking soda is highly alkaline and drinking this water over the course of a few days makes a big difference. Also, even though lemons taste acidic, fresh lemon juice in water actually becomes alkaline in the body during the digestive process. And it's a great way to start your day.

pHinding Balance

Many moons ago in a chemistry lab, between sideways glances at our crush in the front row and wondering if our brother would let us borrow the car later, we learned that pH is a measure of the acidity or alkalinity of an aqueous solution. And when it comes to the human body, our diet and lifestyle choices make all the difference in whether our blood can maintain the balanced pH that it needs for longevity and disease prevention. A healthy blood pH should be slightly alkaline, landing somewhere between 7.365 and 7.45.

As you know, when the body is in trouble, it calls out in the form of symptoms. But before it reaches that point, when there's imbalance, it works hard to right the ship. In an effort to reduce acidity, the body will pull minerals like calcium, sodium, magnesium, and potassium from vital organs and bones to neutralize acids and shuttle them out. Maintaining healthy pH keeps all of our bodily systems happy so we don't experience a host of issues like digestive disorders, heart disease, weak immune function, respiratory infection and allergies, tooth decay (cavities), weak bones and achy joints, acne and skin issues, lack of strength, kidney stones, poor recovery after workouts, and even reproductive issues.

We can maintain a healthful balance and prevent disease by eating more alkaline-forming foods like vegetables, dark leafy greens, sprouts, avocados, and almonds, and less acid-forming troublemakers like processed foods, gluten, energy drinks, dairy, meat, seafood, eggs, sugar, alcohol, coffee, artificial sweeteners, and fruit juices.

Bonuses for YU

I've created loads of free bonus material that's available for *YumUniverse* book owners.

Visit **yumuniverse.com/yu-book-owners** to gain access to cooking classes, e-books, printables, and extra information to help you on your wellness adventure.

Add in More Good Stuff

Plant-powerful is about going after health by adding more real food into our routine. It's about waking up and being an active participant in our wellness. And it's about taking it one step at a time. I admire the folks who can go all-or-nothing, completely changing their diet overnight and sticking with it for life. Bravo. But we all know they're a rarity.

It takes time to revise a lifetime of unhealthy habits — we need patience.

Adding more good into the diet will eventually squeeze out the harmful stuff, but ease into it so we can enjoy the adventure instead of resenting the change.

Celebrate Your Progress and Discoveries

I can't recommend this enough: find a journal and start recording goals, triumphs, and unintended detours. You're on a journey — create a road map for where you've been and where you intend to go. Write in it each day, or once a week. Record how you feel after you eat certain foods. Track how long it takes you to change old habits, what triggers throw you off course, what makes you feel your best, what foods have been surprisingly tasty for you. You'll be astonished how patterns will emerge and how this journal can remind you of insightful, helpful things you've forgotten. When you can see your patterns on paper, you can make changes easier and set new goals for yourself. It will feel good to look back over your progress.

And while we're at it, do the same with this book! It's not like fine china (which is always better in action than collecting dust on a shelf, if you ask me). I made *YumUniverse* so you can use it. I want you to season it with your experiences, notes, spills, and ideas.

Use my thoughts, recipes, and tips as inspiration for creating your own. It's the entire point.

What YU Need

Being accountable for our health includes finding a holistic medical professional who supports our goals — someone who looks to the connection between diet and lifestyle first when they're attempting to heal, someone who can provide you with blood tests and support before you begin this transformation.

Blood work can give us a clear picture of what our state of health is, and where it can go. Find a medical professional who will compare test results with what healthy "normal" is, not the unhealthy "American normal" most results are based upon. It's important that we find a professional who understands the benefits of eating more plants. Your instincts led you to "plant-powerful," so don't let anyone quiet your intuition before you get going. Everyone is different, with unique needs, so begin the journey responsibly by understanding yours. Find support from a professional who won't dismiss your exclusive goals or hopes by simply writing you a prescription.

The following is an overview of essentials and supplements that should be discussed with your doc of choice if you are considering going 100 percent plant-based. Let's begin with the most common question I receive when it comes to a plant-based diet. I bet you can guess what it is...

Where Do I Get My Protein?

Picture a 400-pound gorilla. What does he eat to grow that strong, muscular body? Leaves, stems, roots, seeds, and fruit (okay, and maybe the occasional insect that lives on those foods). But animals like him — giraffes, rhinos, horses, and even cows, when fed their natural diet — grow incredible muscle and athletic ability from plants. Humans can, too. There are even entire websites dedicated to plant-based athletes of all kinds. ThriveForward.com, NoMeatAthlete.com, and VeganBodyBuilding.com, to name a few.

Protein helps form enzymes, hormones, antibodies, and new tissues. It replaces old cells with shiny new ones, and it transports important nutrients in and out of those cells. The human body can manufacture all but 9 of the 22 amino acids that make up proteins. These 9 amino acids are known as "essential" amino acids, and therefore must be derived from what we eat. When a food contains all essential amino acids, it's considered a complete protein. Protein plays many key roles in the way our bodies function, but you need a lot less than you may think.

A FEW PLANT-BASED
SOURCES OF PROTEIN

Raw Hemp Seeds

24 grams per ½ cup

Raw Pumpkin Seeds

19 grams per ½ cup

Cooked Lentils

18 grams per cup

Raw Almonds

16 grams per ½ cup

Cooked Black Beans

15 grams per cup

Cooked Amaranth

9 grams per cup

Cooked Forbidden Rice

9 grams per cup

Cooked Quinoa

8 grams per cup

Cooked Buckwheat

6 grams per cup

Green Peas

8 grams per cup

Avocado

3 grams per cup

Broccoli

3 grams per cup

Sweet Potato

2 grams per cup

Blackberries

2 grams per cup

Almond Butter

5 grams per
2 tablespoons

A PLANT-BASED PROTEIN-RICH DAY

Breakfast

Cereal made with ½ cup cooked amaranth, ½ cup cooked quinoa, 2 tablespoons almonds, ½ cup berries, and 2 tablespoons hemp seeds
19 grams protein

Snack

Apple with 2 tablespoons almond butter
6 grams protein

Lunch

Collard wrap with 1 cup buckwheat, ½ cup black beans, ½ cup avocado, ¼ cup cilantro, ½ cup greens, and ¼ cup pumpkin seeds
25 grams protein

Snack

1 cup snap peas and ½ cup lentil dip
14 grams protein

Dinner

½ cup steamed sweet potato, 1 cup broccoli, and ½ cup sautéed kale served over 1 cup Forbidden Rice
15 grams protein

That's 79 grams of protein right there.

TRY THE FOLLOWING PROTEIN-PACKED RECIPES:

"Cinnamon Toast" Quinoa Cereal page 179

Lentil & Quinoa Tacos page 237

Believe it or not, the S.A.D. is too *high* in protein, and according to the Physician's Committee for Responsible Medicine, the excess can lead to a number of serious health problems.

Kidney Disease: When people overingest protein, they take in more nitrogen than they need. This excess strains the kidneys, which must expel extra nitrogen through urine. Folks with kidney disease are usually encouraged to eat low-protein diets since it reduces excess levels of nitrogen.

Cancer: Although fat is the dietary substance most often singled out for increasing cancer risk, protein also plays a role. Folks who eat meat regularly are at an increased risk for colon cancer, and researchers believe that the fat, protein, carcinogens, and absence of fiber in meat all play key roles. The 1997 report of the World Cancer Research Fund and American Institute for Cancer Research, Food, Nutrition, and the Prevention of Cancer noted that meaty, high-protein diets were linked to certain cancers.

Osteoporosis and Kidney Stones: Diets rich in animal protein promote risk of osteoporosis since they increase calcium excretion through the kidneys. Countries with lower-protein diets have lower rates of osteoporosis and hip fractures. Increased calcium excretion increases risk for kidney stones.

Nearly all plant-based foods contain protein, and nearly all forms of protein contain all protein-forming amino acids in some quantity. If we eat a variety of nutrient-rich, whole foods, our body will work its magic to store what it needs to function optimally. Eat a colorful assortment of grains, nuts, seeds, veggies, and fruit every day and we'll get what we need.

Use this formula as a helpful guide: In the United States, the Dietary Reference Intake (DRI) for protein is 0.36 per pound of body weight (which is 0.8 to 1.0 grams of protein per kilogram of body weight). Weight x 0.36 = protein grams per day. For example, if someone weighs 140 pounds, they need about 50 grams of protein a day. And approximately 10 – 20 percent of our total calories should be from protein sources.

Don't I Need Dairy for Calcium?

As you may have heard, we need calcium to build and maintain healthy bones and teeth, but we also need it for blood to clot, for cell membrane function, for nerve conduction, for muscle contraction, and for regulation of enzymes.[2] The National Institutes of Health (NIH) reports that the average adult fella or lady between the ages of 19 and 55 needs 1,000 mg of calcium per day, while kiddos can need only 800 mg per day. Teens, pregnant or nursing moms, and seniors can require 1,200 mg per day.[3]

Billions of dollars are spent by the meat and dairy industries to convince us that we need milk to build strong bones and animal protein for a healthy body. And they use scare tactics, too: When we hear "osteoporosis," what words come to mind? If you said "calcium" and "milk," then the American Dairy Association has done its job well.

The fact is that science doesn't support these claims. Animal products are actually incredibly acid forming in the body, and regular consumption actually

Let's use the average daily requirement to demonstrate that we can get more than enough calcium from plant-based sources.[5]

A FEW PLANT-BASED SOURCES OF CALCIUM

Cooked Collard Greens

268 mg per cup

Dried Figs

241 mg per cup

Chia Seeds

205 mg per 2 tablespoons

Cooked Turnip Greens

197 mg per 1 cup

Sesame Seeds

176 mg per 2 tablespoons

Cooked Mustard Greens

165 mg per 1 cup

Cooked Cannellini Beans

161 mg per 1 cup

Hummus

122 mg per 1 cup

Cooked Amaranth

116 mg per 1 cup

Raw Kale

100 mg per cup

Almonds

96 mg per ¼ cup

Blackstrap Molasses

82 mg per 2 tablespoons

A PLANT-BASED CALCIUM-RICH DAY

Breakfast

Cereal made with 1 cup cooked amaranth, 2 tablespoons chia seeds, and milk made with ½ cup hemp seed and 2 tablespoons molasses
434 mg calcium

Snack

½ cup hummus, ½ cup broccoli florets, and ½ cup snap peas
104 mg calcium

Lunch

Salad with 1 cup massaged kale, ½ cup dried figs, ¼ cup almonds, 1 tablespoon sesame seeds
405 mg calcium

Snack

Green smoothie made with 1 cup raw mustard greens, 1 pear, ¼ cup cilantro
83 mg calcium

Dinner

One pot dinner made with 1 cup cooked collards, 1 cup cannellini beans, and spices
429 mg calcium

That's over 1,450 mg. More than enough.

TRY THE FOLLOWING CALCIUM-PACKED RECIPES:

Simple Hummus
page 273

Fig & Caramelized Onion Tart page 239

Shiitake
Mushroo[...]

promotes calcium loss from bones. I mentioned this before when I talked about inflammation. See, calcium is found primarily in the bones — it's alkaline, and in an effort to balance an acidic bloodstream, it leaves the bones. After years of this attempt to regulate acidity, diseases like osteoporosis, arthritis, and even cancer emerge.

> *It's interesting (and no coincidence) that the countries that consume the most cow's milk and its by-products also have the highest bone fracture rates.*

In a 1992 study authored by researchers at Yale University School of Medicine, it was found that 70 percent of bone fracture rate was attributable to the consumption of animal protein.[4] And *The China Study* discovered that in rural China, where 90 percent of the protein consumed comes from vegetable sources, the bone fracture incidence is only one-fifth that of the U.S.

Yes, we can get calcium from cow's milk, but we can get all the calcium we need from plants, without the hormones, the antibiotics, and the acid-forming, disease-promoting effects that come with dairy.

Giving up cheese is the biggest hurdle for many of us when it comes to ditching dairy products. I hear "I could never give up cheese" often, and I used to say it myself. Blame it on casomorphines, which are actually Mother Nature's way of bonding mother with infant during nursing. Casomorphines are protein fragments derived from the digestion of the milk protein casein. As casein breaks down in the stomach, it produces trace amounts of morphine, a highly addictive opiate. It creates a normal bond for nursing babies (a calming "milk drunk" effect), but

What About Vitamin D?

Vitamin D and calcium work together to build bones. Vitamin D is essential for calcium absorption, but currently 70 – 90 percent of Americans are lacking in vitamin D, so we need to get enough.[8] Vitamin D is actually a hormone that our body creates when the sun's rays reach our skin cells. About 15 – 20 minutes' worth of pure rays on sunscreen-free chest and arms, three times a week, gives us what we need. But for those far from the equator, or those who cannot benefit from the sun during winter months, we should supplement with plant-based sublingual forms of vitamin D (made from mushrooms).

Mushrooms are a good source of vitamin D and according to mycologist (fungi biologist) Paul Stamets, vitamin D levels in mushrooms can actually be increased by exposing them to sunlight. By placing shiitake mushrooms (gills-up) in the sun 6 hours a day for two days (don't go longer than this or you risk UV overexposure, which can reduce levels — ah, balance), Stamets increased the vitamin D levels from 100 IU/100 grams to 46,000 IU/100 grams! His mushrooms tested a year after exposure still preserved a significant amount of vitamin D. Fresh, homegrown, and even dry mushrooms all respond to sunlight. So try it.

causes an addiction for adults who consume dairy.[6] Casomorphines also act as a histamine releaser — which could explain why so many of us are allergic to dairy.[7]

Carbs Are Your Friends

Carbohydrates are misunderstood, and in some cases downright feared. When most of us think of them, we imagine processed, starchy foods like doughnuts and boxed cereal. Those carbs are processed, harmful, and yes, should be avoided. But carbs from whole plant-based sources provide us with essential fiber and energy (the kind the brain can use) and they actually help us maintain a healthy body weight. They also provide us with health-boosting nutrients galore. Refined carbs (the kind that should instill fear) have had the fiber, protein, vitamins, and minerals removed during processing.

Keep in mind, there are two categories for carbs: simple and complex.

Complex carbs contain three or more sugars (long chain) and can be found in the starch and cellulose of plants, which makes them a fantastic source of fiber. Brown rice, butternut squash, quinoa, buckwheat, beans, lentils, and sweet potatoes are tasty examples of complex carbs — they deliver sustained energy. The starch and fiber that make up these foods helps control blood sugar, lower cholesterol, fill you up, and reduce fat storage.

Simple carbs are made up of one or two sugars (short chain). Natural sources include fruits of all kinds, and unnatural sources include those doughnuts mentioned above — they all deliver quick energy. But whole fruit is the way to go because it provides incredible nutritional value — fiber, phyto-chemicals, antioxidants, vitamins, and minerals. Processed carbohydrates lose most if not all of their fiber and nutritional value many times over during their time at the manufacturing facility.[9]

What About Iron?

There are two types of iron — heme (the kind found in animal foods) and non-heme (the kind found in plant foods). And while heme iron can be better absorbed into the body than non-heme —hang on, don't fret if you're 100 percent plant-based — there are a few things you can do to increase absorption from plant foods. Start by eating iron-rich goodness like lentils and beans, grains like oats and quinoa, nuts and seeds, dark leafy greens, and even molasses and prunes. Also, eating these iron-rich foods with vitamin C foods increases their absorption. So now may be a good time to invest in a cast-iron skillet, which will fortify your foods with beneficial iron. You also want to avoid drinking tea and coffee with iron-rich foods since tannins can block iron absorption.

Fiber Is a Friend, Too

When we think of fiber, we should think of legumes, veggies, and fruit because those are the ways Mother Nature intended for us to get the benefits. If capsules and powders popped into your head instead, there are a few marketing companies out there doing a fabulous job. I bet they also work on those dairy campaigns.

Fiber 101[10]

Fiber is divided into two camps: soluble or insoluble.

Soluble Fiber: Absorbs liquid, turning into a mucilaginous substance that beneficial intestinal bacteria love. Psyllium husk (which you'll see in action as an ingredient in the EAT section), chia seeds, oats, legumes, and berries are examples of soluble fiber. Eat them and not only feel full faster, but regulate blood sugar and lower cholesterol, too.

Insoluble Fiber: Helps to remove toxins from the body and improves digestion and bowel health. It doesn't dissolve, so it adds bulk to toxins that are being removed from the body. It creates productive, healthy bowel movements (which we should be having one to two times a day, at least). Asparagus, celery, nuts, and whole, gluten-free grains like quinoa are excellent sources of insoluble fiber.

Fiber can't operate solo. When upping fiber intake, increase your water intake, too. Water keeps fiber flowing through your body and bowels. How much do you need to drink? We're all different. Some of us eat a lot of raw foods, which contain loads of water, and some of us only get water with coffee through the day. Some folks sit at a desk all day. Some people sweat thanks to two workouts a day. Try dividing your body weight by 2 and drink at least that many ounces of water a day.

Many Americans are chronically constipated, so many pretty much know that fiber supplements taste blech. (FYI, they can be made of ground-up cellulose — aka wood pulp — so there's a reason they taste that way.) And laxatives can turn us into bloated, crampy prisoners since they tend to be habit-forming, which leaves the colon dependent on them for regularity. In general, that's no way to live life. Would you rather get fiber from drinking a beige, flavorless, gelatinous glass of pulp or by enjoying a big, bright, warm bowl of veggie soup flavored with vibrant spices like cumin and coriander? Thought so.

Fiber (again, only found in plant foods) doesn't just boost our digestive health — it curbs cravings by regulating blood sugar levels, it enhances weight loss and prevents colorectal cancer, it removes heavy metals like mercury from the system, and it even flushes excess sex hormones from the body.[11] It literally prevents and reverses disease by soaking up and sweeping out toxins — like our own internal cleaning experts.

Fat

Even looking at the word fills us with dread. We're conditioned.

Like carbohydrates, fat has fallen victim to reductionist fad dieting and marketing hoopla.

We're a confused lot when it comes to fat. Olive oil or no olive oil? Fish-oil capsules for omegas or not? What about coconut oil, isn't that a saturated fat?

We need fat to function optimally — just the whole-food kind. Fat is a major source of energy, and it helps the body assimilate nutrients like fat-soluble vitamins and minerals, and phytochemicals like carotenoids. Evidence is also beginning to show that where a fat came from is more important than the amount consumed (or not consumed). Fats derived from whole plant foods protect health, while fats from animal products and processed vegetable oils are more strongly associated with chronic disease.[12]

The Mayo Clinic breaks it down like this: saturated fat and trans fat are two types that are potentially harmful dietary fats. And monounsaturated and polyunsaturated are two potentially beneficial dietary fats. Of course, some studies out there contradict these guidelines, but for the most part, it's a solid starting point.

Saturated fat comes primarily from animal sources and is known to raise LDL cholesterol levels (the bad cholesterol), which can lead to heart disease and diabetes.

Trans fat can occur naturally in meat and dairy, but most is synthetic, created by manipulating unsaturated fats with the process of hydrogenation. Hydrogenation forces the unsaturated fats to accept additional hydrogen atoms to become partially saturated. Food manufacturers do it to extend shelf life and stability of a product. By now you know, when food doesn't perish, it's a beaming indicator that it's not food. Partially hydrogenated oils don't exist in nature, which is why their consumption leads to a host of degenerative diseases. Trans fats, in general, raise bad cholesterol (LDL), lower good cholesterol (HDL), and promote cardiovascular disease.

Monounsaturated fat is a kind you want, and it can be found in a variety of foods like avocados, nuts, olives, and their oils. Studies show that these fats can improve cholesterol levels, which decreases your risk for heart disease. They may also regulate blood sugar, which is helpful for diabetics.

Polyunsaturated fat is required for growth, reproduction, skin function, cholesterol metabolism, and cellular communication, and lucky for us, it's found primarily in plant foods.[13] These fats regulate cholesterol levels in the blood, decrease the risk of diabetes, and can lower blood pressure. You may have heard about essential fatty acids (EFAs) like omega-3s and omega-6s. They're especially beneficial and essential. Since our bodies cannot produce them, we need to get them from our diet, but in a healthy ratio. Omega-6 is commonly found in animal products and processed foods, so Americans consume an excessive amount. Disproportionate amounts of omega-6 can throw hormones out of whack, and that can actually lead to inflammation and disease. An ideal ratio of omega-6 to omega-3 is 4:1.[14] Try balanced, healthful plant-based sources including flax seeds, hemp seeds, chia seeds, walnuts, pumpkin seeds, and their oils. Cauliflower, leafy green vegetables, seaweeds, hummus, even Brussels sprouts contain good amounts of EFAs. And surprisingly, a "weed" that probably grows in your garden, yard, or the local park every summer called purslane also contains omega-3s — and it's delicious.

Overall, I like to get beneficial fats from whole food sources as much as possible.

My only exceptions are cold-pressed oil from a nut or seed for baking, salad dressings, and sautéing.

What about Coconut Oil?

There's a great debate out there in Healthy Land that you may have heard about: Coconut oil — one of the only plant-based sources of saturated fat — has created quite a stir. Some experts tout its incredible benefits (increases energy, reduces LDL cholesterol, has beneficial antibacterial qualities, reduces inflammation) while some say it's just as bad for you as lard (clogs arteries and promotes cardiovascular disease). The majority of the debate is the fact that coconut oil is composed primarily of unusual fatty acids called medium-chain triglycerides (MCTs), which scientific study demonstrates do not negatively impact cholesterol levels.[15] Their chemical structure is actually easily digested by our bodies. See, most fats are broken down in the intestine and restructured into a form that can be transported in the blood. But MCTs are absorbed intact and taken to the liver, where they are used directly for energy. In this sense, they are processed very similarly to carbohydrates.[16]

Studies have demonstrated that, yes, processed (refined) coconut oil can elevate LDL (bad cholesterol) — but the oil used in those studies contained trans fats, and by now, we all know what those do to our health.[17] Unrefined virgin coconut oil, however, has proved to not elevate LDL (and it has shown to elevate beneficial HDL).[18] Its polyphenol properties (health-boosting antioxidants) may even reduce LDL cholesterol.[19]

The jury, though, is still out. And every *body* is different. So use this conflicting information as an opportunity to find out what works for you. I know many people who exercise four to five days a week and haven't eaten animal products for years and years, but still struggle with high LDL levels. Culprits for increased cholesterol can be genetic and even stress, which, as certain studies have found, takes a toll and increases LDL cholesterol.[20] It even turns out that excessive sitting and sleep deprivation (which is as American as cheeseburgers and fries) makes the body think it's sick, which can weaken the immune system, increase inflammation, mess with hormones, and increases total blood cholesterol.[21, 22, 23]

Get bloodwork done with a trusted professional and see how your body reacts to unrefined, virgin coconut oil. There really is no other way to be more sure.

Many of the recipes in this book call for coconut oil, but almost all of them can be prepared without it.

Every time there's a chance to use an alternative, I will share it with you. That way, no matter where you land in the great coconut oil debate, you can enjoy delicious plant-based meals!

Sleep — Give Your Body a Chance to Rejuvenate

I cannot express enough what a difference getting quality sleep will make in your life. I used to be the quintessential night owl, finding my greatest moments of creativity and energy from 11 P.M. to 2 A.M. For years, I partied late and worked late. Case in point: I had a job for ten years where the culture was built upon it — 2 A.M. worknights for months on end was the norm.

Our bodies are wired to protect us from threats, and it can't tell the difference between a predatory lion about to pounce or an unrealistic deadline at work. Both trigger our fight-or-flight response, and biologically, the reaction is the same. When we're confronted with a threat (a barking dog or an aggressive boss), our adrenal glands release a surge of hormones, including adrenaline and cortisol, to prepare us. Adrenaline's job is to increase heart rate, elevate blood pressure, and boost energy supplies. Cortisol (the primary stress hormone) increases sugars in the bloodstream, enhances the brain's use of glucose, and increases the availability of substances that repair tissues. Cortisol also curbs functions that would be non-essential or detrimental in a fight-or-flight situation. It alters immune system responses and puts the digestive system on lockdown. Ever notice how right before you have to give a big nerve-wracking presentation, you have to hit the bathroom? Or how after a month-long stretch of late nights at the office, right when you're finally going on vacation, you get a "cold"? It's no coincidence. Cortisol also puts a halt on the reproductive system and growth processes.[24] There's no time for making babies or growing when you have to outrun a lion (or meet that deadline).

> *The body is well equipped to prepare us for attack. But in modern times with all of our stress, we're chronically ready for attack, and it leads to all sorts of issues, even disease.*

Sleep is the body's time to rejuvenate. And if we didn't have electricity, television shows to watch, and work to be done 'round the clock, the sun would set and our tiny little pineal glands would kick out the "darkness hormone" melatonin, and we'd in turn get sleepy. Modern demands have us significantly disconnected from the natural circadian rhythm (our biological clock that responds to the sun rising and setting). When our circadian rhythm is out of whack, it can contribute to weight gain and premature aging (gray hair, wrinkles, achy joints) and make us more susceptible to disease.[25] Maybe that's why it's called beauty sleep.

The importance of slowing down and getting quality sleep almost requires its own book, but in a nutshell, let's give our amazing bodies the time to repair and rebuild by getting enough rest. Be asleep by 10 P.M. and watch excess body fat melt off, achy joints disappear—you might even notice less gray hair on your head after a while.

Probiotics

Antibiotics are overprescribed for humans and livestock (used to keep sick cows alive), and they do just what the name says — they kill all bacteria (the friendly with the unfriendly). This is one of the primary reasons why we can't fight off issues like yeast infections, rashes, acne, or colds and flu.

Save Money, Stay Healthy, and Have Fun Making Homemade Cultured Foods

Learn how to make health-boosting probiotic foods easily at home — everything from non-dairy yogurt and kimchi to kombucha — by visiting **yumuniverse.com/tag/fermented-foods.**

When the good guys are few, the bad guys can thrive. Just one dose of antibiotics can wipe out our bacterial system, and it can take years to build back up again. This is why, once we get on the antibiotic train, we can stay ill for months — our system is left with no protectors. We're defenseless and susceptible to more illness.

Bacteria can be our friends. Stay with me. There is such a thing as good bacteria, and instead of wiping them all out, we need to create a non-clinical place for the good guys to dominate. See, the idea of establishing balance also applies to your gut and its microscopic inhabitants. It's funny, but I always picture the rumble scene from *The Outsiders* when I discuss this topic. In my mind, the Greasers are the good guys — misunderstood and doing their best in small numbers to protect their territory — letting the Socs (in my mind, the bad bacteria) know who's boss. If given a chance, the Greasers will prove that they're loyal, caring, and lovable despite the unfair stereotypes.

These beneficial bacteria are known as probiotics, and they're tough stuff — boosting immunity, fighting inflammation, aiding digestion, and bringing the body into harmony so it can prevent and heal from disease. Good and bad bacteria should naturally coexist in our gut — it keeps life (and books and movies) interesting — but we want the good guys to outnumber the bad guys for vibrant health (that happy ending).

Now, the dairy industry pushes yogurt for probiotics, but since the milk is heat pasteurized, the likelihood of having live probiotics is slim. Excessive heat kills life, even the kind we can't see. With yogurt, you also get all of the acid-forming, heath-diminishing qualities of dairy. Instead, buy probiotic capsules or powders in the refrigerated section of the health food store. If refrigerated, odds are better that they are alive and ready to rumble. Cultured and fermented foods are another way to get probiotics into our systems. It's fun and easy to culture foods like spicy kimchi, sauerkraut, miso, kombucha tea, coconut kefir yogurt, and coconut kefir water. Many of these items can be purchased at the health food store, too. Try them all and go to town — you can't consume too much.

B_{12}

B_{12} is an essential nutrient for us humans. It's vital for metabolism, brain health, and keeping the body's nerve and blood cells healthy, and it even helps make DNA. If you're not consuming animal products, and even if you are (meat-eaters can become deficient), making sure we are getting enough vitamin B_{12} is critical for health. The body can store B_{12} in the liver for years, but deficiency in the long term can lead to dementia, anemia, even blindness. But here's the kicker: B_{12} is only found in animal products and fortified foods.

So, if a plant-based diet is so wonderful, why is an essential nutrient like B_{12} unavailable from anything that grows in the ground? Well, bacteria are the only known organisms that manufacture vitamin B_{12} (by converting cobalt salts). And if you read my bit about probiotics above, it could very well be that we live in antiseptic, germophobic times, where even our agricultural soil quality is sterile. The organisms that make B_{12} live in soil and water, and animals can get B_{12} by eating food and soil contaminated with these microorganisms. If we grew food in rich soil, as we once did, we'd also likely get B_{12}.

But you don't have to get your B_{12} by consuming animal products that come with the host of health-diminishing returns. You just have to be smart and proactive about getting B_{12} from quality alternative sources.

Kombu
(Kelp)

> *Whether you're an omnivore or an herbivore, many of us have digestive issues, and this makes B_{12} assimilation a little trickier.*

So, while certain foods are B_{12} fortified, and spirulina and seaweeds contain B_{12}, the jury is still out on whether their B_{12} is bioavailable (meaning, the body can use it).[26] The truth is, there's still quite a bit that science has yet to discover about B_{12}, and what little is known is uncertain. Still, there are many opinions about plant-based sources for B_{12}. Studies show that most of the popular blue-green algae used by many people as supplements predominantly contain pseudovitamin B_{12}, which is unfortunately inactive in humans. Dried green and purple nori, on the other hand, contain substantial amounts of bioavailable vitamin B_{12}, and so do various types of tea, like fermented kombucha. Evidence has also demonstrated that vegans who consumed chlorella and nori had serum vitamin B_{12} concentrations twice as high as those not consuming algae.[27] Bioavailable B_{12} can also be found in fortified non-dairy milks, cereals, nutritional yeast, and energy bars. Just make sure these products are free of any junk, preservatives, or artificial blech.

Recommended amounts of B_{12} vary depending on what expert is doing the recommending: anywhere from 2.4 micrograms to a mere .01 – .25 micrograms a day seems to be the average.[28] If you choose to supplement, find a sublingual (placed under the tongue) form of methylcobalamin B_{12}, because it can be absorbed more directly into the bloodstream. Methylcobalamin B_{12} is the pre-methylated form (a form the body recognizes) that exists in nature. What you should avoid is cyanocobalamin, a pharmaceutical form of B_{12} with cyanide (that's right, poison) added to stabilize the molecules. And it needs to be converted to methylcobalamin before it's absorbed into the body anyway. The cyanocobalamin form is easier to find because it's less expensive to produce. It's the B_{12} most physicians prescribe, but it's not bioavailable for humans.[29]

How do we know we're getting enough B_{12}? Until more substantial studies are performed, get your blood work done. Ramp up some of the bioavailable B_{12} options listed here, and then compare future blood levels to see how you're doing.

Take it seriously, be proactive and responsible about it.

To Soy or Not to Soy?

Soy is a controversial health food, a contentious commodity crop, a debated piece in the animal welfare puzzle, and a disputed petroleum-based product substitute. And even though it's a health food with substantial science-based evidence behind it, the love-soy-it's-good and don't-love-soy-it's-bad camps remain pretty divided.

Proponents of soy champion the cholesterol-lowering benefits, high-quality protein, and cancer-prevention potential. On the other side of the fence, opponents make a compelling case that any health benefits are completely lost in processing, and that soy is one of our most genetically modified foods (along with corn), and it causes all manner of health issues, including digestive complications, thyroid dysfunction, cognitive decline, reproductive disorders, heart disease, and cancer.

Soy challengers also claim that it's high in a health-compromising compound called phytic acid, which can obstruct the absorption of beneficial nutrients leading to malnutrition. Phytic acid is found in pseudograins like quinoa, nuts, and legumes, but soaking reduces and neutralizes the acid in these ingredients (see Section 2). Soybeans, however, have to be fermented to become bioavailable, so soaking alone doesn't work.

Epidemiological, clinical, and laboratory studies into soy consistently contradict each other. Some research demonstrates that the isoflavones (plant estrogens) in soy can interfere with our endocrine system and hormone balance when consumed in large quantities (like we do on the S.A.D.). Excessive soy in the diet has been linked to reduced fertility in women, early puberty, and even male breast development, while other studies show that a lower, more balanced consumption of phyto-estrogens can actually have the opposite effect.[33, 34, 35, 36]

Minimally processed organic, fermented soy-based products (like tempeh) can be helpful transition foods for those who want to reduce their consumption of animal products. There's no doubt about that. And the benefits that come with the fermented options can be great. But it's so easy to overdo it with soy. And we don't want that; we want variety.

Which camp am I in? You won't find recipes using soy in this book because I'm convinced that it's an allergen for me and thousands of others. I'm interested in developing recipes that everyone can enjoy. Soy tends to be a crutch ingredient in the animal-free recipe world, too. Hey, I get it, the price tag is low, it's versatile, and it's easy to use in loads of recipes. But I think we're suffering from soy overkill.

Soy & Hexane

According to a report from the Cornucopia Institute, an "all-natural" energy bar and a certified organic energy bar may look like twins to us (with the exception of price), but if we were to look closely at how the soy ingredients were manufactured, we'd more than likely opt for the certified organic. See, most conventional soy oils and proteins are made using hexane, a by-product of gasoline refining. It's a neurotoxin and a hazardous air pollutant that soybean processors use as a cheap, efficient solvent to extract the oil from soybeans.[30, 31, 32] Federal law prohibits companies who manufacture certified organic foods from using hexane. "Natural," and "all-natural" foods, however, are free to use the polluting neurotoxin petrochemical hexane, and they do so in the spirit of "cheap and easy."

While scientists, doctors, and experts battle (for years, no doubt) over the benefits and dangers of soy, I want to enjoy meals now without the worry.

Remember, the further we get away from the whole soybean, the more trouble we can get into when it comes to health. Miso and soybean oil couldn't be more different despite what the marketing claims say.

Keeping It Simple Is Smart Stuff

As much as I'd like to live to be a spunky centenarian, I have to be honest and admit that I may not. I grew up in a family of smokers. I partied a lot. I've spent more of my life eating crap than the good stuff. Like most folks, I've been surrounded by environmental toxins and emotional stressors from birth. But I care about myself. So, no matter what lies ahead, I can say with great conviction that my life became more rich and exciting when I became plant-inspired. I've experienced the beauty of the body's ability to heal itself and I believe in this approach to wellness. My mind is clear, my heart is happy, my body pain-free. I focus on balance, I eat a variety of foods, and I tune into my body. Every day, I discover something new and improve a bit more.

When it comes to wellness, the closer we stick to Mother Nature and our own intuition, the less noisy, complicated, and frustrating our journey will be. It'll be easier to find the day-to-day happiness we want. And we'll see clearly so we can take that next gutsy step forward.

Remember this: you're only really restricted by walls you build yourself. Don't be afraid of what you don't know; be curious enough to make its acquaintance. Don't believe the hype. Investigate, experiment, and embrace accountability. Take small steps, stay true to yourself, and unlock that power you have inside. It's pretty thrilling.

Dill Weed

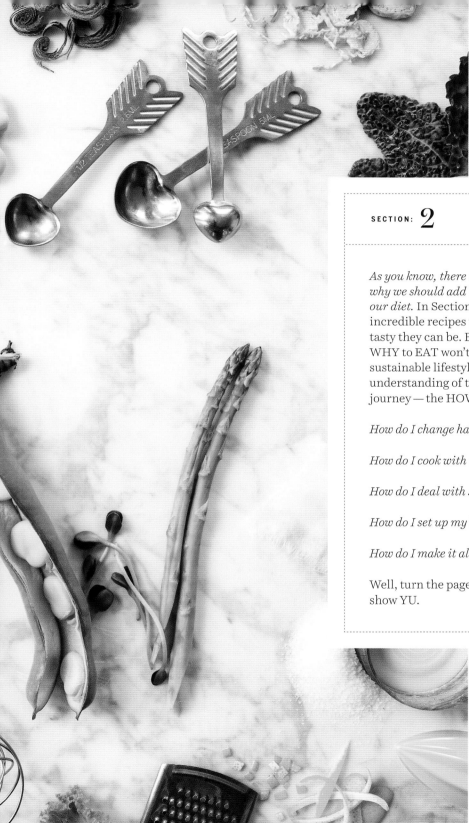

SECTION: 2   *How*

As you know, there are many reasons why we should add more plants to our diet. In Section 3, we'll dive into incredible recipes that prove how tasty they can be. But going from WHY to EAT won't translate into a sustainable lifestyle without an understanding of the heart of this journey — the HOW.

How do I change habits?

How do I cook with new ingredients?

How do I deal with social situations?

How do I set up my kitchen?

How do I make it all work?

Well, turn the page, love, and I'll show YU.

New Adventure, New Outlook

Let's imagine the WHY is a stunning riverside path. When you look across the river, you see another good-lookin' pathway — that's the EAT. You can't simply jump from one to the other though, right?

You'll need a reliable bridge to get to-and-fro. That bridge is HOW. You can know why you want to start a wellness journey and you can collect the recipes you want to try, but building a solid path of understanding to travel along needs to be done plank by plank, lesson by lesson, discovery by discovery.

I remember the very first "healthy" cookbook I bought (Jennifer Cornbleet's *Raw Food Made Easy*). The first time I used dates to make one of her recipes, I left the pits in them. I almost broke my pricey blender. But I didn't know that dates had pits since I had never eaten one. Lesson learned! (Shortly after, I wrote a post about how to pit dates.) Here's another. My grandmother made an incredible chocolate cake — the stuff of local legend. Back when I was a newbie herbivore, I thought I could prepare her recipe simply by swapping coconut flour for white flour. And why not use stevia in place of sugar and omit the eggs? (Hey, experienced vegan bakers, are you laughing yet? I am.) Taken from the oven, my cake deflated like a sad balloon and then crumbled into dust when I tried to cut a piece. I actually looked around the room, wondering if the spirit of my dear departed grandma was witnessing this disgrace. The taste? If licorice and aspartame had a baby… And the sweetness level was off-the-charts intense. Hundreds of baking experiments later, I now know how to make a proper gluten-free, plant-based chocolate cake (page 290).

So my goal with this section is to spare you some blunders, save you some money, and help you maximize your time by sharing what I've learned along the way. Get to building that wellness bridge, folks; I've got some sturdy planks to share.

Embrace Imperfection

First off, let's say a big "no thanks" to the idea of doing this plant-based lifestyle thing perfectly. Because we can't, and we shouldn't try. When we strive for perfection, we miss out on the beautiful details of the journey because we're so focused on some nebulous future outcome. We also fuel unnecessary self-esteem issues along the way. When we strive to be flawless, we're basically saying to ourselves, "I'm not good enough and something's wrong with me, so I have to work harder, faster, and better and then I'll matter." I'll say this: you matter now. We're all imperfect. You deserve health and happiness without the pressure of "perfection."

Imperfection is the perfectly wonderfully way to live. The Japanese have another world view that I'm fond of — *wabi-sabi* — which means finding beauty in imperfection. Lord knows, we've got that beautifulness in all of us.

Be nice to yourself and embrace the vulnerability that comes with this journey — the snafus, the failures, and the unexpected victories. Those moments are where we'll truly grow and learn. And there is no perfect time to start. Read that sentence again. Waiting for the "perfect" time to begin making changes is the same as making excuses. Life is always going to throw a curveball. There will always be a birthday party with cake, unexpected meetings with treats on the table, late nights, rude people, traffic jams, vacations that (delightfully) take you away from your routine, and lack of time. We can choose to let them empower us or disempower us, remember? We need to accept and learn how to dance with these realities instead letting them get in our way.

If you want to achieve your health goals, start with a promise to be kind to yourself on this wellness adventure — that includes letting go of unrealistic, insecurity-feeding expectations. There's nothing wrong with you, especially if things go differently than planned. And there's no better time to start than now.

They're Not Mistakes, They're Opportunities

I'm gonna give it to you straight. I won't say everything's easy on this journey, but I can tell you with great confidence that it's worth it. The sooner you embrace the fact that blunders are just as important (and frequent) as the triumphs, the easier it will be to take that first step and feel great about it. All adventures have bumps in the road. They're what make the trip special, memorable, and exciting.

When my brother and I were in our 20s, we were insatiable road-trip junkies. We'd fly to Seattle (my suitcase filled mostly with mix CDs), rent a car, and spend weeks driving back to Chicago, crisscrossing the wonders of Idaho, Montana, Wyoming, and South Dakota. We'd follow dusty roads to a one-horse town for a legendary Huckleberry Milkshake. Or we'd drive along snowy, guardrail-less fjords in Norway, singing "Judy Is a Punk" instead of paying attention to the (definitely wrong) road we were traveling along. We'd head north for the weekend to explore Canada. Or south, to see a band — or three — in Nashville, Tennessee. When we reminisce about those times, it's not about what we had planned (I doubt either of us can even remember that). We recall with joy the miscalculated turns, the surprises, the derailments, the adventure. Our detours made the biggest impressions and led to our greatest discoveries. Making the uncharted something familiar is what makes the story. And, excitingly, when we were at our most vulnerable was when we felt the most alive.

That speck is me.

I know the daunting thoughts you think when starting your journey: *"I'm a terrible cook, what if I ruin a recipe?" "I don't think my family will hop on board." "I'm afraid to do this alone." "What if my coworkers make fun of me?" "What if I can't follow through?" "What will everyone think of me?"*

Going outside of our comfort zone isn't about learning how to squelch fear, because fear will always come along for the ride whether we like it or not.

But that's okay. A fearful reaction tells us how deeply this matters. In order to maintain momentum so that we achieve our goals, we need to get comfy with fear, dance with him like we do other perceived obstacles. Just put him in the backseat and turn up the good jams to drown out his jabbering when he gets to be too much. You can always take a peek in the rearview mirror to check if he's still there. Try to find comfort in that because if he weren't around, it would be a boring, meaningless ride. Most of the stuff we avoid — confrontation, starting new habits, having to explain our choices to folks at a dinner party — we avoid simply because we're afraid of being afraid. Go ahead and imagine the worst-case scenario. How would you deal with it? Probably like a champ, because it's usually not as bad as we make it out to be. If you avoid fear, you'll stay in neutral and stagnate. If you acknowledge fear, then you can shift into first gear.

Facts: You are going to stand out. So own it. You are going to screw up a recipe here and there. It's an opportunity to improvise and learn. You will have to be a tad selfish. Those who love you will understand (or soon witness that it was worth it). You are going to feel healthier and happier than you ever have before, which may be downright scary for those of us who are used to a lifetime of the opposite.

These feelings may be completely uncomfortable, but they're part of this ride — no way around it. Familiarity is reassuring, yes; but it's also boring and rut-inducing. The unknown is where extraordinary things are waiting for us. We may not be able to see what's ten miles ahead when we sit behind the wheel, but if we know where we want to go, and just keep driving forward, we'll get there no matter how many detours we take.

There is a crack in everything. That is how the light gets in.

—Leonard Cohen, singer-songwriter, musician, novelist

Baby Steppin'

Sometimes the smallest move in the right direction ends up being the smartest of our life. Inch a big toe forward and just take the step.

> *Maintain momentum by taking on change in manageable bites.*

It's easy to get excited and inspired, but once a goal is set, don't overdo it to the point where you burn out. Willpower is a lot like a muscle. It gets tired with overuse, it needs time to rebuild, and incremental change will make it stronger. Here's a great baby step: start by making a green smoothie every day and stick with that one simple addition. Do it until it becomes routine and pay attention to how you feel (or better yet, write about it your journal). After it's routine, maybe move on to replacing dairy milk with almond milk in your coffee and cereal. Stay committed, appreciate how far you've come, and be honest with yourself — deep down you know when you can take on more, when you are making excuses and when you are approaching burnout. If you are resenting the changes, that's a good sign to back off a bit. We all have different thresholds, emotional roadblocks, and habits that can be changed.

A Growing Garden of YU and Me

Humans are social creatures; we crave acceptance, we need to belong, and we need to matter. So when we deliberately walk away from the routines, rituals, and habits that we've known for decades, it's pretty scary stuff. The world is not set up to accept or nurture us plant-inspired folks quite yet — we're a minority — so we need each other more than ever.

As you read this book, know that someone else out there is reading it, too. Someone who wants to live a disease-free, happy life just like you do. Someone else who has questions, fears, victories to share, and challenges to overcome. Being health-minded can feel isolating at times, so I remind you that this journey (and any worthwhile journey) is always better shared with friends. It's why I created YumUniverse.com, and why I recommend that you reach out to our YU community when you need heartfelt support. It's there for us and I encourage you to participate. We can all learn something from what you have to share and no doubt, your question is one that many others want the answer to. So, ask.

Habits

For as long as I can remember, I've had a bad habit of chewing on the inside of my cheeks. It's awful, I know. As with any ingrained habit, though, I don't really realize when I'm doing it — it's automatic. So a while back, I decided to look into habits: why they're formed and how we can change them. Nowadays, I can see that I start nibbling when I am stressed or anxious. It's a coping strategy that's been with me since I was a kiddo. I'm still working on it, but understanding the cycle as it plays out helps me catch myself. And if I can catch myself, I can take a long, deep breath (which is what I really need) and stop stressing. This ability to pause and recognize is the key to habit adjustments of all kinds. Here's how it works.

From an evolutionary standpoint, the more quick and competent our decisions are, the more we increase our chance of survival. And habits are a neurological cycle designed to help us make efficient decisions. In *The Power of Habit,* Charles Duhigg explains that there's a series of three steps that lead to habit development:

(1) *You receive a cue.*

(2) *It triggers a behavior.*

(3) *That behavior results in a reward.*

We remember the reward, so it drives us to perform the behavior again when the cue arises. After enough repetition of a particular cycle, our brain can go on autopilot with these habits.

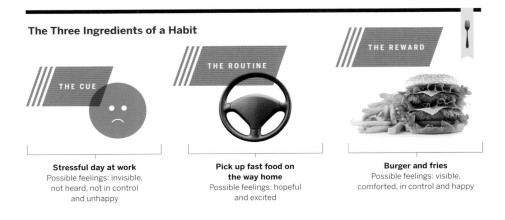

The Three Ingredients of a Habit

THE CUE

Stressful day at work
Possible feelings: invisible, not heard, not in control and unhappy

THE ROUTINE

Pick up fast food on the way home
Possible feelings: hopeful and excited

THE REWARD

Burger and fries
Possible feelings: visible, comforted, in control and happy

Dopamine is the maestro here. It's the feel-good chemical that's released in the brain when we succeed or, as the body sees it, do something that increases our odds of continued existence. It's responsible for desire, decision making, motivation, and memory creation. When we do something the brain perceives as "good," it rewards us with a pleasurable dopamine release, making us want to do it again and again. The more we perform this routine, the more dopamine the brain releases and the more ingrained the cycle becomes. It's a genius system, really. But this is why, even though we read the staggering statistics about our state of health and the dangers of processed foods, change is difficult. We're fighting our own intrinsic survival system, and modern times, modern food, modern drugs, and modern culture conspire to use it against us.

The power to change begins with understanding how this system works. If we're aware of what's happening, we can catch ourselves. So when that cue get tripped, the outcome can be different.

How to make change stick? In a nutshell, keep things simple and start with one habit you'd like to change. Not two habits, one habit.

Open a journal and write it down. In Duhigg's book, he uses an example that illustrates the habit loop well: stress sends an alcoholic to a bar, where the reward is the comfort of drinking with a community. When the habit loop is triggered with a recovering alcoholic, she goes to AA and the reward is attention and understanding from the community there instead.

Pay close attention to what's happening as the habit you want to change plays out, and make a note as the patterns and potential alternatives reveal themselves. What are the triggers for this habit? Does it always occur at a certain time of day? Does the cue come from a person? A location? A feeling? There can be multiple triggers, so write them all down.

How do you feel once you've reached the reward state of the habit cycle? Do you feel safe? Part of the group? In control? Is anxiety calmed? Were you able release pent-up emotion? Does it feel like an escape? Reward is pretty much why habits exist, so really think about this.

Truth time. What new routine could replace one of your old ones while still giving you a satisfactory — even magnificent — reward? You may have to try a few substitutions to see what sticks, but oftentimes you'll find that doing something nice for yourself is simply the self-care that you were looking for all long. It helps to identify potential obstacles before making changes, too. Preparation is powerful. List all obstacles in your journal and also write down how they'll be solved so they don't derail progress when hurdles arrive.

Making healthy improvements isn't only about changing habits that need changin'. It's also about establishing new actions and patterns. Attaching a new goal to an existing cue is a great way to build new daily patterns, minimize stress, and stay prepared. For example, when you walk into the bathroom to brush your teeth every night, leave a note on the mirror to soak some nuts and legumes in a bowl of water while you sleep. Match up that cue with the new routine. Bedtime becomes soak time. In the morning, you'll be rewarded with the gratifying relief of having food at the ready. This will make you happy and excited to cook. You'll be proud that you made the time to take care of yourself. That's a great reward, so the routine gets set.

Share with friends or your new support group what you're committed to changing. That way, you hold each other accountable each week (or daily, if that's what you need). Consistently check in and share what you've learned with each other through the process. And if anyone is feeling weak, make yourselves available to each other — a simple, quick text or IM can work wonders. Positive feedback is über important.

Planning 101

If something is important to us, we'll find a way; if not, we'll find an excuse. We have to be responsible for our action (or inaction), so when we say, "I don't have time to shop, prep foods, and cook in advance," we simply aren't making time. If we truly want to change our lives for the better, we have to reprioritize. Food is a relationship, and relationships take work. They also require forgiveness, connection, and honesty, or they fail. In order to achieve health goals, we have to let go of the conventional notion that cooking should always take 20 minutes or less. It can be, but not always. Get over it.

We have to give more power and respect to the goals we want most, instead of what we want in the moment.

◀ Maybe write this one out to post on your fridge, bathroom mirror, and/or office wall.

Use the schedule on the following pages as inspiration for planning and staying prepared all week long.

Plan & Stay Prepared

DAY 1   *10 – 20 minutes*

Choose a time of day to focus on writing up a meal plan for the week.

Look through favorite magazines and cookbooks. Try adding a few new plant-powerful recipes to your existing meal routine. You don't have to prepare a different recipe three times a day for seven days either. Leftovers are a reality, and keeping prepped individual ingredients on hand (like cooked or sprouted quinoa) means you can create multiple dishes with them each week (quinoa works in a savory wrap and a warm breakfast cereal).

Pick the breakfast recipes you'd like to try this week — smoothies (page 280), granola (page 168), chia pudding (page 164). Add a few lunch and dinner recipes — salads (page 223), soups (page 213), tacos (page 237). Toss in snacks like hummus (page 273), veggies, kale chips (page 33), and crackers (page 188). Write down the amounts needed for everything and double-check them before you leave the house to shop. It's what my carpenter friend told me: Measure twice, cut once.

Chickpeas
aka Garbanzo Beans

DAY 2   THE BIG DAY   *2 – 3 hours*

One day of the week could be dedicated to preparing for the rest of them.

I tend to go for the one big day — I think of it as my self-care day. I go into it knowing it will take time, and I have grown to love this day very much. Don't let anything interrupt your food prep time. If one whole day isn't possible, break up these suggestions into multiple days throughout the week.

Tomatillos

Carve out enough shopping time so you aren't rushing. You want to stroll down the aisles, not spin. If you take time, you can properly investigate labels, punch questions into your phone, and connect with your experience at the store. A mad rush just perpetuates the disconnection-from-ourselves-and-our-food problem. Think of it in relationship terms: if someone you care about was sharing important news with you and you just ran about the room, clearly focused on something else, it would be rude. So don't treat yourself that way. Now, I know how busy life can be, and sometimes I end up racing around the grocery store, too. But the intention is to set aside the one special day, so do your best to make this time for yourself to balance out the crazier times.

When you return home:

Organize & Store

Put on your favorite tunes and unpack the loot. Store produce, herbs, veggies, and other goods properly for maximum lifespan (see page 110 for tips).

Soak

Place the nuts, seeds, grains, and legumes you'll be using for recipes into bowls, fill with water, and soak (see page 138). Maybe even start one bowl for sprouts (see page 142).

Prepare

If I know I have a busy week ahead, I'll use this day to prepare dressings, sauces, and fresh ingredients, like lemon juice, in advance. It takes no time at all to juice a bunch of lemons and put them in an airtight jar in the fridge. One whole lemon will yield about ¼ cup juice and lasts for up to two weeks. Whip up a dressing recipe or two. Pre-mince garlic and store in an airtight glass container (1 clove = ½ teaspoon minced). Usually, during my unpacking, I get a tomato sauce, veggie stock, or non-dairy cheese sauce going as well. All of which are delicious quickly tossed with kale, sautéed veggies, cooked grains, and legumes in a pinch — no recipe necessary.

Peel, dice, and pre-chop vegetables or other ingredients you'll need in the next day or two if you anticipate being pressed for time that week. Think ahead for snacks, too. Cut celery and carrots into sizes for dips (squeeze with lemon juice to protect foods that oxidize quickly). Make a spice mix (page 202) that can easily be sprinkled on a salad or tossed with sautéed veggies.

While freezing can diminish nutrient quality a bit, it's better to have organic veggies and ingredients ready to use than not, so check out page 121 for freezing tips.

Turkey Fig

Mung Bean
Sprouts

DAYS $3-4$ *30 – 40 minutes*

These steps are interchangeable, so plug and play where it makes sense for your schedule.

Drain & Rinse

In the morning, rinse whatever you had soaking overnight. Cook what needs to be cooked, or place the rinsed and drained ingredients in an airtight container in the fridge to cook later. Soaked ingredients will keep in the fridge for about a week, maybe more, depending on the ingredient. Cashews perish sooner, while lentils can last for weeks — use your nose and eyes (Mother Nature's expiration detectors) to determine if all is okay to eat. If making sprouts, follow the sprouting instructions on page 142.

Prepare

If you haven't already, peel, dice, and chop root vegetables, onion, or other ingredients needed in the next day or so. Store them in an airtight glass container in the fridge. Toss more soakable ingredients into a bowl with water if you need to soak some more.

Cook

If some of your soaked ingredients have little tails on them, that's great! That means they are sprouting, which enhances the nutrient profile and digestibility. Taste them and keep them in the fridge as sprouts if you like them raw, or cook them (which will diminish nutrient quality a bit — heat does that). I like to keep cooked quinoa, beans, chickpeas, buckwheat, and lentils in the fridge for easy cereals, soups, and salads. If you make a new recipe or two, store leftovers and your soaked and cooked ingredients in the fridge in an airtight glass container, or freeze for weeks to come.

DAYS $5-7$ *30 – 40 minutes*

Prepare some tasty new recipes if you like, or take it easy and eat some delicious leftovers — you'll have some.

Pomegranate

Marjoram

20 – 40 minutes

Leave Room for Improvisation

There are many weeks where I don't have a plan at all. So when you're super busy, just soak something! I'll often grab a handful of legumes, grains, and nuts and toss them in a bowl to soak, not knowing what I'll do with them. This is planning at its best (leave notes around the house as reminders: "just soak something"). Since there's no plan, I may not have exactly what a recipe calls for when it's time to cook, but here's some good news: Most YumUniverse recipes (with the exception of baked goods) work just as well with alternate veggies, grains, nuts, seeds, and legumes from what the recipe asks for. This is where exploration comes in, the kind of "making do" that will build confidence in the kitchen.

In a pinch, rice, quinoa, and buckwheat can interchange in equal cooked amounts. So can beans, lentils, and chickpeas. Sunflower seeds and macadamia nuts are a great replacement for cashews in sauces (page 208). Nuts of all kinds can easily replace each other in everything from milks to baked goods like. Try the Quinoa "Cinnamon Toast" Cereal (page 179) with buckwheat, the Lentil, Kale & Quinoa Tacos (page 237) with chickpeas (just mash them a bit), or the Chinese Spice Pecans (page 206) with almonds and/or walnuts. Play. This is how to truly discover the ways certain flavors and textures work. Go ahead. Break rules.

Leftover Ingredients & Scraps

Is there one pepper, some mushrooms, and a small container of cooked quinoa in the fridge? Hop on YumUniverse.com, search for specific ingredients, and a whole bunch of recipes will come up that can incorporate those leftovers. When in doubt, sauté an onion and toss it with leftover ingredients for a simple one-pot meal. Season with spices (page 202), sauces (page 208), or simple salt and pepper. Be sure to reference page 122 for tips on using veggie scraps and how to extend shelf life of foods.

Making time for preparing and enjoying meals is making time for ourselves. Eat at the dinner table or outdoors in the sunshine for some vitamin D. Use that time as a break from the constant, disruptive stimulation of electronics. Wellness is about practice. Much like learning a new language, it seems foreign, exotic, uncomfy, and maybe even out of reach at first. But with each new word that we learn, we realize that we can do it. Each accomplishment creates excitement and fuels momentum. One day you'll be fluent in plant-inspired living. Understanding our habits, our bodies, and our potential will change as we continually polish and learn. This journey is about more than what we feed ourselves. It's about nurturing our spirit, too.

Plan Ahead Ideas

The world isn't set up to cater to the plant-powerful quite yet, but that doesn't mean that we have to fall into a victim role or end up lost and hungry when we're away from our kitchen.

If we go elsewhere and they're serving BBQ ribs and cookies but no greens or veggies, we need to recognize that whether we eat healthy or not is decided before we leave the house. It's not someone else's responsibility to feed us, it's ours. Same goes for a day full of errands. Either we choose to plan ahead, or not. Last-minute food decisions made out of desperation are rarely the kind that boost health. I've learned this one the hard way. When I tell myself "just this one time won't hurt," I usually end up feeling worse than I did when I was hungry. Bad food choices are never worth it. If you can remember your phone when you leave the house, you can remember to pack a snack before you head out the door. Try this: at least make one healthy choice to start the day, like drinking a green smoothie (page 280), so if you end up faceplanting into the cake at a bridal shower that afternoon, it's still progress.

I almost always grab some fruit, bottle up a green smoothie (page 280) or a plant protein shake, kale chips (page 33), or an energy bar (page 257) and take one of these two on-the-go recipes detailed here with me when I will be away from home for more than one hour. They keep just fine at room temperature for at least 4 – 8 hours (especially if your salad dressing contains an acid like vinegar or lemon juice).

Also, keep a fork, spoon, and napkins in an "on-the-go" bag or your glove box so you can eat before or after events if you anticipate a tough crowd or unhealthy food. That way, at best, you're pleasantly surprised if it's a colorful spread, and at worst, you have a backup plan. Don't let opinions or lack of options derail your health goals. If you feel silly eating in your car or on public transit, just picture me doing it with you, too, because I just may be! It's called commitment.

On-the-Go Salad

5 – 10 MINUTES TO PREP

Prepare a few jar salads and seal them in an airtight glass container in the fridge for up to 1 week. Take to work or enjoy at home for a quick meal. Just pour the dressing of choice in the bottom of the container and layer the goodies on top (this keeps them fresh until ready to eat). Keep jar upright during transport, then shake and enjoy. If you're not adding dressing to the jar (during plane travel, for instance), find a lemon wedge, pepper, and/or olive oil (check a food court), which makes a nice, simple dressing.

CUSTOMIZE YOUR OWN JAR SALAD WITH THESE STEPS:

Start at the bottom (layer 1) and build to the top (layer 4)

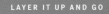
LAYER IT UP AND GO

LAYER 1: DRESSING

Choose one from page 226

2 – 3 tablespoons should do

LAYER 2: HEARTY GOODNESS

These foods hold up and marinate well in liquids.

Radishes

Carrots

Peppers

Red onions

Cooked chickpeas

Cooked beans

Olives

Artichokes

Mushrooms

Steamed or roasted veggies

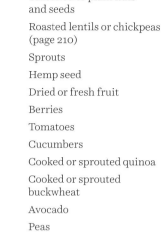

SHAKE AND EAT

LAYER 3: LIGHT & CRUNCHY

Seasoned or plain nuts and seeds

Roasted lentils or chickpeas (page 210)

Sprouts

Hemp seed

Dried or fresh fruit

Berries

Tomatoes

Cucumbers

Cooked or sprouted quinoa

Cooked or sprouted buckwheat

Avocado

Peas

LAYER 4: LEAFY MAGIC

Chopped kale

Mixed greens

Fresh herbs

Arugula

Sprouts

Cabbage

Edible flowers

psst! For heartier greens like collards, mustard, and kale, before adding them raw to the jar, chop and place them in a bowl. Sprinkle with a pinch of sea salt and massage for 1–2 minutes to soften them. Squeeze out excess water, and pack your jar. This quick "massaging" step also minimizes any bitterness inherently in the greens.

5–10 MINUTES TO PREP | # On-the-Go Breakfast

Make a few of this cereal mix, seal in an airtight glass container (canning jars work great), and store in a cool, dry place like the pantry or fridge. Since the ingredients are all dry, it will last for at least 4 to 8 weeks. Take to work, on a plane, or prepare at home for a quick breakfast (snack, lunch, or dinner). Just add hot water or non-dairy milk, stir, and let it sit together for five minutes. This cereal is also yummy cold.

JUST ADD HOT WATER

psst! To save space, especially when traveling, store in a sturdy plastic bag (double bag it for insurance). You can always find a spoon or cup/bowl, and at those odd times that you can't, eat it straight out of the bag and own it. It's better to eat something than nothing when the body needs fuel.

INGREDIENTS:

¼ cup dry, hulled, and sprouted buckwheat groats

(use dry, hulled, and unsprouted if you like; they soften well)

¼ cup rolled oats

1 tablespoon chia seeds

1 tablespoon Sucanat

¼ cup dried fruit

½ teaspoon ground cinnamon (optional)

Pinch ground cardamom (optional)

Pinch fine-ground sea salt

Lead by Example

Healthful living doesn't always resonate with the people who need it. It comes to people who want it and go after it. No matter how many studies we read or how passionate we are, we must understand that we can't make someone join us on this journey unless they choose it.

Almost every time we try to talk others into our lifestyle, we create resistance.

I know how hard it is to watch friends and family suffer from preventable illness. I know what it's like to watch folks discuss their child's health issues as they feed them the probable cause. But we have to let go of trying to convert others, starting now.

While I've always been careful about preaching to folks about the benefits of a plant-powerful diet, when it comes to the peeps in my inner circle — my family and pals (especially the ones suffering from disease) — I'm guilty of desperately pushing. I've spent hundreds of dollars on books, DVDs, and food for them. I've talked until I'm pretty much blue in the face about the dangers of certain foods and unhealthful lifestyle choices. I've tried my best to inspire, encourage, and motivate. And it's not that it has fallen on deaf ears, but I now realize that no one changes unless they want to. Of course, we've all heard that one before, but it's true — we each need to reach that realization on our own, in our own time.

The road to a lifestyle change is unique to each person due to their layers of memory and experience that compounds over time. It's challenging enough to change ourselves, so let's stay focused on that first — it can be a lifelong project.

We only frustrate ourselves, and others, if we push our agenda. Many people prefer to blame anything but themselves for their illness or stagnation. Some folks have been unhealthy and in poor health for so long that the idea of happiness and health scares them deeply.

Humans like to feel like what they're doing is accepted. So you'll notice that even a simple awareness that you eat differently can make others defensive. They may be thinking, "Why is what I eat not good enough for you?" and "Are you judging me?" Or you may be taunted with retorts like, "Mmmm, I love me some bacon." Or my favorite checkout line quip, "Sooomeone's healthy, are you juicing all that stuff?" Stay flexible, and when necessary, put on your invisible force fields and watch any negativity bounce right off. Go ahead, visualize it: Ping! Bonk. Ding! Splat. Expect it so it's not a surprise. Unfortunately, yes, it's somehow socially acceptable for others to openly critique your food decisions if they are healthy ones, but if the tables were turned, well, not so much. Stay confident that you're making a choice that you don't have to justify to anyone but yourself.

Resiliency is also a form of self-kindness you may like to embrace. Over time, as we continue to read about food ethics and eating sustainably, our dietary values may shift. Eating some meat here and there may not be "healthy enough" anymore, and we might want to go 100 percent plant-based. Or maybe we find that instead of being an herbivore, occasionally eating humanely raised animal products (like eggs from your neighbor's happy chickens) feels right.

Don't freak out about changing your mind — making decisions about what we eat is a lifelong practice, and the most important thing we can do is to stay open-minded.

About everything, really. Flexibility is a great friend and change is inevitable. This approach can also avoid perpetuating the unfortunate stereotypes about the plant-powerful — most of us are understanding and confident enough in our choices that we don't feel the need to push them onto others. If you aren't there yet, strive for it. I know this is harder to put into practice when it comes to friends and family, but nothing ruins a good journey like someone who doesn't want to be there for the ride. Lead by example. If you're truly making changes, people will see you becoming happier, leaner, healthier, and stronger — and they'll want it for themselves. And if you make them the recipes in this book, they can experience how tasty it all can be.

Plant-Powering Your Kitchen

One of my favorite tips for successful transitioning is to make the kitchen one of the coziest, most inviting rooms in the home. Over time, my kitchen has become a room full of stories thanks to a mismatched collection of flea-market finds and other special goodies. I adore the unique personality of one-off items — teacups, bowls, plates, glasses. When you enjoy a meal at my house, you're likely to get a special place setting just for you.

I love to see who gravitates toward my grandmother's gold leaf bowl or the trophy plate my mother won as a girl for her horseback riding skills. When I cook for myself, chicory root tea simply tastes better in the teacup my soul sister Marta gave me. And a warm soup is always more fun in the ginormous peek-a-boo owl mug my younger brother found. These are the simple things that make me happy and they fill my kitchen with character and love.

So, find what makes your heart sing. Turn that kitchen into a sacred space, because if you adore your kitchen, you'll spend valuable time there. Preparing meals and experimenting with new culinary ideas will become an effortless, stress-relieving, and enjoyable way to spend time if you're in a happy, nurturing space that reflects who you are and what you want to become.

Clean It Out

Remove anything from the kitchen that will tempt, frustrate, and otherwise hinder progress. This includes junky or expired foodstuffs but also broken appliances, wonky tools, and those dishes, serving ware, and utensils you never use. Have a giveaway party, invite pals over to help unload, and celebrate new goals. Donate goods to someone who can fix or make use of them. Maybe even set out a healthy snack YU made. See what happens.

Get the tempting S.A.D. foods out of the house — they're kryptonite — and if they're not there, we can't eat them. We instantly set ourselves up for success if we junk-proof the kitchen all around. Don't forget about the counters, fridge, pantry, and freezer.

Make room for the good stuff.

Rearrange & Organize

Keep handy the appliances and tools that you'll be using often. Bring them to the front of the cabinets or countertop. Utilize quirky jars and vessels for items like rubber bands and cheesecloths (which you'll end up using more than you think). Make it easy on yourself.

To ensure that I eat a variety of foods, I personally need to see all my options. So my pantry items and spices are out of the cabinets and stacked on open shelves. I'm much more likely to use the red lentils or the mustard seeds if they aren't collecting dust in the back of the pantry where I can't see them. Label them if you need to and group items for easy locating — flours, spices, grains, nuts, seeds, teas, etc. Store bulk pantry items in airtight glass containers — recycle glass jars from tomato sauce, nut butters, or other store-bought items.

Appliances/Tools

These are the tools and appliances that every dedicated plant-based cook should have in their kitchen from day one — they make prep efficient and cooking stress-free, healthy, and enjoyable.

Essentials

A High-Powered Blender

There's one appliance that we'll end up using more than any other: a blender with a powerful motor. It's an investment, so you may hesitate getting one, but once you see what you've been missing, you won't be sorry. And after about one month's use, it'll have paid for itself many times over.

I use mine multiple times a day, more than my pots and pans. And I travel with it. My cooking got easier and my recipes more creative with it. And I hear all the time from folks who held out and now claim that they don't know why they waited so long.

Hop online to research options from every price point. Find a restaurant supply shop in your area to buy one wholesale, pick up a refurbished one, or ask all your family/friends to chip in for it as a birthday or holiday present.

Healthy Cookware

Like everything related to health, we can find just as many proponents of a particular method, tool, approach, or paradigm as we can its opponents. And when it comes to what cookware to use, there are options that have undeniable pros and cons. Here's what you'll find — and won't find — in my kitchen and why.

Cast Iron

I waited too long to add a cast-iron skillet to my kitchen. But now that I have, it's my favorite way to cook. Cast iron adds trace amounts of beneficial iron to foods, evenly distributes heat, browns foods beautifully, and lasts ages.

There's a bit of maintenance that comes with cast-iron cookware, but it's easier than you think. Keeping a cast-iron pan's natural non-stick surface up to snuff is called "seasoning." Modern cast-iron cookware usually comes pre-seasoned, with a soy-based oil that many suspect is genetically modified. When buying a modern cast-iron pan, look for unseasoned and season it yourself. If you find a vintage cast-iron gem at a flea market, estate sale, or online auction, search for a clean, smooth pan without divots or pockmarks. (A rusty pan can be restored, if that kind of project is appealing to you — there's something satisfying about bringing one back to life.)

After some extensive research, I ultimately went for a Griswold #8 — the perfect size for cooking and baking everything. Not too big, not too small. I found her on eBay for $45, and I consider it an investment in my health. I feel confident that I'll be cooking with this same pan as an eccentric, mature lady some day.

Seasoning Cast Iron

You'll want to "season" vintage or unseasoned cast iron when it comes home. Methods differ depending on who you talk to, but here are the basic steps. (Skip directly to step 3 if you found a clean vintage pan.)

1. Scrub and clean the pan well, removing any rust.

2. Dry well.

3. Place clean, dry pan in an oven heated to 400°F for 40 minutes.

4. Remove and, using a natural cloth rag, apply a light coating of avocado oil (or another high-smoke-point oil) to the entire piece.

5. Put back in the oven for 30 minutes. Then turn off the heat and allow to cool in the oven.

6. You can repeat this step a few more times, but once should be enough to last a long while.

Maintenance/Use

A well-seasoned pan is easy to maintain:

After use, rinse with hot water and scrub off food with a plastic or natural dish brush (no metal) and dry well all over (you can even heat it a bit on a low burner to dry). If left wet, it can rust (which you can clean off). Never use abrasive scouring pads or chemicals.

Lightly coat inside of pan with oil, don't rinse off. You'll be able to cook pancakes or veggies without having to add extra oil.

Don't let foods simmer or cook until no oil/moisture is left in the pan — it will cause irreparable damage.

Don't store food in a cast-iron pan — acids from the food can damage the seasoning.

Don't put cast iron in the dishwasher and never soak in water.

Keep thick pot holders nearby when using. This is a serious pan that conducts heat and it requires careful handling!

Acidic foods like tomato sauce or vinegar can make the food darken and taste a bit metallic — they can break down the seasoning. I tend to use another pot or pan for these jobs.

Are Microwaves Unhealthy?

If you choose to use a microwave I'll still love YU — but here are a few reasons why one won't be found in my kitchen. Overall, I don't believe that anyone is too swamped to find the extra 5 – 15 minutes it takes to naturally heat up food or beverages in the oven or on the stove top. If we're that busy, something needs to change. Microwaving perpetuates bad habits — validating the unhealthful and disconnected cultural trance of "too busy."

When it comes to how a microwave heats food, honestly, I'm suspicious. Whole, plant-based foods are "alive" — we just can't see the activity without a microscope. Yes, heating of any kind destroys some living nutrients and enzymes, but instead of heating from the "outside in" with conventional methods, microwaves heat from the "inside out," directly targeting the water molecules and agitating them enough where they generate violent friction to rip apart and "heat" the food. Most convenience foods are packaged in plastics and heated in plastics, and plastics contain carcinogenic compounds. Hospitals won't use microwaves to warm blood for transfusions because they destroy red blood cells, which can be fatal. On a cellular level, whether it's food or blood or water, the microwave deforms molecules. All for what? A few minutes saved?

Of course, I know that we're hit with radiation all day long — phones, computers, wireless gadgets. But I respect my food too much, so the microwave is one thing this busy gal can cut out of her life. If you choose to stop using it, after a few weeks, you won't miss it. Sell it and use the money toward a health-promoting appliance instead.

Stainless-Steel Pots & Pans

I have a love/hate relationship with my stainless-steel skillet — I love that it's not aluminum, but I am not a fan of how it beats up pancakes (use cast iron for this instead). For the most part, though, stainless-steel pots and pans work great for sautéing veggies, cooking grains, and cooking warm cereals and soups. And I use my stainless pots to heat up water in lieu of an aluminum teapot. There are many grades of stainless steel. Some products are made with scrap metals that can leech excessive chrome and nickel into foods, and some are made with surgical-grade stainless, which, proponents claim, is the safest choice. But it's pricey. Save money by looking on eBay for three solid tools: a medium pot with a lid, one large stockpot with a lid, and maybe one skillet.

Maintenance/Use

Don't use metal utensils in this cookware.

Lubricate the pan before adding food, either with oil or vegetable stock.

Don't let liquids boil until dry or foods simmer until dry — it can cause irreparable damage.

Clean with natural soap, water, and a plastic or natural dishwashing scrubber — no metal.

Can go in the dishwasher.

Extended use will result in some minor scratches — this is character! It won't interfere with cooking success.

If food gets stuck on the bottom, pour about 2 – 4 tablespoon baking soda in the pan, fill with water, and soak overnight. Scrub easily the next day with a plastic or natural dishwashing brush. Don't use abrasive scouring pads or chemicals.

Glass Baking, Cookware & Storage

In an effort to keep my foods free of unwanted chemicals, I store them in glassware with airtight lids — never plastic. This goes for leftovers, sauces, juices, and pantry items. We can easily find various sizes, sets, and stackable containers to use for everything from salad dressings to nuts. If leftovers are stored in glass, we can put the container in the oven to reheat and save a little dish duty by eating out of it when heated. (Just make sure the glass gets to room temp before putting in the oven. I've never experienced it, but I hear that extreme temp differences can cause the glass to break.) I love to scour a flea market for vintage storage containers, baking dishes, and bowls — it's a more sustainable and more beautiful way to go. There's a story behind each piece and they can add inspiring color and charm to your kitchen.

Medium saucepan with a lid

9" x 13" casserole dish

9" x 9" or 8" x 8" baking dish

9½" pie dish

5" x 9" loaf dish

Set of nesting mixing bowls

Set of storage containers (round or square, just make sure they can stack)

PFCs and Aluminum

PFCs: Perfluorinated compounds (PFCs) have the ability to make products grease-, stain-, and water-resistant. And we can find them in everything from microwave popcorn bags and food wrappers to furniture, clothing, and carpeting. Studies link PFCs to thyroid dysfunction, preeclampsia, elevated cholesterol, weakened immunity, flu-like symptoms, cancer, liver dysfunction, endocrine disruption, birth defects, developmental delays, and fertility issues.[1, 2]

Teflon cookware — which is ubiquitous because of its ease of use and ease of cleaning — contains PFCs. While manufacturers often warn consumers to avoid high temperatures when using Teflon, tests by the Environmental Working Group (EWG) demonstrate that in just two to five minutes on a conventional stove top, Teflon-coated pots and pans and other non-stick surfaces could exceed temperatures where the coating breaks apart and emits toxic particles and gases.[3]

If you have to continue using non-stick cookware for a while, here are some tips from the EWG:[4]

• Never preheat non-stick cookware.

• Heat non-stick cookware at the lowest possible temperature — don't put in an oven hotter than 500°F.

• Always use an exhaust fan above the stove while cooking.

• Keep pet birds out of the kitchen — the fumes from an overheated non-stick pan can kill a bird in seconds.[5]

• Don't use the self-cleaning oven function. It cleans at high temperatures, which can release toxic fumes from non-stick interior oven parts.

Aluminum: Our risk of excessive toxic aluminum intake comes from many sources — foods, drinking water, medicines (like buffered aspirin and antacids), antiperspirants, food and beverage cans, cosmetics, and yes, cookware. Research suggests that aluminum is linked to an increased risk of cancer, Alzheimer's, respiratory issues, and other serious health problems.[6, 7] Manufacturers claim that anodized aluminum — which is treated with an electrochemical process to harden it — is safer than raw aluminum cookware, while some reports claim that acidic foods and time can wear down this protective barrier, which eventually allows toxic aluminum to leech into the food.

Knives

Starting out, I made more than 400 YumUniverse.com recipes with only one serrated knife and one dull chef's knife. We don't need a bunch of fancy knives to get going, but I do recommend one 8" chef's knife, one serrated knife, and one paring knife (choose good-quality steel on all) — they should cover all of your bases just fine. To make sure knives last a long time and keep their edge, have them sharpened by a pro a few times a year or buy a sharpening steel to keep at home (visit **yumuniverse.com/knife-skills-part-1-of-2** for a helpful knife skills video).

Colander & Strainer

A colander is a perforated bowl used to drain foods like pasta, rice, and grains. It can be used to rinse berries, vegetables, and other ingredients as well. In addition to a colander, pick up a fine mesh handheld strainer or sieve (bonus points for ones with legs that fit over the top of a pot) for rinsing smaller ingredients like quinoa, buckwheat, and grains that can slip through the holes in some colanders. A fine mesh strainer can do the colander's job if you only have the budget or space for one. And it works great for steaming veggies. Go for stainless steel if you can.

Cutting Boards

Keep a few cutting boards made of natural material like wood or bamboo (easy on knives) in the kitchen. A long one will fit nicely over the sink, so scraps can fall away as we cut. A medium 15" x 10" is handy for quick chopping — make sure the length of your longest chef's knife doesn't go over the edge when placed diagonally across the board — for safety reasons, we want the board under the knife at all times. An optional cutting board to pick up is a big 18" x 20" (or around that size). It covers a lot of counter space, fits over the sink, and provides tons of work room.

Maintenance/Use

Keep cutting boards from sliding around the counter by dampening a paper towel or cheesecloth and placing it beneath the board. The moisture will help it stick to the counter, so there isn't any dangerous slipping.

Clean your board after use. Wash it with natural soap and dry well before storing.

Clean boards a few times a month, or even weekly, by sprinkling coarse sea salt on the cutting surface and scrub with a lemon wedge. Use a scraper or silicone spatula to scrape the liquid away. Rinse and dry.

Keep wooden boards from cracking and splitting by "seasoning" them evenly with a coconut, walnut, almond, or olive oil massage once or twice a month. Just rub the oil completely into the board and wipe off excess.

For especially tough staining, scrub with baking soda. (Note that this can sometimes whiten an area, so don't slice your staining beets and berries on a cutting board if it's precious; or do as I do and embrace the permanent stains as the memory of a delicious meal experienced.)

Warping is possible if a board is allowed to take in too much water. This is why drying after each use is so important. If you end up with a warped board, try this: wet all sides and place convex-side up on top of a moderately warm surface like a fridge top or sunny counter. Place a clean, dry towel underneath, and place one large bowl or a few nested bowls (for extra weight) on the board "lump." Let it dry completely (may take a day). If it looks like the curve is flattening out, repeat until it becomes flat again. Then make sure it's always dried off after use.

Veggie Grater

You want a sturdy grater — either box or handheld — to prepare fruits and veggies or all sorts of recipes. If you already own a food processor, you don't need this tool — it will come with a grating blade that saves you quite a bit of time and elbow grease.

Wooden Spoons

Wooden spoons are non-toxic, inexpensive, strong yet soft, and able to adjust well to temperature differences, especially high temperatures. Not to mention, they're pretty. Pick up a few sizes and shapes and make sure at least one of them is a slotted spoon — very handy for removing ingredients from hot liquid. Use the cleaning techniques described for cutting boards to remove tough stains.

Cheesecloth

Cheesecloth is a loosely woven cloth that is traditionally used to wrap and protect dairy cheese while allowing them to breathe. But it can also be used for non-dairy cheese making and a host of other kitchen tasks. Buy one large cheesecloth from the local kitchen supply shop, health food store, or online, and cut it into multiple 8"- 10" squares. They get used often, from straining non-dairy milks and sauces to brewing large batches of tea (just fill and tie off with natural cotton string to steep). Use them to cover sprouting and soaking jars (keeps pests out while letting contents breathe) as well as fermented foods. Muslin, cloth diaper fabric, and natural, sheer curtain fabric work well for these purposes, too, so buy what fits the budget, or look around the house first. These swatches of fabric can be hand- or machine-washed and used over and over. Certain foods will naturally dye them — berries, teas, nuts — again, try to embrace that prettiness. Store cheesecloths in a vintage cookie jar or other vessel that's handy and fun. I store mine in a Darth Vader cookie jar — and I always smile when I pull a cheesecloth from his head.

Measuring Cups & Spoons

There are two different kinds of measuring cups — the kind that measures liquid and the kind that measures dry ingredients. It's a big help when both are in the kitchen at some point, but using one or the other for a while, at first, won't make a big difference with basic recipes, unless we're baking — where exact amounts are crucial. Opt for glass, ceramic, or stainless-steel measuring cups when buying.

Dry Ingredient Measuring Cups

These come in a nesting set of multiple sizes, usually ⅛ cup, ¼ cup, ⅓ cup, ½ cup, ⅔ cup, ¾ cup, and 1 cup. They are flat on top so ingredients can be leveled off with things like butter knives.

Liquid Ingredient Measuring Cups

All measurements are in one clear mini "pitcher" with a pouring spout. It should be marked with line measurements for cups, ounces, and milliliters. When measuring, don't forget to set it on a flat surface to determine amount needed.

Nice to Haves

Add these helpful tools to the kitchen little by little to make time spent there easier and easier. They aren't essentials, but once you have them in your kitchen "toolbox," you'll wonder why the heck you didn't get them sooner.

Enameled Cast-Iron Dutch Oven

These are ideal for prepping acidic foods, making magical soups, and yes, aesthetics. They can come in very bright colors, but there can be certain toxic metals in the enamel in these types of cookware, so you'll want to make sure you buy enameled cast iron from a manufacturer that doesn't use lead or cadmium in the enamel (at least on the interior enamel). Look for manufacturers from the U.S. or Europe over ones made in China to hedge your bet against these contaminants being included. Enameled cast-iron cookware is pretty pricey, so maybe put it on a wish list or registry — it's a quality product that with proper care can last a lifetime.

Don't use metal utensils in this cookware.

Lubricate the pan before adding food, either with oil or vegetable stock.

Don't let liquids boil until dry or foods simmer until dry — it will cause irreparable damage.

Clean with natural soap, water, and a plastic or natural dishwashing scrubber — no metal.

Don't put in the dishwasher.

Keep thick pot holders nearby when using. Like a cast-iron pan, it can become hot and heavy.

If food gets stuck on the bottom, pour about 2 – 4 tablespoons of baking soda in the pan, fill with water and soak overnight. Scrub easily the next day with a plastic or natural dishwashing brush. No abrasive scouring pads or chemicals necessary.

Cherry Stoner/ Olive Pitter

If you ever plan to prepare recipes with quality olives or fresh cherries, spend the $12 and get this gadget — it will change your life. And your cherry-filled recipes. Less mess, less stress.

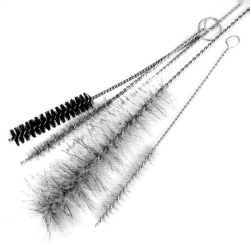

Bottle Brushes

There are lots of hard-to-reach cracks and crevices in appliances and tools, and we'll be using more bottles that need cleaning, too. We'll be more inclined to recycle and reuse a bottle if we can get it clean, and a simple set of these guys will do the trick. Clean the brushes themselves with a good scrub and a soak in a natural antibacterial mixture of apple cider vinegar (1 tablespoon), baking soda (1 teaspoon), and water (2 cups).

Standing Mixer

If you do a lot of baking, a standing mixer can be not only a gorgeous addition to the kitchen, but a necessary one. You'll easily whip creams, make doughs, and cream batters. With the right attachments (purchased separately), a standing mixer can also become an ice-cream maker, a noodle maker, and a grain mill for making your own flours.

Stoneware

Folks have been using it for thousands of years. Stoneware is heavy-duty, toxin-free ovenware that produces some of the most beautifully baked cookies and tarts ever. The more a stoneware piece is used, the more character is gets — stains, dark spots, and marks. That means it's getting the love it deserves, and it will only add more magic to foods. We can find stoneware pizza stones, cookie sheets, muffin tins, and loaf pans. Due to the unique heat distribution, add 5 – 7 minutes to baking times when using stoneware — just make sure to keep an eye on things.

Maintenance/Use

Don't use metal utensils.

Always warm stoneware while you warm the oven; extreme temperature differences can make it crack.

Season it just like cast iron to get a non-stick surface.

Don't ever put stoneware in the dishwasher.

Keep thick pot holders nearby when using. It's heavy and hot.

Scrape it off and wipe it clean until used again.

If you can't get down with not washing it, use natural soap, warm water, and a plastic or natural dishwashing scrubber — no metal. Dry well and re-season if necessary.

Sprinkle 2 – 4 tablespoons baking soda on the stoneware and soak overnight if it gets some pesky stuck-on food. Scrub easily the next day with a plastic or natural dishwashing brush. No abrasive scouring pads or chemicals necessary. Re-season.

Small Spice/ Coffee Grinder

Pick up one for around $12 and it can make al the difference in the texture and taste of the food we prepare. Freshly grind seeds, Sucanat, spices, teas, herbs, and more. It's easy to use, takes up very little cabinet or counter space, and it's a breeze to wipe clean.

Food Processor

The food processor is really a magician — able to take on almost every mundane kitchen task in seconds — grating, slicing, whipping, mixing, kneading, and puréeing, which will get us cooking that much faster, and hopefully more often. It's easy to clean, easy to use, and it makes kitchen time more efficient. In seconds, we can prepare all sorts of ingredients that can be used immediately, throughout the week or later if frozen. People often ask whether they should get a blender or a food processor. The only differences, really, between a food processor and a high-powered blender are cost (a quality food processor is less expensive) and the fact that the blender handles and renders liquids and sauces from nuts and seeds the way the food processor cannot.

Unbleached Parchment Paper

A big roll of unbleached parchment is incredibly helpful for rolling out gluten-free dough (just place between two sheets and roll), tart crusts, crackers, and other goodness, without the mess and stickiness factor. There are a few brands out there that claim to be made from compostable, recycled ingredients and don't use chlorine bleach to whiten their papers, don't test on animals or use animal ingredients, don't use toxic glues, gluten, or non-veggie-based inks, and that's where we should start. However, there isn't a company yet that offers an unbleached parchment paper that isn't treated with silicone (which is where the non-stick magic comes from). I keep a few rolls on hand at all times. The boxes they come in are usually flimsy, making it hard to tear, so I store my rolls out of the box and use kitchen scissors to cut pieces when needed. Reduce waste by reusing pieces a few times. I often roll out crackers, wipe off the paper I used, then roast veggies on it or cut it up to use for muffin liners (http://yumuniverse.com/diy-parchment-cupcake-muffin-liners.). You'll know when it's time for a new piece — it browns and becomes covered in other foods that can't be wiped off. Here's an important "lesson learned" tip: there's a big difference between wax paper and parchment paper — you want parchment for cooking and baking, not wax.

Kitchen Scissors

The kitchen experience becomes more effortless and tidy with a pair of kitchen scissors. They're one of those hidden essentials I didn't realize I needed until I had them. Cut herbs, parchment paper, cheesecloths, food packages (use on self-tear packaging that doesn't really tear well at all), and veggies. Kitchen scissors are also a dream for removing large, green leaves like kale and collards from stems. Sometimes, once I wash and de-stem large-leafed greens and large-leafed herbs like basil or sage, instead of cutting/chopping with a knife, I'll roll them up and use the scissors to cut smaller pieces into soups and other meals. It's a time- and mess-saver.

Is Silicone Safe for Regular Use and Baking?

It's difficult to say because there haven't been enough studies. Silicon (minus the "e") is the natural element found in sand, rock, and quartz, and when bonded with oxygen, you get the synthetic rubber silicone. Most descriptions of it say that it's chemically inert and stable, but using it is a personal choice.

Silicone Kitchen Spatula

This is one of those tools that really should go in the essentials category, but until you experience its benefits firsthand, you may not believe me. The magic here is that the spatula flexes and bends around blender blades, almost-empty jars, and all kinds of bowls, so you can use every drop of your recipe goodness.

Whisk

Mixing ingredients for baking, dressings, sauces, and non-dairy creams is made easier with a nice stainless-steel whisk. 'Nuf said.

Immersion Blender

This'll purée soup, dressings, and sauces on the spot without transferring food to blender. Just place the wand into your pot or bowl and whir away.

Veggie Peeler

We all have one. But we don't always use it to its full creative potential. A peeler can make ribbon noodles out of veggies like zucchini and broccoli stalks, decorative curls out of fruits, and remove tough skin from root vegetables. It also shaves chocolate, removes strings from celery, and can even zest citrus.

Salad Spinner

Speed up the washing and drying of greens with a salad spinner. It gets the leaves dry in seconds.

Apron

Pick up one or five (if you collect them like I do). They help put you in the cooking mind-set and create some kitchen cheer. Plus they'll protect your clothes.

Mandoline

It's your own private produce guillotine. The blade slices fruits and veggies paper thin, making veggie noodles, pies, shaved ingredients for salads, and chips super easy. There are two types of mandoline slicers, a handheld and a standalone, and lovers of one or the other can have strong opinions about which is better. I prefer a standalone mandoline with gripper feet over a handheld because it's more sturdy and comes with an adjustable thickness dial. Watch your fingers when using a mandoline — always use the guard that come with it. Don't learn a lesson the hard way. (Et tu, Marie Antoinette?) This incredibly sharp blade and fast slicing are a dangerous combination.

Dehydrator

I bought my dehydrator years ago so I could make raw recipes, but now I mainly use it to save food before it perishes. Once the water is removed from food, it can last for a very long time, and that's what the dehydrator does: removes the liquid. Almost anything can go in the dehydrator. Slice and dehydrate pears, apples, and other fruit for snacks.

Dehydrate kale stems, greens, carrots, and other veggies to use for a stock (see page 122). Soak and dehydrate sprouts, buckwheat, nuts, seeds, and quinoa, grind up in a coffee grinder, and voilà, your own protein powder. Just store everything in airtight glass containers in a cool, dry place like the pantry or fridge.

A dehydrator is a great way to make healthy, fun snacks like fruit leathers, chips, and crackers. We can also dry out veggies and fruit and grind them into powders to supplement smoothies and soups. (Parents: this is a great way to sneak veggies into food for the kiddos.) One teaspoon of powder can be made with one carrot, and one teaspoon of powder can be stirred into most anything. Get the kids involved in helping make these foods. If they're involved, they're more inclined to eat them.

Tongs

Very helpful for removing items from hot water (especially when blanching) or from the oven without removing the baking sheet (that cookie that you just can't wait for any longer, perhaps?). Also nice for turning items on a baking sheet or in a roasting pan — gives some nice control. Use them for flipping tortillas when steaming, too.

Silicone Ice Cube Tray

It's nice to have a few of these on hand. They're gems: freeze small servings of vegetable stock for sautéing; herbs in oil for sautéing; chili for topping tacos, rice, or noodles; soups for stirring into and quickly flavoring grains, leafy greens and legumes; compotes for cereals; dressings for salads — all sorts of quick solutions for meals that need to be prepared quickly. I prefer the silicone trays because they're deep and freeze up a nice-sized single serving. They also make lovely ice cubes, which can be fancied up for parties if you add some edible flowers before freezing.

Tip for freezing crystal-clear ice cubes:

Boil the water you will be using and allow it to cool. Boil again, allow to cool, and fill your tray — the boiling cleans up the impurities and minerals in the water that cloud up your cubes.

←

Shopping & Storage

Now it's time to get down to business. Happily, cooking goes hand in hand with shopping.

Shopping

True, going shopping can be a chore. But it's also an opportunity to learn something new and have fun — it comes down to the perspective we choose. The grocery store is full of possibilities, colors, textures, flavors — it can even be relaxing. I know there are some of you out there who may be rolling your eyes right now. But the fact is, grocery shopping has to be done, and with some of these tips and resources, no matter what side of the shopping fence we're on — love it or loathe it — we can make it efficient, cost-effective, and enjoyable.

Make a List, Check It Twice, Stick to It

If we shop with a plan, we shop efficiently. Plan recipes for the week and write down what's needed. Check over the list a few times before leaving the house so you don't find yourself preparing a meal and missing a key ingredient. When shopping, stick to the list so foods don't go to waste.

Eat Before You Shop

To make sure we don't overspend, and to steer clear of a cranky experience, go shopping with a satisfied belly. That way, we keep unexpected and unnecessary purchases to a minimum and can stay focused on getting the job done as we cruise the aisles.

The Perimeter Is Where It's At

Packaged, processed, misleading foodstuffs are always in the aisles in the center of the store. Stick to the periphery and find the items that nature designed for us — fruits, vegetables, herbs, spices, and bulk items like nuts, seeds, and legumes.

Frozen or Canned?

Fresh foods are best, but for those transitioning to plant-powered diets or days with busy schedules, sometimes you need a fast solution. If you have to choose between frozen ingredients or canned, go frozen. The dangerous amounts of sodium and aluminum from canned foods should be kept to an absolute minimum. Keeping frozen berries, veggies, stocks, soups, and gluten-free tortillas is helpful on hectic days. Or buy fresh and freeze at home. Buy dry legumes and beans in bulk and soak at home.

Bulk: Save Money and Get the Portions You Need

Contrary to what we may have heard, a plant-powerful diet can be a real bargain. Most ingredients (legumes, nuts, seeds, spices, flours, teas) needed for recipes can be found in custom quantities (e.g., 1 tablespoon of chili powder versus a whole jar) and low prices ($1.25/lb. for quinoa) in the bulk section of most grocery stores. And if not, you can usually talk to a manager at the store and ask them to order in bulk for you, or you can find bulk buying options online (visit **yumuniverse.com/yu-book-owners** for recommendations).

> *Since bulk foods don't have all the pricey (and environmentally unfriendly) packaging, we save.*

Bulk is also great for keeping pantry containers stocked — buy the amounts needed versus a pre-measured box.

Know Who's Growing Your Food

Get to know local farmers and save on organic produce by buying locally from a Farmers' Market or by joining a CSA (Community Supported Agriculture). With a CSA, a farmer offers a certain number of "shares" to the public. Typically the share consists of a box of vegetables (but other farm products may be included). Interested folks purchase a share (aka a "membership" or a "subscription") and in return receive a box (bag, basket) of seasonal produce each week throughout the farming season. It's a fantastic way to save money and infuse some spontenaeity into your life. You support local farms while building confidence in the kitchen with surprising, homegrown ingredients. And the closer we are to the source of our food, the more beneficial they are for us since nutrient value begins to diminish once picked.

Use Coupons

Once we start to find our favorite go-to products, visit the coupon/savings sections of their websites and print out coupons. Also ask the grocery store for their coupon handouts and make sure to visit product websites to sign up for savings, too. Never underestimate the power of double coupon day or the amount of money that can be saved by joining a store's membership rewards program. Subscribe to newsletters for favorite products and connect with them and the stores you frequent on Facebook and Twitter — "like" and follow to learn about daily and weekly specials.

Dirty Dozen & the Clean 15

According to the EWG, consuming certain types of organic produce can reduce the amount of dangerous toxins we intake by as much as 80 percent per day. Using data from the United States Department of Agriculture on the amount of pesticide residue found in non-organic fruits and vegetables (after they had been washed), the EWG compiled two helpful lists for consumers.

The fruits and vegetables listed on EWG's "Dirty Dozen" list, when conventionally grown, tested positive for at least 47 different chemicals, with some testing positive for as many as 67 chemicals. The fruits and veggies on the "dirty" list should always be purchased certified organic. The "clean" fruits and veggies are the ones we can count on having less pesticide residue. For the most up-to-date list, check the website ewg.org.

PLUs

Did you know that you can read the PLU (price lookup code) on produce to shop for clean, organic items? PLUs for conventionally grown produce are usually a four-digit number, currently in the 3000–4999 range. If an item is organic, you'll see a five-digit number beginning with the number "9." If an item is genetically modified, you'll see a five-digit number beginning with the number "8." To remember which is which, use these little rhymes: "9 is fine" and "8 ain't great."

Don't Buy Junk (Not Even as a Just-This-Once Treat)

Don't keep temptation in the house — be kinder to yourself. If you want Chocolate Chip Cookies (page 31) or Vanilla Ice Cream (page 285) or a salty, crunchy snack like chips (page 33), I have mind-bendingly good alternatives for you in Section 3.

Shopping Support

I've created a bunch of helpful charts to help your shopping experience. Visit the appendix for the information you need to access special bonus materials for *YumUniverse* book owners, print them out, and keep them in your wallet or purse at all times for quick and easy reference.

Storage

When ingredients are clean and whole, we need to know how to store them to make them last as long as possible — this makes hard-earned dollars go far and helps us build confidence in the kitchen.

Stackable Glassware

We'll be storing lots of tasty pantry items and goods in the fridge and the freezer, and glass storage containers are a safe, sustainable way to go. Yes, plastic storage containers are unbreakable, "disposable," and prevalent in American homes. But that isn't enough of a reason to use them. Studies demonstrate serious health hazards associated with plastics (even products like baby bottles labeled BPA-free), such as reproductive problems and endocrine disruption, which can cause cancerous tumors, birth defects, and other developmental disorders.[1, 2]

Start saving glass containers and bottles for pantry items and leftovers instead. Have friends and family save them for you, too. Buy a few stackable containers (bail jars are extremely airtight, and canning jars are an economical solution) to get started. Save store-bought glass kombucha or beverage bottles to carry water, protein shakes, and smoothies on-the-go. It's only happened to me only once, but if a glass storage container breaks, it only takes a minute or two to wipe, sweep, or vacuum it up. A broken container is not a solid enough excuse to drink or eat out of plastic.

When using glass in the freezer, just be mindful of extreme temperature differences — let hot glass and contents cool off before placing in the freezer, and allow frozen glass and contents to reach room temp before placing in an oven (this takes about 5 minutes).

Plastic Baggies

If you choose to continue to use plastic baggies, wrap goods in parchment or cloth before filling bags. And definitely save them after each use — plastic bags can be washed over and over again instead of being tossed. Give them a good scrub, turn them inside out, and stand them upside down on a towel to dry out. Only when I have to, I use the same baggies from a box I bought years ago — I just wash after each use and reuse them.

Pantry & Bulk Item Storage

Maximize the value of bulk items by storing them properly so they last a long time. If you have a cool, dry home, store most bulk and pantry items in a cabinet or on a shelf out of direct sunlight. Since mold is attracted to moisture, if you live in a damp, warm climate, or experience humid summers, store these goods in the fridge and freezer.

Eating right is knowing what you're putting into your body. So here's what I use in my recipe — the ingredients, how to store them, and the best way to use them.

BAKING POWDER

9 – 12 months

Baking powder contains sodium bicarbonate (baking soda), an acidifying agent (usually cream of tartar, a by-product of wine fermentation), and a drying agent (cornstarch, potato starch, or wheat starch, so if you have a serious gluten allergy, buy gluten-free baking powder). Make sure to always buy aluminum-free baking powder.

BAKING SODA

(bicarbonate of soda)
2 – 4 years

A leavening agent, it's used in recipes that contain liquids and acids (like vinegar, lemon juice, chocolate, or honey) because it needs them to react (produce carbon dioxide gas) so baked goods rise. It almost always comes in a cardboard box, so transfer it to an airtight glass container for longer leavening power. If you suspect that it may be losing potency, put a sprinkle in a dish and add a squeeze of lemon or a drop of apple cider vinegar. If you see bubbles, it's okay. If not, it's time to buy more.

COCONUT

(flaked or shredded)
6 – 12 months

Lightly toasted, coconut flakes can really elevate the taste and texture of simple recipes like Chia Pudding (page 164). Just stir the coconut flakes constantly in a dry skillet heated to medium, for about 3 – 5 minutes. Now, the first time I tried to toast coconut

Red Quinoa

Mung Beans

flakes, the kitchen almost caught on fire. Don't turn your back even for a second until it starts to brown! Then remove from heat ASAP. It's worth the eagle-eyed attention. Store in the fridge for extra-long shelf life. Look for unsulphured dried coconut (see page 112 for why).

COCONUT AMINOS

6–12 months

This is my preferred gluten-free alternative to soy sauce. It's coconut sap, naturally aged and blended with sun-dried, mineral-rich sea salt, and it contains loads of amino acids (the building blocks of protein). In any recipes where I've listed it, you can substitute soy sauce, nama shoyu, or tamari in equal amounts if soy isn't a concern for you.

CONDIMENTS

6–12 months

Most condiments like hot sauce, Worcestershire, horseradish, coconut aminos, mustard, curry paste, and ketchup will last a long while in the fridge.

EXTRACTS

Indefinitely

Stay away from imitation flavoring — blech — the taste is never as good as the real deal, and that's because it's made from synthetic chemicals. Look for gluten-free extracts if you have an allergy. Or better yet, make homemade. Yay for homemade! (Psst! Makes a nice gift for someone lucky.)

FLOURS

2–3 months in the pantry
4–6 months in the fridge
6–12 months in the freezer

Most gluten-free flours come in small packages that can get used up within 2–4 weeks (unless you're experimenting, then it can be 2–4 days). In this case, a cool, dry pantry is fine for storage. But since the only processing most gluten-free flours go through is basic grinding (thank goodness), they still contain beneficial oils that can go rancid. To ensure that ingredients last as long as possible, remove them from bags and store in airtight glass containers in the fridge or freezer, where pests and moisture can't compromise them.

Almond Flour

Make Homemade Extract

Place 1 cup vodka and flavoring (see below) into a glass jar with an airtight lid (Mason jars work great). Store in a cool, dry place for 8 weeks or longer (shake occasionally). Use as needed. (Keep the flavoring in the jar and strain your serving amount as needed.)

Try these flavorings with the above steps:

Almond Extract

1 cup ground almonds. Add 1 vanilla bean sliced lengthwise for extra flavor.

← Cacao Extract

1 cup cacao nibs (raw bits of cocoa bean that smell divine), roughly chopped. Add 1 vanilla bean sliced lengthwise for extra flavor.

Hazelnut Extract

1 cup ground hazelnuts. Add 1 vanilla bean sliced lengthwise for extra flavor.

Lemon Extract

¼ cup fresh lemon zest (make sure there's little to no white pith, which makes it bitter).

Vanilla Extract

3 vanilla beans, sliced in half lengthwise.

Orange Extract

¼ cup fresh orange zest (also citrus, so make sure there's little to no white pith, which makes it bitter).

Peppermint Extract

¼ cup dry (must be dry) peppermint leaves.

Goji Berries
aka Wolfberries

FRUIT (DRIED)

3–6 months in the pantry
6–12 months in the fridge

Watch for dangerous additives here. Sulphur dioxide is a preservative (a sulfite, which can also be found in wine, shredded coconut, soup, and spice mixes) that makes its way into most dried fruits like raisins, cherries, blueberries, apricots, and figs. Sulfites can be very dangerous for folks with asthma and sulfite allergies as they can trigger anaphylactic shock (a severe, potentially fatal allergic reaction characterized by sharp drop in blood pressure, rash, and difficulty breathing). Studies have found that exposure to sulphur dioxide can result in respiratory diseases, even cancer, so buy organic unsulphured dried fruit when possible.[3] Avoid processed sugars, too. Look for unsweetened products or sweetened only with organic fruit juice.

GRAINS & PSEUDOGRAINS

1 yr+ in the pantry

Grains have always been a diet staple — bulgur, rye, wheat, rice, barley, and corn, to name a few. "Pseudograins" are ancient grains that are actually seeds. Gluten-free grains include coixseed, millet, oats*, rice, sorghum, teff, and wild rice, and pseudograins include amaranth, quinoa (pronounced keen-wah), and buckwheat. (Contrary to its name, buckwheat is gluten-free; buy hulled.) Transfer them from bags to airtight glass containers to protect them from moisture and pests. Keep them cool and dry in the pantry or in the fridge. Older grains and pseudograins require more time to cook.

*Oats are inherently gluten-free, but are sometimes contaminated in the field or processing facility. Make sure oats say "gluten-free" on the package and buy from trusted sources (visit **yumuniverse.com/yu-book-owners** for some recommendations).*

HERBS (DRIED)

1–3 years in the pantry

While most folks keep dried herbs near or above the stove, it's best to keep them away from heat and steam for longer shelf life, so move them to a cool, dry pantry or shelf out of direct sunlight. Use the ratio of 1:3 when substituting dried herbs for fresh ones.

Scarlet Runner Beans

LEGUMES & BEANS

Indefinitely in the pantry

Legumes and beans share a funky catch-22. Legumes are a food classification (a plant with a fruit that grows in the form of a pod), and beans (a seed of a certain variety of plant species) are a type of legume, but not all legumes are beans. Right? For example, peas and peanuts are legumes, but they're not beans. Before using both in recipes, make sure you remove any pebbles, seedpods, leaves, or twigs that may show up. As long as they remain dry, they'll keep for years. Older legumes and beans require more time to cook, so try not to mix newer legumes with older ones or cooking textures can be inconsistent.

MISO

Indefinitely in the fridge

Prized for its medicinal qualities and probiotic benefits for over 2,000 years, miso is an excellent all-purpose seasoning for soups, dressings, sauces, and spreads. Quality miso is alive with probiotic microorganisms like Lactobacillus and digestive enzymes. And thanks to all this bacterial goodness, it aids in digestion and assimilation of foods. Most miso is created with soy or barley, but gluten-free, soy-free varieties can be found made from azuki beans, brown rice, garlic, red pepper, millet, and chickpeas. Whether opened or unopened, miso can keep for years, even indefinitely. It darkens with age, and the taste will be less sweet the older it becomes, but like wine, the more years that pass, the better it is. To maintain the beneficial probiotic action, don't heat miso above a warm temperature — heat will destroy beneficial bacteria. It's best added to raw foods or post-cooking. Store in the refrigerator.

MUSHROOMS (DRIED)

6–12 months in the fridge

Dried mushrooms are full of flavor and meaty in texture. Like fresh mushrooms, they're tasty in soups, sautés, and sauces. But before using dried mushrooms in a recipe, even a soup or a stew, it's best to rehydrate them (plump them up) in hot water, or for extra flavor, hot veggie broth. If you soak them in water only, save the liquid; it makes a delicious stock. Keep them cool and dry in the fridge or freezer until ready to use.

NUT BUTTERS

6 – 8 months in the fridge

They aren't processed with trans fats (yay!), so natural nut and seed butters can separate when they sit on the shelf. The oil on top can be tricky to stir in when you first open the jar, especially for the kiddos. So, here's a fun tip for avoiding a potential mess: make sure the lid is tight and store jars upside down, so all the oil heads upward, which ends up being under all the good stuff when serving. This makes it easier to stir together, too. Store in the fridge.

NUTS ➡

1 – 8 months

Keeping nuts and seeds in airtight glass containers in the fridge or freezer will increase shelf life overall, but if you go through them in about 4 – 6 weeks, save space by keeping most of them in a cool, dry pantry (or on a shelf) instead. Try to buy raw, organic when possible. If you're soaking and dehydrating nuts (read why and how starting on page 138), once bone-dry, store in the pantry (if eating within 1 – 2 weeks) or better yet, the fridge (longest shelf life).

Store and Use Fresh Herbs Like a Pro

If you've overbought or you don't think you'll be able to use up fresh herbs before they perish, try these tricks to make purchases last and your hard-earned dollars go as far as possible.

Dry herbs at home: Wash herbs and pat them dry with a clean towel. Place on a plate and set by a sunny windowsill and allow to dry completely (3 – 7 days). Once crispy and dry, transfer to an airtight glass container. Store like you would any dried herbs.

Create "easy meal" seasoning cubes: These are a real life preserver on busy nights where you have no energy left to cook. It's a great tip for preserving fresh herbs, but it can be used with dry herbs as well. Wash fresh herbs and dry them completely with a clean towel first. Pack ½ teaspoon dry or 1 teaspoon of fresh herbs into the compartments of an ice-cube tray. Fill with olive oil, warm coconut oil, or liquid veggie stock and freeze until solid. Then once frozen, transfer herb cubes to an airtight container and keep in the freezer until ready to use (to protect cubes from freezer burn, transfer them out of trays once solid). On busy nights, when a quick dinner is a must, place an herb cube in a skillet with onion and fresh veggies and sauté. Toss with cooked grains and enjoy in a wrap, in a bowl, or over greens. Try herb combinations like sage, rosemary, and thyme, or marjoram and sage, or chive and parsley, or dill and lemon zest.

Almonds

9 – 12 months
Fridge or pantry

Brazil nuts

6 – 9 months
Fridge or pantry

Fresh, quality Brazil nuts should be more white than yellow.

Cashews

6 – 9 months
Fridge or pantry

Hazelnuts

4 – 6 months
Fridge or pantry

Macadamias

6 – 9 months
Fridge or pantry

Peanuts

6 – 9 months
Fridge or pantry

Heirloom Peanuts

Most peanuts available to consumers are very susceptible to high levels of a carcinogenic mold called aflatoxin. You can find aflatoxin-free peanuts and peanut butters from heirloom peanuts with a quick Google search. Pricey, but nice when you need that peanut-y fix.

Pecans

9 – 12 months
Fridge or pantry

Pine nuts

1 – 2 months
Fridge

Their high oil content makes them a bit more fragile.

Pistachios

2 – 3 months
Fridge or pantry

Pistachios are another nut that's linked with aflatoxin.

Walnuts

6 – 8 months
Fridge or pantry

OILS

3 – 36 months

Oils are extracted from sources like nuts, seeds, and olives. Each has its own unique flavor, nutrients, and role in food assimilation — we need fats for the absorption of fat-soluble vitamins. Oils also improve texture and flavor in foods, but whether they're a part of your diet is your choice.

Some oils can be used for high-heat cooking (usually saturated fats), while others need to be unheated for nutritional benefits (delicate flax and hemp). "Smoke point" is when oil reaches a temperature where it begins to molecularly break down and produce smoke. This is how free radicals are formed and the fats become toxic to the body. Most conventional oils (vegetable, canola/rapeseed, "vegan" and non-vegan margarine, vegetable shortening, corn, cottonseed, soybean) are not only primarily grown from genetically modified seeds, but refined to increase smoke point in a process that takes the oil to dangerous temperatures multiple times. Refining also bathes the oil in hexane solvent (the EPA claims it's a carcinogen), lye, and other chemicals like bleach. Refined oil is deodorized and in many cases hydrogenated (which gives us trans fats), leaving consumers with a flavorless, colorless, lifeless, plastic-like product that has no connection to the natural, beneficial plant origin it originally had.

Always use unrefined oils, and when sautéing, heat the pan first, then add oil. When a pan is warm, a little oil will go a long way. When shopping, remember that if it doesn't say "expeller-pressed" or "cold-pressed" (chemical-free extraction) on the label, the oil was more than likely solvent extracted with dangerous chemicals. There are a handful of natural, unrefined, virgin oils that can be used for a variety of cooking techniques and raw recipes. Store all in a cool, dry pantry or fridge out of direct sunlight unless otherwise specified. *Here's what's what:*

Avocado Oil

9 – 12 months in the pantry
Smoke point 350 – 400°F

Pressed from the flesh of avocados, this nutty, buttery oil is more than 50 percent beneficial monounsaturated fat. High in vitamin E, it can also be used on skin. Its high smoke point makes it good for sautéing, frying, and roasting. It's delicious in dressings, too.

Coconut Oil

1 year in the pantry
Smoke point 350°F

Coconut oil can be liquid or solid — 76°F is the melting point. It's a good substitute for butter in most recipes, but since it's sensitive to temperature, if a recipe calls for liquid, don't add it to cold ingredients or it will firm up until warm again.

Nut & Seed Oils ➡

9 – 12 months in the pantry
Smoke point 350 – 400°F

Best used uncooked in dressings or drizzled over prepared foods since they add a rich, unique flavor, especially if toasted.

Almond Oil

6 – 9 months in the pantry
Smoke point 420°F

Sweet, nutty flavor, good for cooking savory and sweet dishes, as well as cosmetic uses like moisturizer or a base for infused oils for healing balms.

Flax Oil

3 – 6 months in the fridge
Smoke point 255°F

Must be stored in the fridge away from light and heat. A very fragile oil, it shouldn't be used for baking or hot recipes. Good for dressings and drizzling over cooked, warm (not hot) foods.

Grapeseed Oil

3 – 6 months in the pantry
Smoke point 400°F

Slightly sweet oil, with a hint of tart and floral that's nice for dressings, stir fry, roasting, and baking.

Hemp Seed Oil

3 – 6 months in the fridge
Smoke point 255°F

Must be stored in the fridge away from light and heat. Like flax, it's a very fragile oil, and it shouldn't be used for baking or hot recipes. Tasty in dressings and drizzling over cooked, warm (not hot) foods.

Toasted Sesame Oil

4 – 6 months in the pantry
Smoke point 350°F

Its strong toasted sesame flavor is delicious in many Asian-inspired recipes for sauces, noodles, soups, and salads.

Olive Oil

2 – 3 years in the pantry
Smoke point 375°F

The robust flavor is great for low-temperature sautéing, baking, and dressings.

GLUTEN-FREE PASTA AND NOODLES (DRY)

1–2 years in the pantry

Keep pasta lasting as long as possible by transferring it to airtight glass containers until ready to use.

RICE (BROWN, WILD, PURPLE, BLACK, BASMATI, RED)

6–12 months in the pantry

White rice will last for years because it's been refined to remove the wholesome bran layers and fatty acids and nutrients that go with it. The oils in unprocessed rice like brown, wild, purple, black, and basmati, however, can go rancid, so make sure they are transferred to an airtight glass container and used within 4–5 months.

SEA SALTS (CELTIC, HIMALAYAN, FLEUR DE SEL)

Indefinitely in the pantry

Sea salts (naturally dried from saltwater lakes and ocean sources) are full of necessary minerals that our bodies rely on for bone density, circulation, stable blood sugar, and hydration. Conventional table salt (mined from underground salt deposits) has been heavily refined (at upward of 1,200°F), stripped of these minerals, and fortified with synthetic iodine (an attempt to reduce worldwide iodine deficiency) and usually contains anti-clumping agents (calcium silicate, ferrocyanide, silica aluminate, and talc, to name only a few). Real sea salt — the kind that benefits health — will not be white; it will have a pink or gray shade to it and come in textures ranging from coarse to fine-ground. Keep some in a little open dish near your range for easy pinches that you can add to meals.

SEAWEED (AGAR, DULSE, KOMBU, WAKAME, KELP)

2+ years in the pantry

Sea veggies — one of the most nutritionally dense foods in the world — are a great source of minerals like iodine (another reason to skip the processed, synthetically fortified table salt). I like to cut kombu into ½" pieces and fill an airtight glass jar, so when I'm cooking grains, noodles, rice, and pseudograins I can add a piece or two to add beneficial nutrients to foods. This technique tenderizes ingredients as well. Leave the cooked kombu in your recipe or remove it (your call) — taste is not altered at all for savory or sweet dishes. It's also helpful to keep a shaker jar of dulse granules nearby as you cook, too. They can be easily sprinkled into salads, soups, sautéed veggies, and cooked grains for added nutrients without adding a strong sea flavor to recipes. You can also make crispy chip-like snacks out of toasted seaweed (page 263).

SEEDS

Varies 3–24 months

Milks, sauces, salad toppings, and desserts of all kinds can be made from these versatile little beauties. Store all in a cool, dry pantry or fridge out of direct sunlight unless otherwise specified.

Chia Seeds

2–4 years in the pantry

Only in America would we take one of nature's most nutritious seeds and use them for a goofy figurine planter instead of eating them. Remember the jingle? "Ch-ch-ch-chia." Yep, these are the same seeds used to grow green hair on a terracotta Barack Obama, puppy, or turtle. Not only can you eat these sprouts, but the seeds are a fantastic source of fiber, protein, and antioxidants (which increases shelf life and stability). Even though they're high in beneficial omega-3 fatty acids, which are usually more sensitive to light and heat (like in flax and hemp sources), chia seeds are stable and hold up to baking and heat well. If you want to grow sprouts, find some terracotta, soak them, spread them on, and wait. If you have no patience for that, I suggest trying them now in a tasty Cardamom Cream Chia Pudding (page 164) or even a Chocolate & Salted Caramel Layer Cake (page 290).

Hemp Seeds (hulled)

6–12 months in the fridge or freezer

Yes, I had the same silly thought the first time I heard about hemp seeds. But don't worry. You will not get high or test positive on a drug test if you eat them (or use the oil). Gobble up hemp seeds (also called hemp hearts) and reap the health benefits of omega-3 fatty acids, protein, and fiber. They must be stored in the fridge or freezer out of light to protect the beneficial omega fatty acids that can go rancid, becoming toxic if exposed to heat and light for too long. Due to this fragility, it's best to only use hemp seeds in salads (page 223), smoothies (page 280), as a topping for cereals (page 163), and raw recipes. Add hemp seeds to hot dishes, once cooled to warm, not during baking or cooking. They also make a delicious, creamy non-dairy milk (page 276).

Flax Seeds (whole)

6–12 months in the fridge or freezer

In order to get the nutritional benefits of flax seeds (omega-3 essential fatty acids, lignans, and fiber), you must grind them first. Otherwise, they will just pass right on through your body undigested — that hull is virtually indestructible. You can fresh grind seeds in individual servings in a small coffee grinder or grind up a bunch and store in an airtight glass container in the freezer and store for up to 4 weeks. Like hemp seeds, flax seeds can easily turn rancid, and buying pre-ground flax is a gamble, since it may have been in transit longer than 4 weeks, and in hot, sunny or warehouse conditions. Use fresh ground flax seeds in salads, smoothies, cold cereals, and raw foods. It's used often in vegan baking as an egg substitute, but high temperatures can destroy the EFAs, even making them toxic. Sprinkle or add in ground flax seeds to hot dishes, once cooled to warm instead.

Poppy Seeds

3–6 months in the pantry

Due to the high oil content in poppy seeds, it's best to store them in the fridge or freezer. Try them in a homemade non-dairy milk (page 276) before bedtime for restful sleep and make some tasty breadsticks with them for snackin' (page 183).

Pumpkin Seeds (aka pepitas)

3–6 months in the fridge or pantry

Toasted pumpkin seeds are one of my favorite warm cereal add-ons (try them on page 168) and they help make the Super Seed Bread on page 182, well, super indeed. These green seeds contain high amounts of our friends, antioxidants, too.

Sesame Seeds (unhulled)

3–6 months in the pantry

I prefer the heartiness and flavor that come from unhulled sesame seeds (black and gold varieties) especially when toasting them. Hulled sesame seeds perish quicker because their oils are exposed.

Sunflower Seeds (shelled)

6–12 months in the pantry

Sunflower seeds make a great replacement for cashews in cream sauces and milks for those with allergies. They're a fantastic, crunchy addition to salads and roasted veggies, too. Keep shelled on hand for easy preparation.

SWEETENERS (NATURAL)

There are a variety of sweeteners that contain beneficial nutrients — which is great if we're going to have a treat. Keep in mind, sweeteners are not health foods, so they should be consumed in moderation.

Blackstrap Molasses

8–12 months in the pantry

One of the most nutritious sweeteners available, molasses is what remains after the extraction of sugar from raw sugar cane. It's a good source of iron and other minerals like potassium and magnesium. Avoid sulfite preservatives and buy unsulphured molasses. Stir into some Homemade Almond Milk (page 276) with a teeny pinch of sea salt and be reminded of Cracker Jacks.

Brown Rice Syrup

6–12 months in the pantry

Made from cooked, fermented rice, this nutty, caramel-like sweetener contains trace minerals and is an great binder for bars. Always purchase organic to avoid GMO ingredients, herbicides, and pesticides used in rice production.

Dates

3–6 months in the fridge

Most health food stores carry the Medjool (usually contain pits) or Deglet Noor (usually pitted) variety of dates. They're incredibly sweet, are a super pre-workout booster, and make a great binder for bars. Use this ratio to substitute for recipes: 1 Medjool = 3 Deglets. Be sure to pit them before using and always double-check pre-pitted dates (just give them a smush between pinched fingers to feel for a pit); sometimes one will hide in a "pre-pitted" date and you'll hear it in the blender — pit pieces will ruin a recipe.

Honey (raw, humanely harvested)

Indefinitely in the pantry

Unpasteurized, unheated raw honey contains many beneficial vitamins, enzymes, antioxidants, and other nutrients that promote body and digestive health, strengthens the immune system, eliminates allergies (if purchased from a local source), and makes a useful remedy for skin wounds (ahem, like kitchen burns) and all types of infections.

1 – 3 years in the pantry

Nothing beats the flavor of fresh-ground spices or fresh herbs, but it's not always possible to go that extra mile each time we cook (or to lean out the back door to an herb garden), so ground spices and dried herbs are great second-placers to keep stocked. To test the freshness of a spice or herb, rub or crush a small amount in your hand, then taste and smell it. If the aroma and flavor is weak, it should be discarded. Dry herbs are more potent than fresh, so keep this ratio in mind when substituting fresh for dry or vice versa: 1 tablespoon of a fresh herb = 1 teaspoon of dried. Try stocking up with some of these staples (buy whole if you have a spice/coffee grinder and ground if you don't).⬇

Bay Leaf

Makes soups sing and also helpful for reducing pain and inflammation.

Cardamom

Adds floral brilliance to savory and sweet dishes and known to calm digestive issues.

Chili Powder

Adds heat and depth to all sorts of recipes and also reduces inflammation and boosts circulation.

Cinnamon

Look for Ceylon cinnamon for the best quality and know that it helps battle candida, boosts digestion, and can help relieve PMS symptoms.

Cloves

Potent flavor for cereals, teas, and baked goods that doubles as a detoxifier; known to help remove environmental pollutants from the body.

Coriander

Don't ever make tacos without this sweet, lemony spice that regulates blood sugar and can help insomnia sufferers finally get some shut-eye.

Cumin

The spice that gives Taco Seasoning (page 202) its distinct flavor, cumin is a great source of iron and helps control blood sugar levels.

Fennel Seed

A mild, licorice-like flavor that's great for teas and dishes of all kinds, fennel kicks up digestive "fire" and can help with various digestive disorders.

Nutmeg

Warm, sweet, and spicy, nutmeg is known as a brain stimulator and pain reducer.

Paprika

Warm, peppery paprika reduces inflammation and is known to brighten and tighten the skin.

Rosemary

A little goes a long way with this piney-scented spice that reduces muscle pain and boosts memory.

Thyme

Slightly minty thyme is tasty in savory and sweet dishes, and it's connected with relieving respiratory problems like coughs and chest congestion.

Turmeric

Bright yellow turmeric is slightly buttery with a touch of horseradish and bitterness — it's one of the most powerful anti-inflammatories around.

Health-boosting honey should be opaque, not clear, translucent, or syrup-like (which is how most honey on the shelves looks due to extreme processing and combinations with non-honey, lookalike sweeteners). Wild-harvested honey collection uses methods that do not harm or anger the bees, their hives, or their land, so look for that label.

Maple Syrup (Grade B)

2+ years in the fridge

Most "maple" syrups in traditional grocery stores contain preservatives, cellulose gums (derived from wood pulp), caramel color (aka ammonia-sulfite process caramel), sodium benzoate, chemical flavorings, preservatives, sodium hexametaphosphate (used to make soap, detergents), and (gulp...) high fructose corn syrup. Google those ingredients to see how scary they all are. Whenever maple syrup is called for in a YumUniverse recipe, I mean 100 percent pure — the kind that is made simply by boiling sap from a tree. While Grade A sounds like it would be a better choice, Grade B maple syrup actually contains more beneficial nutrients since it's the least processed. It's also sweeter, richer, and bolder in maple flavor — we'll need to use less than we would Grade A. Once opened, store in the fridge for extended shelf life.

Stevia (natural)

6–12 months in the pantry

While I'm not a huge fan of the flavor of this sweetener (too abrupt, artificial-tasting, and licorice-like for me), if you do choose to use it (many do), know that it should be green, which means that it hasn't been bleached, processed, or packaged with fillers like the white and liquid varieties found in grocery stores (processed and preserved, with harmful bulking agents). If stevia is green, it's simply dried and ground stevia leaves that didn't go through a lab (and all beneficial phytonutrients are still intact).

Sucanat

1–2 years in the pantry

A dry sweetener, similar to brown sugar in taste, Sucanat maintains its beneficial molasses nutrient content, since it's simply crushed sugar cane that is heated, then air dried. It's excellent in everything from Caramel Sauce (page 296) to Banana Bread Muffins (page 189). Sucanat is actually a brand name that stands for **Su**gar **Ca**ne **Nat**ural.

TEAS

6–12 months in the pantry

There are so many healing combinations and tasty recipes (page 163 for some breakfast goodness) that you can make with teas. Make sure when you buy tea — bagged or loose leaf (which is my preference) — that it's just organic tea without flavorings or additives, since these unnecessary additions are likely from a lab.

I love the healing benefits that come with certain teas (for centuries it's been used to treat everything from cancer to constipation), so I choose to drink them — but usually on their own (not with meals). I ferment them into probiotic kombucha tea (see **yumuniverse.com/how-to-make-kombucha-tea** for directions) and use them to make cereals (page 176), and lattes (page 278). Some of my favorites include Rooibos, which is an antioxidant-rich tea. It's a caffeine-free immunity booster that contains extra minerals like magnesium. If you're trying to kick coffee, try rich, dark, detoxifying chicory root — it's a friend when it comes to stress. It protects the liver and kidneys and can reduce cortisol levels (stress hormone that messes up sleep and adds belly fat and other unpleasantries). For more liver and kidney support, try roasted dandelion root tea, hot or cold. Transfer loose-leaf tea to airtight glass containers and keep in the fridge to really extend shelf life.

YEAST (NUTRITIONAL)

12–24 months in the pantry

Nutritional yeast (not to be confused with fresh or dry yeast, brewer's or bakers yeast) is a yellow inactive yeast that's grown on molasses, then washed, dried, and heated to deactivate it. A nutty, cheesy flavor makes it a favorite ingredient for plant-based recipes. It's also loaded with amino acids and beneficial B vitamins, even B_{12} (make sure you read the label; some are, some aren't). If you have Candida problems, nutritional yeast is safe to consume and won't contribute to overgrowth because it's deactivated, unlike other culinary yeasts.

4 – 12 months in the fridge or pantry

All whole foods are super in their own way but there are certain supplements that are nice to keep on hand since they pack a special nutritional punch. Many times, they come in powders, so they store similarly to flours. If you have a cool, dry home, store most flours and powders out of direct sunlight. To reduce intake of herbicides, pesticides, and GM ingredients, buy certified (or farmers' market) organic when you can. Store all of the following in the fridge for long life unless otherwise specified.

Acai Powder

2 – 4 months

Pronounced "ah-sigh-ee," this purplish black berry from South America is full of antioxidants, omega fatty acids, protein, and fiber. It's delicious in smoothies, cereals, desserts, and even chili — its flavor hints of cacao.

Cacao/Cocoa Powder

1 year

Cacao powder is loaded with antioxidants, iron, and magnesium (why chocolate cravings usually occur with menstruation — the body wants this mineral). Raw cacao is made by cold-pressing unroasted cocoa beans, which keeps enzymes and nutrients intact. Cocoa, on the other hand, is roasted at high temperatures, which can reduce nutrient value and enzyme content. I find that taste-wise, the two are pretty interchangeable in recipes in equal amounts.

Chlorella Powder

1 year

This freshwater algae can be found in powder, tablet, and liquid form as a supplement known to remove heavy metals from the body. It's full of vitamins, chlorophyll, protein, omega fatty acids, and minerals and can be added to smoothies or taken as a supplement daily.

Gluten-Free Flours

4 – 5 months

Since whole grain, gluten-free flours haven't been highly processed, oils and nutrients still in them can make them susceptible to spoilage. Read the ingredients since some gluten-free flours and blends can contain dairy products. Always store in the fridge, or in a cool, dry pantry if they'll be used within a few weeks. Transfer them out of bags and into airtight glass containers.

Green Superfood Powders

6 – 12 months

Green superfood powders are a nice addition to smoothies. They're full of beneficial enzymes, nutrients, chlorophyll, and antioxidants. If you won't go through a container in 2 – 4 weeks, store in the fridge or freezer for maximum shelf life.

Maca Powder

6 – 12 months

Maca (pronounced "mah-kah") is a Peruvian root from the radish family. It can boost energy, clear skin, balance mood disorders, regulate hormones, reduce symptoms of menopause, PMS, and cramping, boost sexual function for men and women, and provide us with beneficial vitamins and minerals. It has an earthy, malty flavor that's yum paired with chocolate, smoothies, cereals, and baked goodies.

Plant Protein Powders

6 – 12 months

Plant protein powders come in a variety of flavors and formulas like brown rice, hemp, and blends. Choose GMO-free products with recognizable ingredients. They're a nice addition to smoothies, great on their own or baked into cookies, bars, and muffins. Look for added beneficial enzymes, nutrients, probiotics, chlorophyll, and antioxidants. If you won't go through a container in 2 – 4 weeks, store in the fridge or freezer for maximum shelf life.

Spirulina Powder

1 year

Spirulina is a high-protein, nutrient-rich algae powder that makes a nice addition to smoothies. It's high in antioxidants, iron, calcium, protein, and EFAs, especially omega-3. Store in the fridge or freezer for maximum shelf life. It has a strong sea flavor, so if you can find spirulina flakes, it's the tastiest — yum in anything chocolate.

Fruit & Vegetable Storage

According to an August 2012 report by the National Resources Defense Council, Americans throw away 40 percent of the food they buy — that ends up being about $2,275 a year per family of four. That's a vacation or two lost. If you store produce properly, every bit of it can be enjoyed either now or in the future.

One of the first steps to mastering produce storage is understanding the power of the ripening hormone ethylene. Ethylene is a naturally occurring gas that is produced by certain produce when ripening begins — changing texture, softness, and color. Learn to discern the differences between ethylene producers and the fruits and veggies that are compromised by ethylene. Certain produce are bigger ethylene offenders than others, so storing ethylene producers near non-ethylene producers can either kick-start ripening or speed up decay, so learn the difference. Use ethylene to your advantage.

ETHYLENE PRODUCERS

If any of these items make it home less than ripe, just seal them in a paper bag for 1–3 days to ripen (ethylene gets trapped and speeds things up). Placing ethylene producers together on the counter will also help, but keep them separate if you want them to last longer. Also know that the warmer it is for produce, the faster the respiration (ripening) process will take place.

- Apples
- Apricots
- Avocado
- Bananas
- Blueberries
- Cantaloupe
- Citrus fruit (not grapefruit)
- Figs
- Grapes
- Green onions
- Honeydew
- Kiwi fruit
- Mangoes
- Melons
- Mushrooms
- Nectarines
- Papayas
- Passion fruit
- Peaches
- Pears
- Peppers
- Pineapple
- Plums
- Prunes
- Tomatoes
- Watermelon

Honeydew Melon

ETHYLENE SENSITIVE

- Asparagus
- Broccoli
- Brussels sprouts
- Cabbage
- Carrots
- Cauliflower
- Cucumbers
- Eggplant
- Green beans
- Kale
- Kiwi fruit
- Leafy greens
- Lettuce
- Parsley
- Peas
- Peppers
- Potatoes
- Romaine lettuce
- Spinach
- Squash
- Sweet potatoes
- Watercress
- Yams

Graffiti Eggplant

Countertop Storage

These items prefer to be stored at room temperature at least until ripe, but move them to the fridge toward the end of their shelf life to extend it a bit more. Keep all of these items out of plastic or paper bags unless indicated otherwise. Sometimes, they're even freezable. When freezing is called for, store in an airtight glass container.

APPLES

If you like the crisp, cool snap of a cold apple, by all means store in the fridge, but they can keep on the counter for 2 weeks or more. For the fresh apple pickers: store a bounty of apples for up to five months in a fridge, fruit cellar, cool basement, or garage. Just keep their temp between 30 – 35°F with about 80 – 90 percent humidity (pick up a humidity meter for around $20).

Freezable? Yes. Core, slice, or dice, and toss with fresh lemon juice before freezing to minimize any oxidation (browning). They're excellent in smoothies — makes them nice and frosty.

APRICOTS

They range in color from yellow to deep orange to even dark purple, but when buying look for fruit with no green. Flesh should yield to gentle pressure, but avoid bruised, soft, or mushy fruit. Once ripened, move to the fridge for no more than 2 days.

Freezable? Yes. Rinse, cut in half, and remove pit first.

Try chilled Granny Smith apple slices topped with Homemade Almond Butter (page 269) and a pinch of sea salt — my fave snack!

Freeze It

Lack time in the evening to make a decent meal? Become BFFs with the freezer. Most cooked meals and ingredients will last one to two weeks in the fridge, but they can last months if frozen. And if you have something that's nearing its expiration, don't waste it! Freeze it. For individual ingredients (like broccoli florets), prepare them and then freeze on a baking sheet. After a few hours, easily transfer to an airtight glass container.

Pre-Cooked Meals & Leftovers

Prepare cooked gratins (page 249), lasagnas, soups (page 213), chilis (page 214), quinoa taco meat (page 237), veggie burgers (page 244) and veggie cakes (page 197), cookie doughs (page 31), pie crusts (page 288), even tarts (page 239, precut for easy single servings) and freeze them for later meals. Just make sure that everything is sealed well in an airtight glass container and has cooled to room temperature before it goes into the freezer to minimize ice crystals.

Ready-to-Cook Ideas

When I can't eat up all the veggies I've bought, and I have enough saved for making stock, I will chop, dice, and mince what I have, toss it all into a bowl with fresh herbs, seasoning mix, and/or a sauce, transfer it to an airtight glass container, and freeze it (in either big or individual serving sizes). On nights where I need to make dinner quickly, I'm very happy to reach into the freezer and only have to empty a container into a hot skillet or baking dish for roasting or sautéing. You're basically making frozen dinners you can trust.

Cooked Grains, Legumes, Beans & Pseudograins

Soak, cook, and freeze hearty legumes, beans, and grains like lentils, quinoa, rice, buckwheat, chickpeas, black beans, and millet. Make sure you allow the cooked grains to cool completely before freezing in airtight glass containers — and think ahead, freeze them packed into single-serving cubes in your ice-cube trays and/or by the cup for your favorite recipes.

Homemade Veggie Stock

SAVE VEGGIE SCRAPS

Always save veggie scraps! Onions, peppers, herbs (wilty ones and just stems, too), lemon peels, garlic, potato skins, broccoli stalks, kale stems, mushroom stems — all of it — to make homemade veggie stocks. The scraps don't have to be pretty, but they still have so much flavor. I keep a large glass bowl (that I have a lid for) near me as I cook and all scraps go in that bowl. I pack 'em down, seal it up, and put the bowl in the freezer until I cook again. Once it's full, I prepare a homemade stock following these steps:

STEPS:

1. Fill a large stockpot to the brim with veggie scraps and water. If there isn't onion, garlic, a slice of lemon, or a bit of herbs in the mix, add some.

2. Bring contents to a boil. Reduce heat and simmer for 15 minutes.

3. Add more water to fill pot and turn off heat. Place a lid on stockpot and let contents cool for 1 – 2 hours.

4. Strain and season to taste with sea salt and pepper. Refrigerate and/or freeze stock.

psst! For a heartier, less watery stock, spoon one cup of scraps and one cup of liquid into the blender and blend until smooth. Add this purée back to stockpot with remaining strained stock — this creates a creamier, richer texture.

Freeze stock in ice-cube trays for single-serving sizes perfect for sautéing veggies and making quick sauces.

AVOCADOS

Unripe, firm, or green avocados will ripen on a room-temperature counter-top in 4 to 5 days. If you cut open an avocado and it's unripe, sprinkle with fresh lemon juice, place the two halves back together, and wrap tightly in parchment, then a plastic or paper bag. In a few days, it should be temptingly ripe and delicious.

Freezable? Avocadoes don't hold up well in the freezer — they are best enjoyed fresh. But you can puree or mash them with lemon and freeze to use later for spreads, dressings, dips, and smoothies.

BANANAS

Choose bananas based on their degree of ripeness and when you'll be using them. Green bananas will take about five days to ripen, yellow bananas are ripe and ready to eat, and yellow bananas with brown spots are ripe, sweeter, and should be eaten within a few days. Now, if you have a banana or three in a bunch and they are looking like they may not make the end of the week, put them in the fridge. The peel will turn black but don't fret, the fruit inside is A-OK to eat and use in recipes.

Freezable? Yes. When freezing bananas, peel them before freezing and place them in an airtight freezer container. There's nothing trickier than trying to peel a frozen banana. They're excellent in smoothies — and it makes them nice and cool.

BASIL

One of the only herbs that once cut prefers room temperature (the fridge can make leaves turn black). Store in a glass of water on the counter — it will make the kitchen smell wonderful. Change the water every few days and it will last for 2 – 3 weeks.

Freezable? Yes, but freeze leaves in an ice-cube tray filled with coconut oil or veggie broth for quick and easy seasoning cubes. Otherwise, dry them and store in the pantry for the best flavor. Plain frozen leaves blacken but taste fine cooked into soups, blended into sauces, or added to smoothies.

BUTTERNUT SQUASH

Choose a firm, heavy, evenly colored squash when shopping and know that this hearty vegetable can last in a cool basement or garage for months, even a year if the conditions are right (somewhere between 50 – 60°F and 60 percent humidity). Sometimes, I will cut only a piece off a large squash to steam for a quick meal. Rub the open end with sea salt or lemon juice to protect it from bacteria, wrap in parchment, and secure with a rubber band, then move it to the fridge until you need a bit more. The longer the neck, the more seed-free squash you have to work with, so look for long over round.

Freezable? Yes. Peel and cut to size before freezing.

CANTALOUPE
(AKA MUSKMELON)

Oh, how my grandfather loved cantaloupe sprinkled with fresh pepper (see page 295). The best way to choose a tasty cantaloupe is by its fragrance. A nice cantaloupe should smell sweet and fruity. It should feel heavy and have a thick-netted rind that yields a smidge when pressed. Once cut, store in the fridge for up to 5 days (give it a squeeze of lemon to extend shelf life).

Freezable? Yes. Remove seeds and rind, cut into pieces (or use a melon baller), then freeze.

CITRUS FRUIT
(CLEMENTINES, GRAPEFRUIT, KUMQUATS, LEMONS, LIMES, ORANGES, TANGERINES)

The workhorses of the kitchen ingredients, citrus zest and juice can transform flavors and even help preserve thanks to their acid content. Choose firm, heavy fruits since this means more juiciness. Will keep on the counter for one to two weeks. Transfer to the fridge to extend shelf life, but they will be juicier and sweeter if enjoyed at room temperature.

Freezable? Yes. Freeze citrus juice or wedges, but peel first. If juiced, use an ice-cube tray to freeze cubes of juice for single serving use (thaw into a recycled jam jar and keep in the fridge every week). Very handy.

If juiced, use an ice cube tray to freeze cubes of juice for single-serving use (thaw into a recycled jam jar and keep in the fridge every week). Very handy.

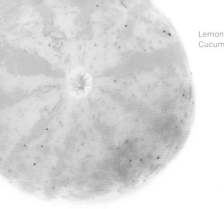

Lemon
Cucumber

CUCUMBERS

Most folks store cucumbers in the fridge, but they're susceptible to chilling injury (especially if you have an old fridge that tends to flash-freeze), so it's best to store them on the counter. If moved to the fridge, keep them on the top shelf, where it's usually warmest, and eat them up in 3–5 days.

Freezable? Not really, they're too watery to hold up well in the freezer. They lose their flavor and vitality when frozen, but if you do freeze, use them in smoothies.

EGGPLANT

My mother used to grow eggplant in her garden on my childhood farm. And now I see their beauty and ability to transform into all sorts of dishes — like the eggplant crisps on page 211 or the curry on page 241. Cold temperatures can damage the texture and flavor of eggplant, so keep it on the counter. If you store in the fridge, eat it up within 1–3 days.

Freezable? Not really, they're too watery to hold up well in the freezer and lose their flavor.

HONEYDEW

Choose a fragrant honeydew melon that is heavy and the color of butter. Once cut, store in the fridge for up to 5 days (give it a squeeze of lemon or lime to extend shelf life).

Freezable? Yes. Remove seeds and rind, cut into pieces, then freeze.

MANGO

Choose fruit that yields to gentle pressure and is blemish-free. Give it a sniff and opt for fruit that has a fragrant aroma.

Freezable? Yes. Peel, dice and freeze. Excellent for smoothies.

ONION
(GARLIC & SHALLOTS, TOO)

If eaten within 4–6 weeks, onions can be stored in hanging baskets, bowls, or on countertops. Store green onions (aka scallions) in the crisper drawer of your fridge. For a little Onion 101, visit **yumuniverse.com/ yu-book-owners.**

Freezable? Not really, they're too watery to hold up well in the freezer and lose their flavor.

PAPAYAS

Select fruits that are primarily yellow with a bit of green on them, and let them fully ripen on the counter at home — at which point the skin will be bright yellow. Ripe fruit will be firm, but yields to slight pressure and will smell sweet. Once ripe, transfer to the fridge, where it will keep for about 1 week.

Freezable? Yes. Seed, peel, slice, and dice first.

PEACHES
(PLUMS, PRUNES & NECTARINES, TOO)

Stone fruits that are picked prematurely will never sweeten properly (even though they will continue to ripen), so select mature fruit to bring home. They should be unblemished, firm, but yield to gentle pressure and smell fragrant. Once ripened on the counter, transfer to the crisper drawer in the fridge to extend life for up to 7 days.

Freezable? Yes. Rinse, cut in half, and remove pit first. And then just toss 'em in the freezer.

PEARS

Ripe pears will be fragrant and have a slight softness around the neck. Russeting (corky, netlike texture that occurs on skin mainly due to weather) is fairly common and doesn't affect the fruit inside the skin — it may even give it a nice, nutty flavor. Unripe pears will ripen on the counter. Once ripe, transfer to the fridge for up to 7 days. Try them in my all-time favorite Pear & Cilantro Smoothie on page 280.

Freezable? Yes. Core, slice, or dice and toss with fresh lemon juice before freezing to minimize any oxidation (browning).

PINEAPPLE

Since pineapples don't continue to ripen after they're picked (even if the skin color changes at home), it's important to know how to select a sweet, juicy one. Leaves should not be dry, shriveled, or wilty. The fruit should smell fragrant, be heavy, and yield a bit to pressure. If a pineapple is vibrant green with yellow coloring, no white patches or brown spots, pull on one of the leaves. If it comes out easily, the fruit is ripe. Once cut, store in the fridge for up to 5 days.

Freezable? Yes. Peel, core, dice and freeze.

PLANTAINS

They look like bananas, but bite into one and we'll see that they're not. Plantains are delicious cooked and taste like a cross between a banana and a potato. Plantain color will change from green to yellow to black during its ripening, but each stage can be enjoyed. The greener the plantain, the more neutral the flavor; the darker the plantain, the sweeter it will be. Peeling is easier the more ripe it is. Move to the fridge once ripe to extend shelf life.

Freezable? Yes. Peel before freezing. Place them in an airtight freezer container.

SWEET POTATO & YAMS (LE GRANDE MIXUP)

Even though they are often mislabeled, sweet potatoes and yams are two different species of root veggie. Sweet potatoes have a smooth purple, gold, white, or copper skin with orange or white

flesh, while true yams will have a tough, dark bark-like texture and white, purple, or red-orange flesh (they're sweeter, too). Store both on the counter for weeks and in a cool basement or garage for months.

Freezable? Yes. Peel and cut to size before freezing.

TOMATOES

When buying, look for richly colored, smooth-skinned, heavy tomatoes that smell earthy, sweet, and tomato-y. They shouldn't be puffy (a sign of weak flavor) and they should yield to slight pressure. Never refrigerate whole tomatoes unless you want mush.

Freezable? Yes. Slice, dice, peel, or purée for all kinds of meals and sauces.

WATERMELON

To find a ripe one, look for a shriveled stem. Also peek at the underside of the melon, where it lay on the ground. It should be a bit yellow there, not white, which could indicate that it was picked a tad early. Once cut, store in the fridge for up to 5 days (give it a squeeze of lemon or lime to extend shelf life). And for the love of all fruits and veggies, get one with seeds — nature designed watermelon with seeds. A lab designed the ones without seeds. It's not that hard to cut around them or spit them out.

Freezable? Yes. Cut into rind-free pieces then freeze.

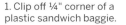

Fruit Flies

Oftentimes, especially in warmer climates and during summer months, produce left out on the counter attracts pesky fruit flies. If they arrive, move all produce to the fridge, empty your trash, wipe the counters to remove any juice, and make this simple chemical-free trap.

1. Clip off ¼" corner of a plastic sandwich baggie.

2. Pour about ½ cup of apple cider vinegar into a drinking glass.

3. Point the cut corner of the bag down inside the glass so it's just above the vinegar, fold excess baggie over rim of glass, and secure with a rubber band.

4. The flies love the vinegar and climb down inside, but can't get out again. Empty it once a week and fill with fresh vinegar. Make multiple traps if you need to until all the flies are gone.

Fridge Storage

Cold temps slow the respiration process for fruits and vegetables, so refrigeration is a great way to extend shelf life for most produce. If certain fruits and veggies are ripening too fast on the counter, or have reached ripeness, move them to the fridge (but keep them away from ethylene-sensitive foods) to extend their life. These are the fruits and veggies that should always be stored in the refrigerator. If you have an older refrigerator, keep delicate foods like greens toward the front door or in the crisper — old fridges can flash-freeze and soggify greens. Resist the temptation to wash fruits and veggies before storing them (unless otherwise indicated). The added moisture from washing invites mold and spoiling. Line crisper drawers with clean paper towels to absorb any excess moisture — it helps produce last longer. Keep some unbleached paper lunch bags on hand to replace plastic bags that are used for storage — they're reusable and non-toxic.

ARTICHOKES

Select heavy globes with a deep green color and tight leaf formation. Press leaves against each other. If you hear squeaking, that's the sound of freshness.

Freezable? Yes. To protect flavor and texture, cook them first. Then transfer to an airtight glass container.

ASPARAGUS

Select firm, straight, bright green stalks with tightly closed tips. Stems should be smooth, since ridges indicate old age. The more uniform the size of the stalks, the more control we have with cooking times. To store, trim the bottom ends and place bundle upright in a sturdy glass or ramekin (small dish used for baking and serving a single portion of food) filled with about ½" water.

Freezable? Yes. To protect flavor and texture, blanch first. Before blanching, hold each spear at either end, and bend it until it snaps. Save the ends for veggie stock (see page 122) and blanch the spears that are left. Then freeze and transfer to an airtight glass container.

BEETS

Select small to medium firm beets with taproot intact (the tapered root at the bottom). If beet greens are still attached (which is the best way to tell if beets are fresh), they should be bright green with no signs of wilting. Large beets with hairy taproots indicate a woodier, tougher texture. When you get home, trim greens 2 – 3" from beet and save them for salads, smoothies, or homemade veggie stock. If you leave the greens on, they can sap moisture from the beetroot. The crisper drawer is the best place for beets. Try the Beet, Apple & Onion Gratin (page 249).

Freezable? Yes. Cut to size before freezing.

BERRIES (BLACKBERRIES, BLUEBERRIES, STRAWBERRIES, RASPBERRIES)

When shopping, look for plump, bright berries. Always check the bottom of the container — you want to see firm, berries, not soggy, mushy, or moldy ones. When you get home, remove any sad ones that snuck by and treat healthy-looking berries with homemade fruit and veggie wash (visit **yumuniverse. com/yu-book-owners** to get the easy recipe that will make berries last for weeks), then soak and dry them gently but thoroughly. Place them back in their container in the fridge for seven to ten days so you can use them in recipes like Warm Lemon & Blueberry Kasha (page 172) or Mixed Berry Fruit Salad (page 36).

Freezable? Yes. Freeze whole or slice into smaller pieces. They're great for cereals, sorbets, compotes, jams, pies, tarts, ice creams, granitas, and smoothies.

BROCCOLI

When buying heads of broccoli, look for tight green florets and firm stalks — no dried, browning stems or yellowing on florets. The bundle should feel heavy for its size. Store in the crisper in an open container or paper bag. Save stalks for delicious homemade veggie stock or veggie noodles (just use a peeler). If buying pre-cut florets, make sure florets look crisp, bright, and green with no sogginess or yellowing. Get them out of the plastic bag and into a dry paper bag or glass container when you get home. Try the Broccoli & Red Pepper Macaroni (page 236). If broccoli is starting to wilt in the fridge, make a fresh cut on the bottom of the stalk and place in a glass of water — it will perk right up.

Freezable? Yes. Cut to size before freezing.

BRUSSELS SPROUTS

If bought on the stalk, leave them on the stalk until ready to cook. If bought loose, store them in a glass container. Either way, sprouts should be firm, tight-leafed, and brightly colored (not yellowing). Keep them in a dry open or sealed glass container and try them seared (so tasty!) and tossed with Miso Dijon Sauce on page 195.

Freezable? Yes. Blanch before freezing.

CABBAGE

Regardless of the variety (green or red), we want to select cabbage with bright leaves that are tight. The cabbage head should be firm, showing no signs of rotting or discoloration. Keep it unwrapped or in a paper bag in the crisper drawer — it's very hearty and can last

for weeks. Usually, wilty leaves on the outside can be removed to reveal fresh ones underneath. Save softer (but not rotten) leaves for veggie stock. Head to page 231 right now for an incredibly simple and tasty Asian Cabbage Salad.

Freezable? Yes. Cut to size before freezing.

CARROTS

When shopping, look for smooth form and rich color. When you get home, trim greens 2 – 3" from carrots — they're full of nutrients, but a tad bitter. Use them in salads, smoothies, or homemade veggie stock. Don't leave the greens on; they can sap moisture from the carrots, leaving them wilty. The crisper drawer is the best place for carrots either wrapped in a paper bag or free. Resuscitate limp carrots by peeling them and then soaking them for a couple hours in ice water. They'll soak up the fresh water and regain some snap.

Freezable? Yes. Cut to size before freezing.

CAULIFLOWER

Coming in colors like green, orange, purple, and, most common, white, cauliflower in any color should be firm and tightly closed with no dark spots or signs of softness. Keep in the crisper drawer wrapped in a paper bag or loose. Cauliflower makes a healthy, tasty alternative to cream sauce so check out page 208.

Freezable? Yes. Cut to size before freezing.

CELERY

Firm, tightly packed stalks with fresh, bright leaves (no yellowing) is the kind of celery we want to bring home. Leave stalks attached to the root until ready to serve and store wrapped tightly in parchment or a paper bag — it can become soft if left unwrapped. As with carrots, you can soak in cold water for a minute or two to help it regain some crispness. Keep it in a warmer spot in the fridge; if it gets too cold, it can flash-freeze and become soggy due to its high water content. To remove the fibrous strings in celery, simply make a thin cut on the inside of one end of a stalk, bend back cut piece and pull downward — the strings should come with it. Save the root and strings for stock and be sure to cook with the leaves, they're loaded with nutrients and flavor.

Freezable? Celery is not the best veggie to freeze, but if you do, you can use it in cooked dishes like soups or stuffing once thawed.

CHERRIES

When buying dark, red cherries look for a rich depth of color. Note that Rainer cherries are yellow and red — this color doesn't indicate a lack of ripeness. If the stem is intact, the brighter green, the fresher the cherries. They should feel firm. Store in the coolest part of your fridge in a paper bag or open bowl — the crisper is a great spot for cherries.

Freezable? Yes, remove pits and stems before freezing. They're great for smoothies, compotes (page 200), and tasty tarts.

A Few More Freezer Tips

If produce is reaching the end of its shelf life (or if you have unexpected travel or overbought), freeze it for later use in soups, stews, pies, sauces, warm cereals, desserts, and smoothies. *Follow these tips:*

- Before freezing any produce, wash well and dry completely. For diced and sliced produce, use a cookie sheet to initially freeze, and then once solid, transfer frozen bits to a freezer-safe glass container or baggie. This way, you don't get a brick of broccoli, or a football of berries.

- For produce that oxidizes like apples, pears, and avocado, squeeze a little lemon juice over it before freezing to keep browning to a minimum. Why? Lemon juice is full of antioxidant power, and remember, browning is oxidation. Also the juice reduces the pH of the exposed fruit and makes it difficult for oxidation to occur.

- Utilize ice cube trays for single-serving portions of soups, sauces, purees, cooked grains, juices, herbs, stocks, and more. Freeze in the cubes and immediately once solid, transfer to an airtight container for long-term storage. If left in ice cube tray too long, frozen goodness is likely to freezer burn.

- Freeze most herbs on their stems, peel, and chop once thawed.

- Prepare fruits into individual cobblers and freeze. Simply bake when you want a treat.

COCONUT (YOUNG)

Young coconuts are harvested while the skin is still green. Before it makes its way to the store, that skin is removed, leaving a white cylindrical husk with a pointy top. Inside this softer husk is the hard shell that most folks are familiar with. And inside that shell is nutritious, soft coconut meat and coconut water (not to be confused with coconut milk, which is the water blended with meat). A cleaver or strong knife is recommended to open them — this task is a bit of a character builder, visit **yumuniverse.com/ yu-book-owners** for a video lesson — but it's worth the effort. The water can be enjoyed right away and the meat can be easily scooped out and used to make dairy-free probiotic yogurt, ice cream, and puddings.

Freezable? Yes. Both the water and coconut meat are freezable. They both make great additions to smoothies.

FIGS

They're fragile and don't continue to ripen after harvesting, so choose ripe (not fermented) smelling figs with soft skin, but firmness that yields with slight pressure, but no mushiness. Stem should be firmly in place. They can begin to spoil hours after harvest, so store immediately in the fridge in a glass container, but not piled high — that can bruise and smush these delicate fruits.

Freezable? Yes, but the texture can become mushy once thawed. Best used in baked tarts and smoothies.

GINGER ROOT

When buying, pick a ginger root with a fresh, spicy fragrance and a smooth skin. The root should feel firm, solid, and heavy. It can last for up to 4 weeks in the crisper drawer stored in a paper bag.

Freezable? Yes. Cut to size and peel if you like first.

GRAPES

Look for plump, unblemished, evenly colored grapes attached to a flexible stem. Store in a paper bag in the fridge.

Freezable? Yes. Frozen grapes make a nice treat (like baby Popsicles) and addition to smoothies. They also make delicious compotes and jams. Wash well, remove seeds, and de-stem before freezing.

GREEN BEANS

Quality green beans should be crisp and firm with uniform bright green coloring. Store in a paper bag in the crisper drawer.

Freezable? Yes, cut to size, remove strings, and blanch before freezing.

Grab a hole puncher and ma your own.

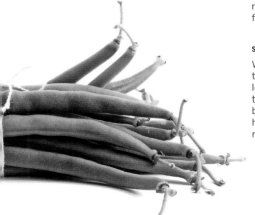

GREENS & HERBS (ARUGULA, CILANTRO, CHARD, COLLARDS, KALE, MARJORAM, MINT, MIXED GREENS, MUSTARD GREENS, PARSLEY, ROSEMARY, SAGE)

Keep in the crisper drawer (except basil). Do not ever wash until ready to use. If bunched greens and herbs are starting to wilt in the fridge, make a fresh cut on the bottom of the stalk or stem and place in a glass of water — most will perk right up.

Freezable? Yes, for herbs and hearty greens. No, for mixed greens, arugula, and softer leaves (unless they will be used for smoothies). For kale, chard, collards, spinach, and mustard greens you can remove stems before freezing. Woodier herbs can stay on the branches and leaves can be removed once thawed, or they can be prepped before freezing.

KIWI

Look for large, plump kiwi fruit without blemishes. It should be firm and yield to gentle pressure. (Leave kiwis on the counter if they need more time.) Once ripe, store in the fridge loose or in a paper bag.

Freezable? Yes. Peel first and cut into desired pieces.

MUSHROOMS

Select firm, evenly colored mushrooms with smooth, dry skin (no wrinkles, slime, bruises, or fishy smell). They need to breathe, so store them whole, dry, and unwashed in a perforated paper bag (use a hole punch) or open bowl in the fridge. Mushrooms are sponges, so don't soak them unless marinating them for a cooked dish. Simply wipe them clean with a dry or slightly damp paper towel before using them in a recipe.

Freezable? Mushrooms can be frozen, but I recommend using them for soups and stews or hot stir fry when you thaw them. Mushrooms can get a slightly mushy texture once frozen.

PEPPERS

Did you know that red bell peppers are actually mature green bell peppers and yellow and orange bell peppers are sweeter, different varieties altogether? Yep. No matter what kind you are buying (habañero, poblano, jalapeño, banana, chili), look for firm, deeply colored, glossy peppers without wrinkles. Store them in a paper bag or loose in the crisper drawer.

Freezable? Yes. Remove seeds, ribs, and stem and cut to desired pieces before freezing. Remember, save ribs and seed-free scraps for stock.

SPROUTS

When buying sprouts from the store, we want them to look fresh and dry from root to sprout — no sogginess or browning. When you get home, give them a cool rinse — it's like a drink of water for them since they're still growing — and drain them thoroughly. Transfer them to a clean, dry glass lid-less container or bowl with a paper towel at the bottom. Allow them to breathe. Every day or so, rinse and drain to extend their life. These tips work for home-sprouted babies, too.

Freezable? Yes, kinda. Their nutritional benefits (like all frozen foods) will diminish a bit with freezing, but you can use them in smoothies once thawed.

SUGAR SNAP PEAS & SNOW PEAS

Look for crisp, firm pods with uniform bright green color. They shouldn't bend; they should snap. Store in a paper bag in the crisper and try the Sautéed Snap Peas recipe on page 196.

Freezable? Yes, just remove stems and strings before freezing. Pods can stay on snap peas.

YELLOW SQUASH & ZUCCHINI

The larger they are, the more bitter in flavor, so try to select vegetables that are 8" or less in length, firm, and brightly colored with healthy stems (no sogginess or breakage). Store loose in the crisper drawer, or in a paper bag.

Freezable? Not so much. They're too watery and lose their flavor and vitality when frozen.

Social Situations

What we choose to eat is a highly personal choice. Sometimes, the folks around you (family, pals, co-workers, the waiter taking your modified order) won't understand your journey, but that's alright because it's your adventure, not theirs.

Too often, nothing can challenge our resolve like the opinions, comments, or influence of others. It's our lizard brain in effect — we want to be accepted because it helps insure our survival. So, as you consciously choose to go against mainstream thinking when it comes to what you eat, be considerate, be kind, lead by example, and simply share good food. These are my favorite tips for those times you venture out of the acceptance and comfort of your own kitchen.

Be a Considerate Guest

When you're invited to a dinner party, it's considerate to let the host know about dietary needs in advance so he/she can prepare, and the meal doesn't become about your not eating. If your host isn't familiar with plant-based dishes, suggest some ideas, send them links to a few recipes that fit with their evening's menu or theme, and offer to bring a dish if that makes it all easier for them.

Be a Considerate Host

When having friends or colleagues over for an event or meal, use the opportunity to introduce how flavorful and beautiful plant-inspired foods can be, without trying to convert or preach. Make it fun and delicious. Focus on catching up, sharing stories and ideas, and connecting. If the food is tasty, it will speak for itself, and those who are curious will reach out to us for more explanation later on.

> *Whether certain recipes are labeled plant-based and gluten-free doesn't really matter when it comes to taste — good food is good food.*

The only exception is when it turns skeptics into believers. Those truly are magical moments that'll make you beam with plant-powerful pride.

YUM
UNIV—
ERSE

Speak Up

When a group of pals or colleagues is getting together at a restaurant, speak up. Suggest a venue that will make everyone happy. Most Thai, Indian, Mexican, and Ethiopian restaurants have plant-based options on the menu. Even sushi restaurants offer veggie rolls, salads, and soups. If these folks are up for a new experience altogether, suggest a terrific vegan restaurant. Have an opinion and voice it. The final destination doesn't have to revolve around our dietary choices, but if we don't speak up, instead of looking at a menu from a Mexican restaurant where a black bean burrito looks good, you may end up at a steak house with a sad iceberg salad as your only choice.

Don't Preach or Perpetuate Unfortunate Stereotypes

At a restaurant or food-based event at someone else's home (or your own), try your best to avoid having conversations about your dietary choices during meal times. It can put others on the moral defensive. And often enough, they'll go there without us having to say a word anyway — just glancing at our plate can trip inquisitiveness. Tell them you'd be happy to explain your journey so far, but you'd prefer to do it after dinner. Then crack a joke or ask a question of someone else to change the subject. Briefly explain your stance when necessary, and let friends and family draw their own conclusions.

Enjoy Yourself

Time spent with others is time spent living a well-rounded, healthy life. Connecting, sharing stories, laughing, and loving is what it means to be human — it's some of the best wellness mojo around, so find the fun in it. If you do succumb to the office pizza party or auntie's chocolate bourbon cream Thanksgiving pie, don't ruin a good time by beating yourself up about it. It's just proof you're human, and you'll get back on track at your next meal. Being plant-inspired can happen at many levels, not just all or nothing.

Start a Recurring Plant-Powerful Get-Together

Pull together a lovely group of veg-curious and veg-committed people to share recipes, discoveries, and ideas once a week, once a month, or every few months. Throw a tea party, a brunch, a five-course supper club. Maybe establish a theme to encourage everyone to try new things. Create a supportive tribe of like-minded people so everyone can geek out over plant-based recipes — it's comforting and inspiring and really can help you stay motivated and on track.

Stay Committed

I have a friend who worked super hard for months, discovering, playing, and really getting a handle on a plant-powerful diet. She lost over 20 pounds, started exercising again, and was really beginning to master the day-to-day. Then she went home for Thanksgiving.

I'm sure you can imagine the rest. Nothing can derail a healthy effort like an aggressive or passive-aggressive partner or family pressure, teasing, and emotional bonds to tradition. Business meetings can also set up a difficult dynamic. We want to make a client or boss happy, but we don't want to compromise our goals by going to a burger joint every night of the business trip. It can be challenging enough to quiet our own negative inner voices, much less those of others.

 Tell me and I forget, teach me and I remember, involve me and I learn.

— Chinese Proverb

If you have to, make a Top Ten list of reasons why you are making the health changes you are. Keep this list in your wallet or purse and when pressure is on, sneak away for a moment, take a deep breath, and read your list.

Picture me and the rest of the YumUniverse community there in spirit cheering you on, because we are.

Prep, Cooking & Baking

Prep

So, we've planned. And shopped. And stored. Now let's move on to tackling basic food prep techniques and the tricks that will make time in the kitchen enjoyable, easy, and fun.

Cooking Lingo & Techniques

Become fluent in basic kitchen speak before you get going. It makes instructions in a recipe familiar so you can confidently get to work. These are the basics:

AL DENTE

Pasta that is cooked to a point where it is a bit firm, not soft.

BAKE

To cook food (covered or uncovered) in an oven.

BEAT

To make a mixture smooth by whipping or stirring briskly with a fork, spoon, whisk, or mixer.

BIAS

To slice on a 45-degree angle.

BLANCH

To partially cook foods in boiling water or steam to intensify and set color and flavor. After 30 seconds in boiling water, the fruit or vegetable should be removed quickly and plunged into ice water to stop the cooking action. This is an important step in prepping certain foods for freezing as well as loosening skins on nuts or produce like peaches and tomatoes.

BLEND

To mix or fold two or more ingredients together, often-times with a blender, to obtain equal distribution throughout the mixture.

BOIL

To cook food in liquid (water or stock) at a temperature that causes bubbles to form in the liquid and rise in a steady pattern, breaking at the surface. A rolling boil is a vigorous boil, when liquid cannot be stirred down to below boiling point.

BROIL

A quick oven-cooking method where the highest temperatures are used to brown food.

BROWN

To cook a food in a skillet, broiler, or oven to add flavor and aroma. Develops a rich color on the outside and moistness on the inside.

CHIFFONADE

A French word meaning "made of rags." Chiffonade refers to thin strips of fresh herbs or leaves. Usually leaves are stacked on top of each other, rolled, then sliced to achieve strips.

CHOP

To cut foods into smaller pieces with a knife, cleaver, or food processor.

A "large chop" means that each piece is about the size of a nickel. A "medium chop" is about half that size. Chop equal-sized piece so food cooks evenly and at the same time.

CORE

To remove the tough, center part and seeds from fruit.

CRUMBLE

To break apart into smaller pieces, usually by hand.

A "small chop" is also known as "diced." ¼" on all sides is your goal here.

DICE

To cut food into cubes.

FOLD

A method of gently mixing ingredients without decreasing their volume. To fold, use a rubber spatula to cut down vertically through the mixture from the back of the bowl. Move the spatula across the bottom of the bowl, and bring it back up the other side, carrying some of the mixture from the bottom up over the surface. Repeat these steps, rotating the bowl one-fourth of a turn each time you complete the process.

GRATE

To rub foods like vegetables, or whole nutmeg or ginger, across a grating surface to make very fine pieces. A food processor also may be used.

GREASE

To coat a baking pan or skillet with a thin layer of oil. A pastry brush works well or you can use your fingers.

JUICE

Liquid extracted from fruits and vegetables.

JULIENNE

To cut food into short, thin strips, like matchsticks.

LINE

To cover a dish, pan, or baking sheet with unbleached parchment paper.

MARINATE

To coat or immerse foods in a liquid ingredient to add flavor before cooking.

MINCE

To chop food (like garlic) into very fine, tiny pieces.

Make the smallest dice possible — itsy bitsy.

MIX

To stir or beat two or more foods together until they are thoroughly combined. May be done with an electric mixer, a rotary beater, or by hand.

PEEL

To remove the outer covering or skin of a fruit or vegetable with a peeler or knife.

PINCH

A small amount of a dry ingredient (the amount that can be pinched between a finger and the thumb).

PIPE

To force a semisoft food, such as frosting, through a pastry bag to decorate food.

PIT

To remove the seed from fruit like dates or peaches.

PREHEAT

To heat an oven or a utensil to a specific temperature before using it.

PURÉE

To process or mash a food until it is as smooth as possible. This can be done using a blender, food processor, sieve, or food mill; also refers to the resulting mixture.

REDUCE

To decrease the volume of a liquid by boiling it rapidly or simmering to cause evaporation — to thicken and intensify flavor. A reduction is the rich-flavored result and it can be used as a sauce, as a dressing, or as the base of a sauce.

ROAST

A cooking method using high heat (oven or open flame), to enhance flavor through caramelization and browning.

ROLL / ROLL OUT

To form a food into a shape. Dough, for instance, can be rolled into ropes or balls. The phrase "roll out" refers to flattening a food, usually a dough or pastry, with a rolling pin.

SAUTÉ

To cook food by stirring in a small amount of oil or broth over medium to high heat in an open, shallow pan. Cut food into uniform sizes for best results.

SCORE

To cut narrow slits through the outer surface of a food to make it more flexible, to decorate it, or to help it absorb more flavor or allow oil, marinade, or sauce to seep into it as it cooks.

SIFT

To put one or more dry ingredients, usually flour, through a sifter or sieve to remove lumps and incorporate air.

SIMMER

To cook food in a liquid that is kept just below the boiling point; a liquid is simmering when a few bubbles form slowly and burst just before reaching the surface.

SLURRY

A mixture of arrowroot and liquid (usually water or stock) used to thicken a sauce or soup. A slurry should be mixed together first, then added to a sauce to thicken without chunks.

SPROUTING

Soaking nuts, seeds, and legumes to kick-start the germination process, which results in a sprout or tail growing from the ingredient. Sprouting boosts nutritional value and digestibility of seeds, psuedograins, nuts, and legumes.

STEAM

To cook food in the vapor given off by boiling water.

STIR

To mix ingredients with a spoon or other utensil to combine them, to prevent ingredients from sticking during cooking or to cool them after cooking.

TO TASTE

Usually starting with ¼ teaspoon of salt, pepper, or recommended ingredient, and then seasoning the recipe to your liking — adding more if needed.

WHIP

To use a wire whisk, rotary beater, or electric mixer to beat food lightly, but rapidly to incorporate air into the mixture and increase its volume.

ZEST

The colored outer portion of citrus fruit peel. It is rich in fruit oils and often used as a seasoning. To remove the zest, scrape a grater or fruit zester across the peel. Avoid the white membrane (the pith) beneath the peel, because it's bitter.

Cooking Up Confidence

I encourage experimentation and coloring outside the lines — it's how we learn and how we can build kitchen confidence. Use my recipes as inspiration and adapt them to create your own.

Measuring Schmeasuring: Don't worry about perfect measurements except when baking (always measure exactly when baking, it's a science). Learn what certain measurements look like in your hand so you can eventually skip the measuring cups and spoons. This way, you let your palate determine if a recipe needs more of this or more of that. Build trust in your taste buds, they're great guides.

Mix & Match: When it comes to savory recipes, it's pretty much all about the sauce or seasoning. And in almost every case, the noodles, the legumes, the grains, the psuedograins, and the veggies act as a vehicle or partner for that flavoring. So play! Swap whatever veggies/legumes/grains you have on hand.

Break Some Rules: When it comes to labels like "sauce" or "dips" or "dressings," know that we can create our own definitions here. My Chipotle Sauce recipe (page 209) not only makes a great salad dressing, but it's also a tasty veggie dip. It can be tossed with quinoa and sautéed veggies for a one-pot meal, too. Picking up what I'm putting down here? If it's yummy, we can use it how we want and call it what we will.

Soaking

Enzyme inhibitors and phytates (phytic acid) are a few of the defense mechanisms that protect plants.

Ever hear someone complain of gas and bloating when they eat beans? Well, in the simplest terms, that's a plant's survival system doing its job.

Plants don't have jaws, or a stinger, or the ability to run, but they do have antinutrients (compounds that interfere with nutrient absorption) like enzyme inhibitors and phytic acid, which basically make us uncomfortable so we don't eat them again. They also protect the seed of the plant so it passes through our body undigested and unharmed (complete with fertilizer!). Phytic acid can block the absorption of minerals like calcium, magnesium, iron, copper, and zinc in the digestive tract, which can lead to osteoporosis, tooth decay, and other mineral deficiencies, while enzyme inhibitors can interfere with the absorption of proteins.[1]

But aren't we supposed to eat more plants?! Yes. Yes. Stay with me. See, in order for us to reap the nutritional benefits of plant foods like seeds, legumes, nuts, grains, and pseudograins, it's recommended that we soak them to minimize or eliminate antinutrient substances. Personally, I notice a significant difference in how my body reacts to and digests soaked foods — no more heavy feeling in my belly, no swelling. And fun to note, since I stopped eating processed foods and wheat (very high in phytic acid) and started soaking, I haven't had a single cavity (almost a decade as I write this) because the minerals my body needs to build strong bones and teeth aren't being consistently intercepted by antinutrients. I was always told poor dental health is simply "in your genes." It's not.

Soaking isn't a new idea; it's a traditional practice of food preparation — thousands of years old — that has unfortunately been replaced with modern food processing and the belief that "quick, convenient, and easy" is better. But we suffer from more acid reflux and digestion issues than ever before thanks to the latter. Let's go back to traditional practices of food preparation — everyone can find the time it takes to soak health-promoting foods.

When we soak nuts, seeds, legumes, grains, and pseudograins before eating them or using them in a recipe, phytic acid is broken down, enzyme inhibitors are neutralized, and beneficial nutrients and enzymes (like phytase, which breaks down phytic acid) increase dramatically because the once-dormant seed is now preparing for growth. The nutrition door is opened when we soak. It also creates the desired texture for certain non-dairy sauces, milks, cheeses, and spreads. And it can help bring out flavor in certain ingredients like almonds and walnuts, too.

Yes, it takes more time than opening a can, but soaking not only rewards us with optimal nutritional benefits, but the flavor and texture of fresh prepared ingredients simply can't be compared to foods that soak in aluminum and sodium until used.

Soaking is incredibly easy. The only challenge at first is making it a routine. My favorite tip is to soak while you sleep.

How to Soak

Always soak ingredients in a glass container or bowl with filtered, pure water. No plastic, no metal — toxins from these vessels can leech into the food. Start with raw ingredients, so you know they are "alive" with nutrients.

1. Rinse "soakables" very well and drain. Remove any debris like tiny stones.

2. Place seeds, legumes, nuts, grains, and pseudograins into separate bowls.

3. Fill bowls with pure water. Leave about 4" of water above ingredients since they will expand as they soak (especially legumes). If they expand beyond the water during soaking, simply add more water so they're covered during the entire soak time. You can cover the bowl with a clean towel if you like (let soaked goods breathe), but it isn't necessary unless you have a fruit fly problem. If you do, secure the towel with a rubber band.

4. Place a little bit of acid — 1 teaspoon — into the water to help break down phytates. A squeeze of lemon or apple cider vinegar will do without changing the flavor. Also add a pinch of sea salt to the water. The opinions vary about whether sea salt actually helps reduce antinutrients, but it can't hurt because in the end, it helps tenderize them.

5. Drain the soak water and rinse well once soaking time is reached. Don't consume soaking water since it contains the antinutrients we're trying to reduce. Have a tightly woven strainer or a cheesecloth available to strain small "soakables" like sesame seeds, amaranth, and quinoa — don't lose seeds down the drain.

6. At this point, once drained and rinsed, soaked goodies can be refrigerated or frozen (for later cooking), dehydrated, cooked, toasted, or sprouted.

Soaking Times

These are average soaking times to use as a guide. Even if you soak them for twenty minutes, it's better than nothing. And all is not lost if you go to bed and wake up in the morning to see that you "oversoaked" your cashews. Just rinse them well. Also know that a purple/gray color is normal on some nuts and seeds when soaked longer than recommended, but they're still perfectly edible.

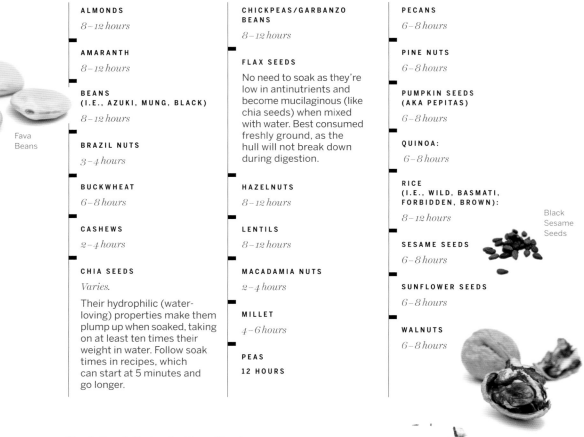

Fava Beans

ALMONDS
8 – 12 hours

AMARANTH
8 – 12 hours

BEANS (I.E., AZUKI, MUNG, BLACK)
8 – 12 hours

BRAZIL NUTS
3 – 4 hours

BUCKWHEAT
6 – 8 hours

CASHEWS
2 – 4 hours

CHIA SEEDS
Varies.

Their hydrophilic (water-loving) properties make them plump up when soaked, taking on at least ten times their weight in water. Follow soak times in recipes, which can start at 5 minutes and go longer.

CHICKPEAS/GARBANZO BEANS
8 – 12 hours

FLAX SEEDS

No need to soak as they're low in antinutrients and become mucilaginous (like chia seeds) when mixed with water. Best consumed freshly ground, as the hull will not break down during digestion.

HAZELNUTS
8 – 12 hours

LENTILS
8 – 12 hours

MACADAMIA NUTS
2 – 4 hours

MILLET
4 – 6 hours

PEAS
12 HOURS

PECANS
6 – 8 hours

PINE NUTS
6 – 8 hours

PUMPKIN SEEDS (AKA PEPITAS)
6 – 8 hours

QUINOA:
6 – 8 hours

RICE (I.E., WILD, BASMATI, FORBIDDEN, BROWN):
8 – 12 hours

Black Sesame Seeds

SESAME SEEDS
6 – 8 hours

SUNFLOWER SEEDS
6 – 8 hours

WALNUTS
6 – 8 hours

Post-Soak Dehydrating/Drying

Completely dry out soaked ingredients to store in the pantry for later use. Spread a single layer of soaked goodies on a tray and dry in a dehydrator set to a temp of 95°F – 110°F or on a baking sheet in an oven set to the lowest temperature (probably 170°F) for 12 – 24 hours. Soak and dry a bunch of ingredients to keep on hand for quick meal prep in the future. Before storing, make sure seeds, legumes, nuts, grains, and pseudograins are 100 percent dry — any moisture will invite mold. To test, bite into dried ingredients. They should be crispy and snap.

Digestive Enzyme Support

Enzymes are substances that can be found in every cell of living organisms, including us humans. They're catalysts for biochemical reactions like breathing and metabolism — they break down foods into building blocks that can be absorbed and put to use by the body. The number of enzymes each cell contains is limited, and when we eat, if the foods we consume don't contain digestive enzymes, our bodies make a withdrawal from the "enzyme bank" to break them down. We can eat all the nutrient-rich foods we want, but if our bodies can't absorb them and make use of the nutrients, we miss out on the health benefits.

The S.A.D. is very deficient in digestive enzymes. And frying, microwaving, high-heat baking, roasting, cooking, drying, freezing, irradiating, and other preparations can compromise the enzymatic power of raw foods. When eating cooked foods and foods containing high amounts of antinutrients like phytates, take digestive enzymes (capsules or powder) before and after your meal — help your body break down and assimilate what it needs to be healthy.

Look for the following enzymes and enzyme classes on the label when shopping. It's best not to compromise on price here (poor-quality product is a waste of moolah) and look for non-animal-sourced enzymes if that's a concern for you. If a label doesn't say "contains no sugar, gelatin, salt, wheat, gluten, soy, milk, egg, shellfish, or preservatives," assume that it does.

Protease: breaks down proteins

Lipase: breaks down fats

Amylase: breaks down carbohydrates

Phytase: breaks down phytic acid

Post-Soak Cooking

Once soaked ingredients are drained and rinsed well, cook immediately or store in an airtight glass container in the fridge to cook at some point (before 4 – 7 days) or the freezer (4 – 6 weeks). If they start sprouting tails while stored in the fridge, no worries, this is a great sign of nutrient power! Just cook as you planned or enjoy them raw.

Roasting/Toasting

It's possible to toast soaked seeds, legumes, nuts, grains, and pseudograins. Either start with soaked and then dried ingredients to toast, or skip the soaking altogether and toast without soaking and drying first (but now we know there are fewer health benefits with this route). Direct toasting unsoaked ingredients can and will neutralize *some* enzyme inhibitors (and it brings great flavor and texture to recipes), but it won't do the job that soaking will (so take digestive enzymes to help the body out anytime unsoaked seeds, legumes, nuts, grains, and pseudograins are consumed).

Sprouting

Sprouting—the transitional stage between seed and plant—is the practice of soaking, draining, and then rinsing seeds, legumes, and pseudograins at regular intervals until they germinate, or sprout. It's a little like kitchen science, so it brings some serious fun and reward to your kitchen routine. Sprouts are rich in fiber, digestible energy, bio-available vitamins, minerals, amino acids, proteins, health-promoting enzymes, and phytochemicals. These nutrients are contained in the seed and remain inactive until sprouting, when enzymes convert them into the food a baby plant needs to grow quickly. These activated nutrients are also essential for human health. Sprouts are not only fresh, cleansing, alive nutritional powerhouses, but they are inexpensive to produce. They're also considered to be a pre-digested food since the enzymes in the seed have done most of the work of breaking down nutritional complexities.

Sprouting is easier than you think, and in most cases, we don't need any fancy gadgetry like sprouting jars or trays to get going (unless we're soil-sprouting, which I won't discuss here since it's more involved). We just need a glass bowl, a glass jar, and a cheesecloth to easily sprout at home.

It's important to discuss that there are varying opinions about sprouts and toxicity out there, but concerns primarily involve commercially grown sprouts. So, if buying sprouts, buy organic. It's also important to note that we should never eat sprouted, raw kidney beans. They're high in lectins, another antinutrient that protects the plant and harms humans, in this case, by attacking the cells in our stomach lining, which can result in diarrhea and vomiting. Soaking and cooking eliminates these lectins, so you can enjoy kidney beans, just never raw sprouted.[2] Follow the recommendations in the "Sproutables to Try" list, since certain sprouts take longer to reduce antinutrient content like lectins, enzyme inhibitors, and phytic acids. We can absolutely cook sprouts into soups, one-pot meals, etc. Just know that heat will diminish some of the nutrient benefits.

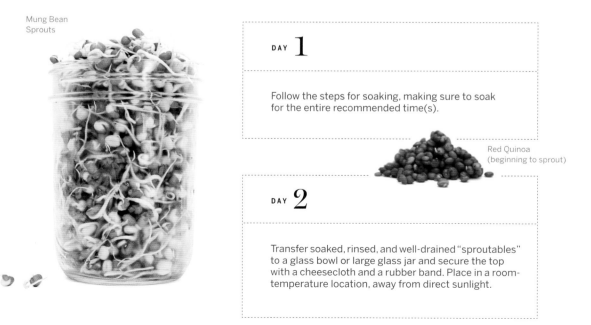

Mung Bean
Sprouts

DAY 1

Follow the steps for soaking, making sure to soak for the entire recommended time(s).

Red Quinoa
(beginning to sprout)

DAY 2

Transfer soaked, rinsed, and well-drained "sproutables" to a glass bowl or large glass jar and secure the top with a cheesecloth and a rubber band. Place in a room-temperature location, away from direct sunlight.

Buckwheat
Sprouts

DAY 3

You may see some tails on "sproutables" at this point. If so, "harvest" them by giving them a taste. If they are sweet and crunchy and to your liking, rinse, draining them well and transferring to the fridge in their glass container secured with a cheesecloth. The cool temperature will slow the sprouting process but not stop it, so don't be surprised if sprout tails continue to grow. Sprinkle them into soups or salads or eat them by the handful. The shorter the tail, the sweeter the sprout. If there aren't tails at all, rinse, drain, and let them sit on the counter for another day. You can keep the sprouts in your jar, filling with water through the cheesecloth. Making sure your rubberband is secure, simply turn jar upside down to drain. Then, flip back over — you're basically just giving your baby sprouts a quick drink.

DAY 4 – 8

Follow Day 3's steps every day until sprouts are ready to harvest — use your tastebuds to decide. The longer the tails, the less sweet the sprout.

You can keep your jar upside down for a few minutes to drain. Just make sure it's on a surface that isn't completely flat (try a plate). You want air to circulate through the cheesecloth at all times, and a place for liquid to escape to.

Lentil Sprouts

Sproutables to Try

I have found the following to be the tastiest sprouts enjoyed plain and added to recipes, salads, wraps, and soups. They are also the most foolproof to sprout. Visit **YumUniverse.com** for helpful sprouting how-to videos.

Buckwheat

Rinse often as buckwheat, like chia, will take on a gelatinous coating.

Start with: ½ cup dry, hulled buckwheat groats yields ½ – ¾ cup sprouted

Sprout time post-soak: 1 – 2 days

Taste & Texture: nutty, plump, tender

Lentils

Start with: ½ cup dry lentils yields 1 – 2 cups sprouted

Sprout time post-soak: 4 days

Taste & Texture: sweet, crunchy, a tad earthy

Mung Beans

Start with: ½ cup dry mung beans yields 1 – 2 cups sprouted

Sprout time post-soak: 4 days

Taste & Texture: sweet, earthy, crunchy

Cooking

> " Cooking is like love. It should be entered into with abandon or not at all.

—**Harriet van Horne,** *American journalist*

Cooking Legumes, Rice, Beans, Grains, and Pseudograins

All of these ingredients should be soaked (and maybe dried if you need to store them) before they are cooked. Soaked, undried grains take less time to cook since they're already hydrated. If preparing for a savory dish, instead of water for cooking, use equal amounts of vegetable stock for incredible flavor.

THIS IS HOW YOU COOK GRAINS, RICE, LEGUMES, BEANS, AND PSEUDOGRAINS.

1. Place soaked, rinsed, and drained goodies in a pot.

2. Fill the pot with water or stock so it covers the soaked ingredients.

3. Toss in a piece or two of kombu.

4. Bring to a boil.

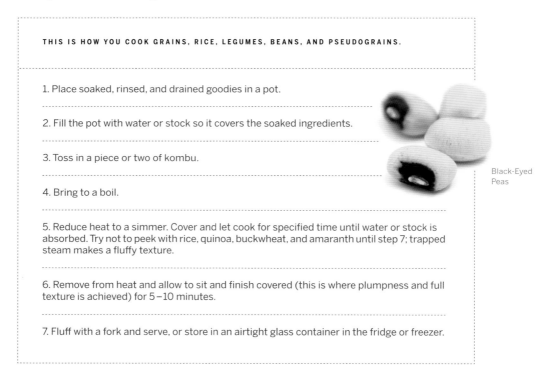

Black-Eyed Peas

5. Reduce heat to a simmer. Cover and let cook for specified time until water or stock is absorbed. Try not to peek with rice, quinoa, buckwheat, and amaranth until step 7; trapped steam makes a fluffy texture.

6. Remove from heat and allow to sit and finish covered (this is where plumpness and full texture is achieved) for 5–10 minutes.

7. Fluff with a fork and serve, or store in an airtight glass container in the fridge or freezer.

When cooking chickpeas, lentils, and beans, peeking is okay and actually recommended. Taste every 10 minutes starting at the 10-minute mark for lentils and the 40-minute mark for chickpeas and beans. They should be firm, but soft and creamy inside. Once that texture is reached, drain any excess liquid, serve, or store in an airtight glass container in the fridge or freezer.

It's important to keep ingredients from drying out while cooking. One burned chickpea, lentil, or bean can ruin the entire batch and stink up the kitchen. In my home, I'm famous for this. Now I set timers every ten minutes. Add more liquid as you cook if they need more time to reach desired texture (and intended taste). Leftover liquid can always be drained off.

What's that foam on my boiling chickpeas and beans? Protein. It doesn't have to be removed; skim it off or stir it back in, chef's choice.

Yields & Cook Times

Start with dry ingredients, then soak, then cook, then enjoy — the formulas below assume that ingredients are soaked (don't use soak water to cook, use fresh). Keep in mind, if you aren't soaking ingredients first, cook time will be 10 – 20 minutes longer.

BEANS

Cook time: 45 – 90 minutes

1 cup beans ✚ 4 cups water or stock ═ 3+ cups cooked

BUCKWHEAT (HULLED GROATS)

Cook time: 10 – 15 minutes

1 cup buckwheat ✚ 2 cups water or stock ═ 2 cups cooked

BROWN RICE (BASMATI, SHORT AND LONG GRAIN)

Cook time: 20 – 25 minutes

1 cup brown rice ✚ 2 cups water or stock ═ 2+ cups cooked

CHICKPEAS

Cook time: 45 – 60 minutes

1 cup chickpeas ✚ 4 cups water or stock ═ 3+ cups cooked

FORBIDDEN BLACK RICE

Cook time: 25 – 40 minutes

1 cup Forbidden Black Rice ✚ 3½ cups water or stock ═ 2+ cups cooked

LENTILS (RED, GREEN, BROWN, FRENCH, BELUGA)

Cook time: 10 – 20 minutes for all except red, which takes 7 – 10 minutes

1 cup lentils ✚ 2 cups water or stock ═ 3+ cups cooked

QUINOA

Cook time: 10 – 15 minutes

1 cup quinoa ✚ 2 cups water or stock ═ 3 cups cooked

PEAS (GREEN & YELLOW)

Cook time: 40 – 70 minutes

1 cup split peas ✚ 4 cups water or stock ═ 1½ – 2 cups cooked

Cook time: 45 – 60 minutes

1 cup whole peas ✚ 6 cups water or stock ═ 2 cups cooked

How to Steam

You will need a large pot with a steaming basket or colander that will fit inside or nestle on top of the pot. Fill up the pot so the water almost reaches the steaming basket or colander and bring to a boil. Add veggies to the basket or colander and cover with a lid, but leave a little bit open so steam can escape. For even cooking, it always helps to make sure your diced or sliced vegetables are in equal sizes. Depending on the veggie, it can take 2 – 25 minutes until ready. Peas, broccoli, and cauliflower may only need 3 minutes, butternut squash may need 15, and sweet potatoes need about 25. You want vibrant color. And a fork should easily pierce foods; they should be soft, but not mushy when done.

Simple Efficiency

Keep a large freezable bag, paper grocery bag, or container near you to collect food scraps as you work. I learned this trick from a chef pal of mine, and it really saves time, minimizing trips to the trash bin. Save scraps and freeze to make veggie stock (page 122). Or toss in the compost bin.

How to Roast

Preheat your oven to 325°F. Line a baking sheet or roasting pan with unbleached parchment paper (for super easy cleanup) or grease a glass roasting dish. Scatter veggies on the sheet or in the pan and make sure they have space around them to cook evenly. The denser the veggie, like a sweet potato, the longer the roasting time needed. Roast vegetables uncovered for 20 – 60 minutes, until easily pierced with a fork, but not mushy.

Gluten-Free Wraps

Use gluten-free tortillas or collard greens to make wraps of any kind. To make sure that you get a nice, crack-free wrap with gluten-free tortillas, steam them first! One to two minutes on each side gives us a seamless roll and some stickiness to help seal up all the goodness. For collards ➡, you want to score the stems by gently running your knife down the length to create a cut that doesn't go all the way through. Then fill and roll. Extra step: steam for 1 minute before filling to reduce any bitterness (if you're new to raw, dark, leafy greens).

Stay Prepared

All we need is one day a week, or a handful of 20-minute chunks of time throughout the week, to set ourselves up for success for months at a time.

Freeze Homemade Sauces

Make some of the sauces on page 208 and store in the fridge or freezer for last-minute meals (better yet, freeze them into ice-cube trays for single-serving magic). A busy night doesn't have to be an unhealthy one. Simply sauté veggies and/or greens like kale, toss with cooked plant proteins and a thawed sauce, and dinner is served in 15 minutes. Thaw sauces and use them as a salad dressing. Add them to a stockpot with sautéed veggies and broth (maybe some rice or noodles) for a soup.

Make a Bunch of Seasoning Mixes (page 202)

Keep homemade dry seasoning mixes in the fridge or freezer (for longer life). When time is not on your side, just throw what you've prepared for the week into a bowl and season it according to the night's preference — keep a variety on hand for options.

Soak While You Sleep

Every night before you go to bed, put some lentils, quinoa, buckwheat, beans, or legumes in a bowl and soak overnight. In the morning rinse well and drain (don't store soaked goodies in water). Either cook immediately (and then store in the fridge) or cook later, but keeping some sort of plant protein cooked and prepared (or easily "preparable") ensures that we're more on track to cooking nutritious food versus ordering carry-out.

Salting to Taste with Sea Salt

Sea salt adds trace minerals and reduces bitterness in recipes, which allows the other flavors and aromas to come through. It's why pastry chefs almost always include a pinch of sea salt in their recipes. And also why, if a dish is lacking depth of flavor, adding a pinch or three of sea salt may do the trick before adding more spices will. Salting to taste is more about making the other flavors bright, not about achieving saltiness (which is more what we'll get with processed table salt). Sea salt will expand flavors as a dish cooks, so start with less and add a little bit at a time, every few minutes as you cook, until desired flavor profile is reached. This as-we-go approach also applies to seasoning to taste and adding pepper to taste. We can always add more, but we can't really remove it once it's added.

Oops! Oversalting & Overseasoning

It can ruin a dish, true, but all is not lost if we were heavy-handed. Simply adding more ingredients like stock and veggies will take on the excess and even out flavor. In times where I've oversalted a soup, for example, I'll freeze half and add more fresh ingredients and stock to dilute the remaining batch. When I thaw out that frozen, salted batch later on, I'll do the same thing — add more unsalted ingredients. If we oversalt, it's one of those happy mistakes that really yields twice the food in the end, and we'll get a frozen meal prepped because of it.

Baking

Gluten-free baking is an opportunity to learn because it's one of the most challenging processes to master — it's truly a science. When we get away from a simple cup of overly processed wheat flour and eggs, we can play, becoming acquainted with a variety of fresh flavors and outcomes. Gluten-free baked goods won't taste like conventional baked goods made with wheat flour, processed sugars, and butter; they'll taste like a new world of goodness. Flavor profiles will be deeper and richer, and textures will be more natural — this is because nutrients are still intact.

With gluten-free, dairy-free baking, it's very important to keep the wet and dry ingredients separate until you're ready to bake. Once mixed, a chemical reaction begins between leavening ingredients and acids to "fluff" the batter. So leave it till the last minute; when your baking dishes are lined, the oven is pre-heated, you have a spoon ready and a silicone spatula on hand for folding, then mix up wet and dry ingredients. Once muffins are in the oven, no opening the oven door (aka peeking) until the timer goes off. This kind of baking is sensitive, and it's important to keep the temperature consistent. If you peek, you may end up with muffins or cake with a sunken center, still tasty, but aesthetically compromised.

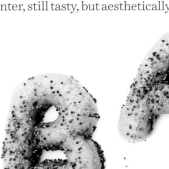

Use the muffin batter from page 189 to make tasty baked doughnuts. Drizzle with some salted caramel from page 296 and sprinkle on a bit of toasted coconut.

Crunchy Onion & Poppy Seed Breadsticks (page 183)

Flours

Combining is the name of the game when it comes to gluten-free flours. They each have their own personality, texture, and flavor, and they work best when partnered with differing personalities.

Easily make flours using a food processor (oats and buckwheat work well), and then if necessary to get a dustier, finer texture, use a coffee or spice grinder for dense nuts and seeds. Just make sure you don't overprocess and end up with a butter (which could be a delicious, happy accident if you don't need the flour). A grain mill (best option) processes grains, nuts, and seeds beautifully (and can be purchased as a relatively small attachment if you have a standing mixer). Grinding your own flours also allows you to soak and dry ingredients first for optimal nutrient assimilation.

One of my favorite tips for using gluten-free flours, particularly ones with an earthy, grassy taste like quinoa and amaranth flour, is to toast them for about 7 minutes before incorporating into a recipe. Toasting rounds out sharp flavors and adds a nice richness to flour.

There are numerous options out there, but after countless successes and failures, these are the flours I prefer to bake with at the moment:

ALMOND FLOUR

Nice moisture content and texture for muffins, cakes, and breads. Blanched almond flour works best and partners well with a more fine-textured, dry flour for balance. Try it in crackers (page 188) or cake (page 290).

BUCKWHEAT FLOUR

Contrary to what its name implies, this unique, dark flour is gluten-free. It's nutty and earthy in flavor and loaded with nutrient benefits. It makes great pancakes, cookies, muffins, and crackers.

OAT FLOUR

Nothing comes as close to the taste and texture of conventional baked goods as oat flour, but it's so important that we use certified gluten-free, especially if diagnosed with sensitivity or celiac. If you can't find reputable gluten-free flour, get oats from a trusted source and grind your own. Oat flour has a slightly nutty flavor and chewy texture that makes incredible Walnut Chocolate Chip Cookies (see page 31).

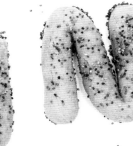

ARROWROOT STARCH/FLOUR

Not only does this fine, starchy flour make a fantastic cornstarch replacement for sauces (page 296) and gravies, but it can lighten the heavy mouth feel that comes with dense flours like almond. It also creates a nice crumb with baked goods and helps make a pliable, gluten-free crepe (page 175).

GARBANZO FLOUR (AKA GRAM OR BESAN)

A creamy, dense, bean-flavored flour that works very well mixed with the sweetness of almond flour (sifting helps lighten texture before baking). Alone, it makes fantastic crepes and flatbreads (that can be twice-baked into pizza crust, see page 184). Garbanzo & fava bean flour (aka garfava) can be substituted in equal amounts for garbanzo.

RICE FLOUR

Brown rice contains the nutritious bran and germ, and white rice does not (thanks, processing). Brown rice flour is nutty and sweet and has a gritty texture that'll result in a denser baked good. White rice flour is a bit more neutral in flavor with the same gritty texture. Sweet rice flour, sometimes called glutinous rice flour (even though there is no gluten present), can add necessary chew to baked goods.

SORGHUM FLOUR

Paired with moist flours like almond, sorghum can really replicate the flavor and texture that most folks are used to with conventional baked goods. It's up there with oat flour in my book and has a sweet flavor and relatively smooth texture (an almost undetectable bit of grit). If oat flour is unavailable, substitute it in equal amounts with sorghum in cake (page 290) or muffins (page 189).

Make cupcakes with the batter on page 290. Frost using the coconut cream from page 175 whipped with the natural dyes mentioned on page 288.

MILLET FLOUR

Mild, sweet flavor that works well in combinations with moist ingredients since it creates a nice, crumbly texture.

Replacements

Many of us have favorite recipes that we'd like to "healthify." Shoot, most of my recipes are plant-based versions I loved as a kid. Here are some tips for making simple swaps that won't compromise the tastes and memories we love.

For a complete list of how-tos and videos ranging from peeling garlic to opening coconuts to popping amaranth (it's teeny tiny popcorn, go check it out!), visit: yumuniverse.com/topics/blog/resources/how-to-resources.

Secrets, especially with cooking, are best shared so that the cuisine lives on.

— **Bo Songvisava,** chef

BUTTER

When sautéing or roasting, use coconut oil to replace the flavor of butter. If it's less about replacing butter flavor and more about having a liquid to sauté veggies in, try vegetable stock to cook. Coconut oil also makes a very butter-like spread on crackers, pancakes, muffins, and baked goods sprinkled with a pinch of sea salt. In baked goods, banana, and sometimes avocado, can add a dense, rich texture similar to butter; so can coconut oil. Know that vegan, non-dairy butter replacements are usually highly processed and contain genetically modified soy and canola ingredients and/or unsustainable ingredients like palm oil. They're pretty junky, so stick with simple.

EGG REPLACERS

Since every flour is unique, and every combination then has its own textural properties and flavor profile, there isn't really a healthful one-solution-fits-all egg replacer. However, these are the formulas I find to work the most consistently with baked goodies if you're game for experimenting.

The chia egg:

1 dairy egg = 2 tablespoons water + ¾ teaspoon chia seeds

The psyllium egg:

1 dairy egg = ¼ cup water + ½ teaspoon psyllium husk powder

Psyllium is a plant rich in soluble fiber and when it comes into contact with moisture, it becomes gelatinous. It gives a "stretch" to gluten-free, dairy-free baked goods and an egg-like, springy bind to veggie cakes and burgers. I prefer psyllium powder (which is ground husks) because it dissolves evenly, but both work.

1 tablespoon of husks = 3 teaspoons of powder

To get the suplhur-y flavor that comes with eggs, use India Black Salt, also known as Kala Namak salt (not to be confused with black lava salt). It's a pinkish, fine salt that has a distinct sulpherous taste and odor (but not in that way). I often will add it to breakfast farinata (page 165), breakfast scrambles (page 170), quiche (page 177), and baked goods (page 181) for egg-y flavor.

MILK AND CREAM

Soaked nuts and seeds blended with water can make fantastic, flavorful cream substitutes, sauces (page 208), and milks (page 276).

Try a nuts/seeds to liquid ratio of:

1:2 for creams

1:4 for milks

Along with them, vegetables like squash and cauliflower can be puréed and added to sauces and soups for creamy texture and depth (page 208).

Try a veggies to water ratio of:

1:2 for cream sauces

Simply use more or less liquid to achieve the texture needed for each recipe—start with less liquid because we can always add more. Experiment with combinations and play! For a sourness or cheesiness, a splash of apple cider vinegar and/or lemon juice can really replicate the flavors of sour cream and buttermilk. And nutritional yeast can add a nutty, cheesy taste.

SMOKINESS AND MEATINESS

To add a smoky depth of flavor to chili, sauces, and soups, liquid smoke and smoked sea salts (particularly applewood) work quite well. Ume plum vinegar (look in the Asian foods section) has a slightly "beefy" flavor. For texture, lentils and chopped mushrooms work well in tomato sauces and gravies. Lentils, mushrooms, chickpeas, and buckwheat add meaty, sausage-like textures to veggie burgers. Buckwheat's mucilaginous properties make it a great binder for burgers and veggie cakes, too.

GELATIN

Gelatin is made from the hooves and bones of animals, so I prefer to use a relatively flavorless seaweed called agar instead.

1 tablespoon of agar flakes = 3 teaspoons of powder.

To set 1 cup of liquid, use 1 teaspoon of agar powder. It should always be dissolved in liquid, then heated or brought to a boil. As it cools, it firms up like gelatin.

Beluga Lentils

CORNSTARCH

Corn is a top allergen for most folks, and since the majority of it tends to be genetically modified, I use arrowroot flour (starch) to thicken sauces and gravies instead. Arrowroot is gluten-free, and like other pure starches, is a light, white powder—feeling like the crackling of newly fallen snow when rubbed or pressed.

1 teaspoon thickens 2 cups of liquid to a gravy consistency.

For liquid uses, it should be made into a slurry first so it doesn't clump in your recipe—just whisk together with a little water until thoroughly dissolved, then add it to your sauce, bring to a boil, then simmer. As it cools, sauce will thicken.

Is Carob a Chocolate Replacement?

There's an ingredient you may have seen out there called carob. It's been used for years as a dairy-free chocolate replacement in vegan foods, and while it can replace it in many recipes, let me tell you, it's not chocolate. It won't satisfy a chocolate craving because the only thing it really has in common with chocolate, aside from a mild cacao flavor and "meltability," is the color brown. Let's free carob from its association with chocolate—it deserves praise as a tasty and unique ingredient. It's sweet, a tad earthy in flavor, and works well with any fruits, spices, and nuts that would pair well with raisins—that's the flavor it's closest to. Not chocolate.

Try it in this Carob Spirulina Chews Recipe: yumuniverse.com/carob-spirulina-chews

Prep, Emotionally

When we make extraordinary decisions that aren't part of the mainstream or accepted by family, friend, or coworker culture, it's important that we focus on building a healthy foundation of confidence instead of engaging in attempts from others to take us off course.

There will be naysayers who are determined to challenge our beliefs. Prepare for them. There will be pushy folks who insist that we eat a particular unhealthful food. What's worse? Being "rude" to our own bodies and eating junk to make someone else happy, or calmly stating that we have an allergy and can't (which isn't a lie, we're all allergic to junk)? When other humans feel like what they're doing isn't accepted (and simply eating a different diet can imply this, no matter how low-key we try to keep it), they may try to devalue our progress and choices (consciously or subconsciously) to make themselves feel better about theirs. When this happens, simply take a long, deep breath before you respond. Maybe take two. Okay, three. Think, "Is this person really going to be receptive to any explanations I may provide? Is it worth it to battle it out?" It usually isn't. Take a moment to create a space between the comment and your reaction. In that space, we can find our commitment again and remind ourselves why we are really making changes. We can either focus on the individual waves, letting them knock us around, or we can rise above it all, out of the ups and downs that limit our vision, and see the entire ocean instead — it's calmer and more expansive from that view.

Let's stay confident, doing our best to spend less time with the folks who drain us and most of our time with people who bring out the best in us. The truth is that nobody knows what's good for you except you. Not your mother, your best friend, your partner, your coworker, or the gal behind you in line at the grocery checkout.

In order to make a great life, we have to be willing to shake things up a bit.

People may say we're "crazy" or "extreme," but if they do, that can be a pretty good indication that we're on to something brilliant.

And those who were seen dancing were thought to be insane by those who could not hear the music.

— **Friedrich Nietzche,** philosopher

Whole Thought

In T. Colin Campbell's book *Whole,* he shares a story that I often think about in the context of having necessary (sometimes frightening) realizations and then finding the courage to make significant change.

> *Think of a fish swimming in the ocean, blissfully unaware of other environments. Once she's caught in a net, hoisted in the air, and then dropped on the deck of a ship, she has no choice but to confront the inadequacy of her old belief that the entire world was water. Suppose she wriggles free of the net and flops back into the water. How can she describe what she has seen to her fellows? What would be their likely reaction, if they were anything like us? "Poor Dori has gone mad. She's babbling and making up lies." What's happened, of course, is that Dori now sees the ocean for what it is: one environment among many.*

There's a lot of discovery to be had out there — things we can't imagine. We just have to be bold enough to venture beyond our comfort zones to find the great rewards and enriching lessons that make a healthy, happy, and rewarding life.

We now know **Why.**

We now know **How.**

I'd say it's time to celebrate, so let's **Eat!**

Time spent cooking is never time wasted, because enjoying (and sharing) nurturing meals is an investment in our overall wellness. For centuries, people made food preparation a priority, gathering around the table to enjoy their hard work, sharing stories, laughter, and love with each nourishing bite. These moments feed not only the body, but the spirit. Sadly, modern times have disconnected us from these practices. We rush preparation, we rush cooking, and we rush eating (usually in front of a TV or computer).

Respecting what we eat, and how we eat, is respecting ourselves. I know very well that certain foods and traditions are connected with important memories, and I'm not asking you to say goodbye to those comforting feelings. I'm inviting you to create new memories and methods for triggering the old faves. I know comfort food. I was raised on it. I missed it terribly when I went plant-based, and as you now know, it's one of the reasons I started developing recipes. These days, I just don't feel like I'm missing out on anything tasty because there is plenty of tasty in my life. You can feel confident knowing that the following recipes delight even the toughest meat-eatin', dairy-lovin', bread-noshin' critics. It's simply beautiful, delicious food all around, so grab a fork and get to work! Nom nom nom...

Details, Details

Remember to always read a recipe entirely before planning, shopping, and cooking. That way you have everything you need, or a Plan B ready if not.

There are a few things to consider when certain ingredients or preparations are called for in the following recipes. Here's a breakdown.

Flag with a sticky note or dog-ear the steps for soaking (page 138); cooking legumes, beans, grains, and psuedo-grains (page 145); roasting (page 146); and steaming (page 146) ingredients — you'll reference them often. After a while, though, with enough repetition, you'll know how to do it all by heart. And that's the plan!

Buy organic ingredients when possible.

Start with raw, dry beans, grains, pseudograins, nuts, and seeds unless otherwise indicated in the ingredient listing with "soaked" or "cooked." For steps and tips, refer to page 138 for soaking and page 145 for cooking. You can always skip soaking, but promise me that you'll read why it's important first (page 138), so if you skip it, you do so in an informed fashion.

Anasazi Beans

Use unrefined, cold-pressed virgin coconut oil. Never refined coconut oil.

Use fresh herbs unless otherwise indicated. You can use dry with the ratio of 1:3, dry:fresh.

Lemon Thyme

Unless otherwise indicated, "sea salt" means fine-ground sea salt.

Nothing beats fresh-cracked pepper from a pepper mill or spice grinder. It's not a deal-breaker, though, if you choose to use pre-ground. I often call for black pepper "to taste" in recipes. This is because I love the flavor it brings to dishes and because it's also known to help digestion.

When using oats or oat flour, purchase certified gluten-free products from trusted sources.

I love the flavor that toasted nuts, seeds, flours, and coconut can bring to a recipe. When a recipe calls for toasted nuts and seeds, start with raw (ideally soaked then dried, see page 138) and unsalted. Heat a dry skillet to medium and stir ingredients constantly for 3 – 7 minutes until they brown a bit. Or preheat an oven to 325°F, and spread ingredients on a parchment-lined baking sheet for 3 – 7 minutes. Keep your eye on coconut — it needs the least amount of time. On all recipes, toasting is always optional, so skip this step if you like.

Dried fruit and coconut should be unsulphured and unsweetened, or sweetened with juice only.

Do your best to use filtered clean, pure water.

Use unsalted, raw nut and seed butters (tahini, almond, cashew).

Wild or humanely harvested raw honey is recommended when a recipe calls for honey.

Use unbleached parchment paper, as it's chlorine-free.

Grade B maple syrup has the most nutrients and what I recommend when "maple syrup" is called for.

Use fresh lemon, lime, or orange juice — squeezed right from the fruit by your lovely hands (or a juicer).

One cannot think well, love well, sleep well, if one has not dined well.

—Virginia Woolf, novelist

Recipe Key

OPTIONAL INGREDIENT

I prefer this recipe best with the optional ingredient, but know that you can confidently prepare a delicious version without it if you like.

**MAKE IT RAW
(OR HIGHLY RAW)**

This recipe is raw, can be prepared raw, or can be cooked up with mostly raw ingredients. Add vegetables to this dish at the end of cooking time to retain more nutrient and enzyme power. Skip the sauté or roasting steps and try it raw. Use fresh berries instead of dried or cooked. Or instead of baking, if you have a dehydrator, use that to retain as many beneficial nutrients and enzymes as possible. When you see this icon, think, "How can I change this up?"

OMNIVORE OPP

This recipe can be prepared as-is, and with a simple addition of meat or dairy, it can accommodate all the dietary needs at the table. This reduces the extra work necessary for a mixed-diet household or dinner party. For example, the Multi-Bean Chili on page 214 is hearty, rich, and delicious, Once prepared, put the servings you need for the meat-eaters in a second pot and simply stir in pre-cooked ground beef, sausage, or shredded chicken (most grocery stores carry these items, especially a roasted chicken). When making a Buckwheat Breakfast Scramble like the one on page 170, prepare as I call for, transfer the servings you need for plant-based folk to a serving bowl, leave the amount you need in the skillet for the omnivore, and quickly scramble in an egg or two. Or try adding an egg to pancakes (page 167) or goat cheese to salads (page 223). All YU recipes are loved by herbies and omnis (confidently serve them as-is), but if you have to add meat or dairy to some, prepare the recipe and just ask yourself, "What could I easily add here?"

MAKE IT OIL-FREE

For savory applications, especially sautéing or roasting, use veggie stock or water instead of oil if you like. For sweet applications, try some banana, apple, or pear. If the oil is used to grease a baking dish, simply line that dish with parchment instead so food doesn't stick.

YU CLASSIC

This recipe has been a community favorite for years, or it's an updated version of a YU classic recipe. The kind that receives reviews like "my husband says if all plant-based food tasted this delicious, he'd go vegan." So, when trying out recipes on skeptics, start here.

Real food doesn't 'have' ingredients. Real food IS ingredients.

—Jamie Oliver, chef

SWAP OPP

Time to experiment. If you see this icon with a recipe, substitutions can be made in equal amounts. This is helpful if you don't have certain ingredients on hand or you just want to change things up. For example, in a swap opp recipe, look for the following and try substitutions in equal amounts, a little more, or a little less.

If it's a savory recipe: buckwheat, chickpeas (garbanzos), lentils, and quinoa can easily replace each other.

If it's a sweet recipe: buckwheat, brown rice, and quinoa can replace each other here.

For baking: sorghum, millet, oat, and all-purpose gluten-free flour can replace each other just fine.

Cashews and sunflower seeds can replace each other.

Dark leafy greens like kale, mustard, and collards can replace each other.

Homemade nut and seed milks can replace each other (see page 276).

Berries can replace each other, or use a combo of berries instead.

Apples and pears can replace each other.

Try a different sauce (page 208) or seasoning mix (page 202).

In savory dishes: carrots, sweet potatoes, or butternut squash can swap.

Black bean, Anasazi, yellow eye, cannellini, black-eyed peas, great Northern beans, red kidney, chickpeas, or pinto beans can replace each other.

If the recipe calls for Portobello mushrooms, try white, cremini, or baby bellas instead.

No flaked coconut? Try shredded.

Dried cranberries, blueberries, raisins, and cherries can be substituted for one another.

Raw honey can be replaced with brown rice syrup or Grade B maple syrup.

ONE-POT MEAL

Start and end this particular recipe in one pot. Easy peasy.

ALMOND—CARDAMOM CREAM CHIA
PUDDING WITH FRESH BERRIES

Breakfast & Brunch

Also see: On-The-Go Breakfast on page 91.

Almond-Cardamom Cream Chia Pudding *with* Fresh Berries

INGREDIENTS

½ cup chia seeds

Cardamom Cream

2 cups water

1 tablespoon almond butter

8 Deglet Noor dates, pitted

¼ teaspoon vanilla extract

½ teaspoon ground cardamom

Pinch sea salt

Toppings

1 cup of your favorite berries

Shredded coconut, toasted*

Hemp seeds*

2+ SERVINGS (PHOTO PREVIOUS PAGE)

This recipe is a staple in my kitchen — it's easy to prepare, full of beneficial nutrients, and it can be adapted with all sorts of fresh fruits, nuts, seeds, and other goodies. Try it for breakfast, as a snack, or as dessert.

STEPS

1. Place chia seeds in a large glass bowl.

2. In a blender, blend together Cardamom Cream ingredients until smooth and pour into bowl with chia. Stir well.

3. Cover chia mixture with a clean towel or lid, and allow to stand for 15 minutes—chia seeds will "plumpen" into pudding.

4. Once set, stir the pudding and spoon it into an adorable bowl. Top with fresh berries, coconut, and hemp seeds.

---

psst! This is also tasty unsweetened (without dates), especially if you use 2 cups of Thai coconut milk instead of the cream listed above.

—

Some folks like thicker chia pudding than others. If a batch is too thick for you, simply add more cardamom cream (or non-dairy milk or water). If it's too thin for you, add more chia seeds.

—

Substitute 5 Medjool dates for Deglets.

—

Make a "fruit pie" chia pudding parfait by layering this pudding with baked crumbled Pretty Pretty Pie Crust (page 288) and warm fruit compote (page 200) — yum!

Mushroom Sausage Farinata

4–6 SERVINGS

Growing up, my grandfather, aka "Daudie," used to bring us sausage from the local farmers' market on the weekends. I remember the zesty spices fondly. He'd make sausage sandwiches on buttery homemade bread he baked the day before. And my brother, cousins, and I would just smile at one another eyes wide, mouths full, cheeks puffed out, because no doubt we were loved and this proved it. I wanted to bring back those memories with this dish — I think my grandfather would've been proud.

STEPS

1. For the Farinata: In a large glass bowl, whisk together the chickpea flour, salt, and water. Cover with a towel and let batter sit for 4 – 8 hours.

2. Preheat oven to 325°F.

3. Heat a large skillet (preferably cast iron) to medium-high and then add 1 tablespoon coconut oil. Sauté shallots and red bell pepper for 5 minutes, stirring often. Add mushrooms and sauté another 5 minutes. Add garlic and sauté for 3 minutes.

4. Stir all remaining ingredients into cooked veggies for 2 – 3 minutes. Remove from heat.

5. Whisk Farinata batter, and if using cast iron to cook Mushroom Sausage, simply pour batter into skillet and transfer to the oven to bake for 20 – 25 minutes. If not using cast iron, transfer veggies to a greased baking dish, then pour batter into veggies, and bake for 20 – 25 minutes. Serve warm.

---

psst! You can skip the soaking step for the batter, but I recommend it for the right texture and digestibility.

INGREDIENTS

Farinata

1¼ cups chickpea flour

¼ teaspoon sea salt

1¼ cups water

Mushroom Sausage

1 tablespoon coconut oil*

1 cup shallots, diced

⅔ cup red bell pepper, diced

4 cups Portobello mushrooms, chopped

3 tablespoons garlic, minced

1 teaspoon paprika

1 teaspoon fennel seed, rough chopped

1½ teaspoons Sucanat

1 tablespoon sage, chopped

2 teaspoons marjoram, chopped

¼ teaspoon red pepper flakes

⅛ teaspoon liquid smoke

1 teaspoon sea salt

1½ teaspoons black pepper

Heck Yeah, Banana Pancakes

INGREDIENTS

Dry

½ cup chickpea flour
(aka garbanzo flour)

½ cup brown rice flour

½ cup almond flour

1¼ teaspoons baking powder

¼ teaspoon sea salt

Pinch ground cinnamon*

Wet

1 ripe banana

1 cup water

1 tablespoon maple syrup*

1 tablespoon almond butter

1 teaspoon vanilla extract

2–4 SERVINGS

These fluffy pancakes are delicious topped with classic maple syrup, but try taking them to the next level (adding antioxidants and rich flavor) with a blueberry compote (adapt the Sweet Cherry Rose Compote recipe from page 200).

STEPS

1. In a large bowl, whisk together all dry ingredients. Set aside.

2. Mash banana into a smooth paste, then whisk or blend together all wet ingredients until ultra-smooth. Pour wet ingredients into dry and whisk together.

3. Heat a skillet to medium-high and then add a dollop of oil. Using a ladle, pour batter into the hot pan. When the edges of the pancakes start to dry and the tops have bubbles, flip. Cook other side for 2 – 3 minutes and serve warm.

psst! For fun shapes, place cookie cutters down into your skillet and fill with batter (use a piping bag for precision). Let batter dry around edges and on top before lifting up the cutter. Flip and brown on the other side.

—

Fold ⅓ cup fresh or frozen fruit or nuts into batter.

Orange & Pepita Granola

10+ SERVINGS

Anyone who grew up eating boxed, processed cereal remembers how fruity and delicious the milk tasted when you got to the bottom of your bowl. Well, bottoms up! This nutritious granola has the same nostalgic taste without the harmful chemicals, dyes, and flavorings. It doubles as a tasty snack that travels well, too.

STEPS

1. Preheat oven to 300°F.

2. In a small bowl, stir together wet ingredients.

3. In a large bowl, toss together dry ingredients.

4. Add wet ingredients to dry and fold well.

5. Line two baking sheets with parchment paper (or just one — you can split the batch, baking one half at a time).

6. Bake the granola for 20 – 25 minutes. Granola should look slightly browned and toasted.

7. Remove from oven and repeat if you are splitting your batch. Granola will harden as it cools.

INGREDIENTS

Wet

¾ cup maple syrup

1 teaspoon vanilla extract

Dry

3 cups rolled oats

1 cup shredded coconut

1 cup pumpkin seeds

1 cup almonds, roughly chopped

Zest from 2 navel oranges

1 teaspoon sea salt

Pinch ground cardamom*

psst! Don't overcrowd your baking sheet — you want granola evenly spread across the sheet about ¼" tall. Overcrowding leads to uneven toasting. If you bake and the edges of granola are browned but the center is not, you may have overcrowded the pan. Simply remove the toasted granola, spread the untoasted around the pan, and bake longer.

—

I made a version of this granola to serve the Art Campers at Camp Wandawega in Wisconsin one summer and added 2 teaspoons of orange blossom water to the wet ingredients before baking. I highly recommend it if you can find some — *wowza.*

—

Serve over Easy Vanilla Bean Ice Cream (page 285), Chia Pudding (page 164), or with homemade non-dairy milk (page 276).

Herbed Carrot &
Sweet Potato Hash

4+ SERVINGS

Back in my party-girl days, my pals and I would hit the bars till closing time (4 A.M.!), then head to a diner for breakfast before going home. One of my favorite greasy-spoon joints used to serve hash browned potatoes with fresh rosemary. I've created a more veggie-tastic version here that reminds me of laughs, love, and urban adventure with old friends.

STEPS

1. Heat a skillet to medium-high heat and add oil and all vegetables. Stir occasionally for 15 – 20 minutes. Around the 10-minute mark, add the rosemary and start seasoning to taste with salt and pepper. Serve warm.

---

psst! Try this hash all nestled in a crepe (page 175) with fresh greens and drizzled with Balsamic Reduction (page 227).

—

Make it a collard wrap. Add cooked buckwheat or quinoa and a sauce from pages 208 – 209.

—

In this photo, I used one cup of purple sweet potato and one cup of regular for extra color.

—

Instead of cooking in a skillet, you can roast this recipe in an oven set to 325°F for 25 – 35 minutes.

INGREDIENTS

2 tablespoons coconut oil

½ cup carrots, diced

2 cups sweet potato, diced

1 cup red potato, diced

1 yellow onion, diced

1 cup red or yellow bell pepper, seeds and ribs removed, diced

1 tablespoon fresh rosemary, chopped

Sea salt and black pepper to taste

Buckwheat Breakfast Scramble

2–4 SERVINGS

Do a Google search for "vegan breakfast scramble" and you'll see that the majority of them are tofu-based. Which leaves those of us not eating soy wondering what to do for this classic American breakfast staple. Buckwheat has a plump, soft texture that works well as a scramble, especially if you can find India black salt (not the same as black lava salt), which tastes a bit like eggs. Neat!

STEPS

1. Place sauce ingredients in the blender and mix until smooth. Set aside.

2. Heat a skillet to medium-high and then add oil.

3. Sauté onion and pepper for 7 minutes, then fold in cooked buckwheat and sauce. Toss for a minute or two and serve hot. Season with pepper to taste.

---

psst! India black salt is a specialty item, I know, but it's a fun one I think you'd like. If you can't find any, regular sea salt is a fine substitution.

—

Try adding a large handful of chopped kale when you fold in the cooked buckwheat.

INGREDIENTS

Sauce

¼ cup cashews, soaked

1 tablespoon nutritional yeast

¾ teaspoon India black salt

Scramble

1 teaspoon coconut oil*

½ cup yellow onion, diced

¾ cup yellow bell pepper, seeds and ribs removed, diced

2½ cups buckwheat groats, cooked (1 cup dry)

Black pepper to taste

Beautiful Breakfast Patties

2–4 SERVINGS

Instead of using fake meat, these breakfast patties are a beautiful combination of whole, nutrient-rich pseudograins, veggies, and herbs. They make delicious sandwiches with Super Seed Power Bread (page 182) or Chickpea Flatbread (page 184), salad crumbles, and meaty texture for sauces like Easy Tomato Sauce (page 209).

STEPS

1. Heat a large skillet to medium-high and then add coconut oil. Sauté shallots and red bell pepper for 5 minutes, stirring often. Add mushrooms and sauté another 5 minutes. Add garlic and sauté for 3 minutes.

2. Stir in paprika, fennel seed, Sucanat, sage, marjoram, red pepper flakes, liquid smoke, sea salt, and black pepper into cooked veggies for 2 – 3 minutes. Remove from heat.

3. Transfer veggies to a food processor fitted with the s-blade. Add ½ cup cooked buckwheat and pulse 15 – 20 times. You want chunky texture, not a paste.

4. Transfer to a bowl, and fold in quinoa, remaining buckwheat, and psyllium husk powder until well mixed.

5. Heat skillet to medium-high and add a dollop of oil. Form 2 – 3" patties and cook for 5 – 7 minutes on each side until browned.

---

psst! Psyllium is a great egg replacer (page 150) and binds patties well. If you skip it, be gentle when flipping.

—

Make extra patties and freeze for future meals.

—

Fold in 1 cup chopped kale for some green action.

—

Prepare this recipe as a savory crumble (skip psyllium if you go this route), cooking over medium-high heat for 10 minutes stirring often. Crumble onto a pizza (page 240) or add to a wrap (page 248).

INGREDIENTS

1 tablespoon coconut oil

2 large shallots, diced (1 cup)

⅔ cup red bell pepper, seeds and ribs removed, diced

4 cups chopped Portobello mushrooms

3 tablespoons garlic, minced

1¼ teaspoons paprika

1¼ teaspoons fennel seed, roughly chopped

1½ teaspoons Sucanat

1 tablespoon + ½ teaspoon sage, chopped

2 teaspoons marjoram, chopped

¼ teaspoon red pepper flakes

⅛ teaspoon liquid smoke

2 teaspoons sea salt

1½ teaspoons black pepper

1 cup buckwheat, cooked (⅓ cup dry)

1 cup quinoa, cooked (⅓ cup dry)

2½ teaspoons psyllium husk powder*

Warm Lemon & Blueberry Kasha

2 SERVINGS

As a munchkin, I would pick every blueberry out of blueberry pancakes and shove them to the side of my plate. I completely missed the point. Now, as a fan of this antioxidant-rich little gem, I like to develop recipes where I can add in all the little blue dudes I dissed during my childhood, starting with this comforting cereal.

STEPS

1. Place all ingredients except almonds into a pot heated to medium-high and stir together for 5 – 7 minutes until a few blueberries begin to pop.

2. Serve warm and top with toasted almonds.

---

psst! Try making this cereal with diced apples.

—

Use strawberries, blackberries, or raspberries instead of or in addition to blueberries.

—

Serve with extra almond milk if you like.

—

Top with hemp seeds for essential fatty acids like omega-3.

—

You can use frozen berries instead of fresh.

INGREDIENTS

1½ cups buckwheat, cooked (½ cup dry)

1 cup blueberries

1 cup almond milk

2 tablespoons Sucanat

2 teaspoons chia seeds

1 teaspoon lemon zest

1 teaspoon lemon juice

Pinch ground cinnamon*

Handful of almonds, chopped and toasted*

Cranberry & Almond Breakfast Cookies

12+ SERVINGS

You know what's great about breaking the rules? Cookies for breakfast! You know what's great about breaking the rules in plant-powerful fashion? Our cookies taste good and they're good for us.

STEPS

1. Preheat oven to 325°F.

2. Combine all dry ingredients in a large glass bowl and set aside.

3. Toss wet ingredients in the blender and mix until smooth. Pour into dry mixture. Fold until well mixed.

4. Line a baking sheet with parchment and grab your favorite cookie cutters.

5. Place cookie cutter on parchment paper-lined baking sheet and fill ¼" high with dough — press into cookie cutter shape, lift and repeat until you fill baking sheet.

6. Bake for 35 – 40 minutes, or until dry and slightly browned. Remove from oven and allow to cool.

---

psst! You can also add 1 teaspoon lemon zest or orange zest.

—

If you can find Ceylon cinnamon, use that — traditional cinnamon pales in comparison when it comes to fragrance and taste.

INGREDIENTS

Dry

1 cup rolled oats, toasted

½ cup flaked coconut, toasted

¼ cup dry buckwheat groats, toasted

¾ cup almonds, toasted

¼ cup sunflower seeds, toasted

½ cup dried cranberries

Wet

1 cup red apple (any kind you like), cored and diced

2 tablespoons coconut oil*

¼ cup water

1 tablespoon chia seeds

1 teaspoon Sucanat*

1 teaspoon vanilla extract

½ teaspoon sea salt

¼ teaspoon ground cinnamon

Pinch ground cardamom*

Ginger & Pear Crepes

INGREDIENTS

Glaze

¼ cup water

3 tablespoons Sucanat

1 tablespoon ginger, minced

½ teaspoon vanilla extract

2 teaspoons lemon juice

Pinch sea salt

Pinch cinnamon*

Crepes

1½ cups water

1 teaspoon almond butter

2 tablespoons coconut oil

½ cup chickpea flour

¼ cup millet flour

½ cup arrowroot starch/flour

½ teaspoon psyllium husk powder

¼ teaspoon sea salt

Fillings/Toppings

1 ripe Bartlett pear

Handful of almonds, toasted

Handful of hemp seeds

2–4 SERVINGS

Figuring out how to make thin, light, egg-y crepes that didn't crack or taste sad and dry was one of my proudest kitchen victories. These guys open up a whole new world of possibility for breakfast and dinner. Fill them with fruits, nuts, seeds, berries of all kinds, or Sweet Cherry Rose Compote (page 200). And for a savory crepe, try loading it with roasted veggies (page 192) and/or topping them with fresh greens and a drizzle of Balsamic Reduction (page 227).

STEPS

1. In a saucepan, whisk together Glaze ingredients over medium heat.

2. In a large bowl, whisk together Crepe ingredients.

3. Heat a skillet to medium-high and add a dollop of oil. Using a ladle, pour some crepe batter into the pan. Tilt the pan and carefully swirl to spread the batter out nice and thin.

4. When the top appears to be drying, run a spatula around the edges of the crepe and carefully flip. Cook the other side for one minute and repeat until you use up all the batter.

5. Slice pear however you like — matchsticks, thinly on a mandoline, or into wedges.

6. On a plate, lay out crepe, fill with pear, drizzle with glaze, and roll up. Top with almonds and hemp seeds for good measure.

psst! Easily make a coconut whipped cream to top your crepes simply by refrigerating a can of Thai coconut milk (not reduced fat) overnight. The cream settles at the top of the can and firms up nicely when chilled. Just scoop out the cream on top, save the liquid for smoothies (page 280), and whip it a bit with a fork or whisk (add some vanilla bean or a splash of extract if you like). You can also use the cream to frost cake (page 290) or Banana Bread Muffins (page 189). Fold in vanilla bean seeds, extracts, or fine citrus zest for extra flavor.

Comforting Chai Power Cereal

2+ SERVINGS

Chai tea is a powerful immunity-boosting blend of herbs, spices, and tea leaves (usually black, but it can be made with Rooibos for a decaf version, visit YumUniverse.com for info). This recipe turns that comforting, fragrant drink into a warm, nourishing cereal.

STEPS

1. For the Chai Tea Latte Sauce, bring water to a boil, remove from heat, and steep tea for 7 – 10 minutes.

2. Transfer tea to blender and mix with other Chai Latte Sauce ingredients until smooth.

3. Warm a saucepan to medium and add cooked pseudograins. Stir in chia seed toppings if using. Add Chai Tea Latte Sauce until warmed throughout.

4. Serve with other toppings.

---

psst! For extra flavor, cook pseudograins in chai tea. Just use steeped tea like you would water when cooking.

—

This cereal can be made with just one pseudograin if you like, or try it with oats.

INGREDIENTS

Chai Tea Latte Sauce

1½ cups water

6 chai tea bags or ¼ cup of loose chai tea

1 tablespoon almond butter

6 Deglet Noor dates, pitted (or 3 Medjool)

½ teaspoon vanilla extract*

Pinch sea salt

—

1½ cups quinoa, cooked (½ cup dry)

½ cup amaranth, cooked (3 tablespoons dry)

½ cups buckwheat, cooked (3 tablespoons dry)

*Toppings**

1 tablespoon chia seeds

¼ cup almonds, toasted and chopped

Flaked coconut, toasted

Hemp seeds

Mushroom, Caramelized Onion & Artichoke Quiche

6–8 SERVINGS

My fitness trainer Paula is also a health-food geek, and in between each burpee or pullup, we talk shop. As one of my recipe taste-testers, I believe she was extra-skeptical about this eggless quiche. But after she tried this version, she sent me a text that read "That quiche was so quiche-y and amazing! I guess I like artichokes now." Success!

STEPS

1. Follow the instructions on page 288 to prepare pie crust. Prebake in an oven set to 325°F for 20 minutes. Leave oven on.

2. In a skillet heated to medium-high, add coconut oil. Sauté onion and Sucanat for 5 minutes and then add mushrooms for 7 – 10 minutes.

3. Blend together water, cashews, agar, sea salt, lemon juice, and black pepper until smooth.

4. Lay some artichokes in the bottom of the pie shell. Fill with mushrooms and onion.

5. Pour in cashew blend and top with a few artichokes.

6. Bake for 70 minutes. Broil for 1 – 2 minutes to brown top (optional). Allow to cool a bit and serve warm.

---

psst! This is an opportunity to use India black salt for egg-y flavor.

—

You can absolutely use a store-bought gluten-free pie crust if you like.

—

Agar is a neutral-flavored seaweed that firms up the quiche. If you can't find agar powder, use 4 tablespoons agar flakes for every 1 tablespoon powder. You can prepare this quiche without agar. The taste will still be delicious, but the texture may not be as firm.

—

I used 2 cups cremini and 2 cups white mushrooms. You can also use Portobello, baby Portobellos, or a combination of all of these.

—

Make mini quiches: Press crust into 4 – 5" ramekins. Prepare and bake according to the steps above.

INGREDIENTS

Crust

One 8 – 9" pie crust prepared *without* Sucanat (page 288)

Filling

1 teaspoon coconut oil

1 cup yellow onion, diced

2 teaspoons Sucanat*

4 cups mushrooms, sliced

2 cups pure water

¾ cup cashews, soaked

1 tablespoon agar powder

2 teaspoons sea salt

1 tablespoon lemon juice

Black pepper to taste

1 10-oz. jar artichoke hearts (about 1 cup)

Quinoa "Cinnamon Toast" Cereal *with* Toasted Pecans

INGREDIENTS

1½ cups quinoa, cooked
(½ cup dry)

2 teaspoons coconut oil*

½ teaspoon ground cinnamon

Pinch ground cardamom*

1 – 2 tablespoons maple syrup

¼ teaspoon sea salt

2 – 3 tablespoons
dry cranberries

¼ cup pecans, toasted

1 tablespoon hemp seeds

2+ SERVINGS

My grandmother "Maudie" (better half to "Daudie") used to make us grandkids the best cinnamon toast. She'd slather warm, toasty white bread with butter and then layer cinnamon sugar about ⅛" thick on top from a green Domino "Sugar N' Cinnamon" shaker shaped like a little man. I had completely forgotten about this treat until I took one bite of this tasty creation for the first time. Then like a lightning bolt to the memory bank, I could see her smile, her perfectly coiffed hair, her sunny, happy kitchen, and a plate of sparkly toast just for me. I think her loving spirit just may have helped me create this breakfast treat.

STEPS

1. In a saucepan heated to medium, stir together cooked quinoa, coconut oil, cinnamon, cardamom (if using), maple syrup, and salt until warm.

2. Transfer to a bowl and top with cranberries, pecans, and hemp seeds.

psst! Try adding some other goodies like toasted coconut, diced apple, and/or chia seeds.
—
Serve with fresh almond milk (page 276) for extra creaminess.

Baked Goodness

Toasted Super Seed Power Bread

INGREDIENTS

½ cup sesame seeds

1 cup rolled oats

½ cup pumpkin seeds

½ cup almonds

¼ cup sunflower seeds

½ cup chickpea flour

½ cup poppy seeds

¼ cup chia seeds

3 tablespoons psyllium husk powder

1 teaspoon sea salt

1 tablespoon Sucanat

2 tablespoons coconut oil

2 cups water

---

psst! If you can only find psyllium husks, use ¼ cup in this recipe instead of powder.

—

The toasting step can be skipped, but I recommend it for incredible flavor.

—

Fold in ½ cup fresh or dried cranberries for pops of sweet tartness.

—

Use kitchen scissors to cut two sheets of parchment paper to size to run vertically and horizontally in (and slightly out of) your loaf pan for a wrinkle-free bread loaf.

12+ SERVINGS (PHOTO PREVIOUS PAGE)

Sometimes, you just want a sandwich. Or a piece of toast with some Raspberry & Chia Jam (page 205). This bread recipe is inspired by ancient methods and it's loaded with wholesome nuts, seeds, and fiber, unlike the nutrient-deficient gluten-free options you'll find in stores today. Its dense, toasty, slightly sour flavor is positively divine topped with Chickpea, Tarragon & Cranberry Salad (page 253) or sliced thinly, spread with coconut oil, a pinch of salt, and toasted for a Beautiful Breakfast Patty (page 171) sandwich.

STEPS

1. Preheat oven to 325°F and line a baking sheet or two with parchment paper. Place the sesame seeds, oats, pumpkin seeds, almonds, and sunflower seeds on the sheet and toast them in the oven for 7 – 10 minutes, then transfer to a large bowl.

2. Add remaining ingredients to the bowl. Mix well. (Feel free to use your hands.) Form the dough into a ball and cover with a towel. Let sit overnight, about 10 – 12 hours.

3. The next day, preheat oven to 325°F and line a loaf baking dish with parchment paper (allow ½" of parchment paper to exceed the top edge of loaf pan so you can easily lift out the bread once baked).

4. The dough will be very firm. Using your hands and a little effort, shape into a rectangle and press the dough into parchment-lined loaf pan, making sure it reaches all four corners.

5. Bake for 30 minutes and remove from the oven. Lift loaf out of pan by the parchment paper and set onto a baking sheet. Flip your loaf, making sure parchment paper is flat underneath, and bake another 45 – 50 minutes. Allow to cool. Slice and experience heaven. Store in an airtight glass container in the refrigerator.

Crunchy Onion & Poppy Seed Breadsticks

8+ SERVINGS

This is the perfect savory crunch factor to enjoy alongside creamy soups like Roasted Red Pepper & Tomato Bisque (page 217) or a Nectarine & Fresh Lemon Salad (page 229).

STEPS

1. Preheat oven to 325°F.

2. Sauté onion in ½ teaspoon coconut oil for 10 minutes until browned. Set aside.

3. In a large bowl, whisk together flours, arrowroot, baking soda, and salt. In another bowl mix together water and apple cider vinegar.

4. With a fork, cut in 2 tablespoons coconut oil into dry mixture until it becomes crumbly, then add water and apple cider vinegar mixture. Form a ball of dough with your hands.

5. Dust a flat surface with oat flour and roll out dough into 6" lengths about ½" wide.

6. Pour some poppy seeds onto a plate and roll your 6" lengths through them, or just sprinkle seeds on top.

7. Place on a parchment-lined baking sheet and bake for 20–30 minutes, until edges are just starting to brown.

INGREDIENTS

½ cup white onion, diced

2 tablespoons + ½ teaspoon coconut oil

1½ cups almond flour

1½ cups oat flour

2 tablespoons arrowroot starch/flour

1 teaspoon baking soda

1 teaspoon sea salt

¾ cup water

1 tablespoon apple cider vinegar

Poppy seeds

---

psst! Have some fun: roll these breadsticks out into letters or shapes like you see done for the "baking" letters on page 148 and 149.

—

Skip the onion and make this poppy seed recipe sweet. Use 2 teaspoons of lemon zest and 2 tablespoons of Sucanat instead of onion.

—

Instead of poppy seeds and onion, fold in 1 tablespoon of Herbes de Provence (page 203).

Chickpea Flatbread

4+ SERVINGS

In Italy they call it farinata, in France it's socca, and in India it's pudla besan. This simple flatbread is made with chickpea flour (aka garbanzo flour, aka besan) and it can be enjoyed solo, flavored with herbs. Or you can top it with all sorts of delicious options — savory and sweet. It also makes a nice gluten-free pizza crust. The possibilities are truly infinite with this one. Here's the base recipe and some ideas to try.

INGREDIENTS

1 cup chickpea flour
(also known as garbanzo flour)

½ teaspoon sea salt

1¼ cups room-temperature water

2 tablespoons coconut oil or
avocado oil (plus more for the pan)

STEPS FOR PLAIN FARINATA

1. In a glass bowl, whisk together the chickpea flour, sea salt, and water.

2. Cover with a towel and let it sit on the counter for 4 – 8 hours. (It's nice to let the batter soak because the flour really absorbs the water, and it even ferments a bit if left to sit longer, which adds a nice sourness, but you can skip this step and still end up with a decent farinata.)

3. Preheat oven to 450°F.

4. Place an empty, ungreased cast-iron skillet or 9" x 9" or 9" x 13" baking dish into oven for 5 minutes.

5. If needed, gently warm coconut oil on the stove top to make it liquid. Whisk oil into batter.

6. Remove hot baking dish(es) from oven and add a dollop of oil and quickly spread it around entire bottom of pan with a pastry brush or spatula.

7. Reduce oven temperature to 325°F.

8. Pour batter into dish(es) and bake for 10 – 20 minutes, until flatbread is firm and edges are browning.

9. At this point, if you want to fancy up the looks of your flatbread by browning, you can place it under the broiler for a few minutes, but keep an eye on it so it doesn't burn.

10. If you are loading with toppings and then baking (see variations on opposite page), note that you may need to add cooking time, and once removed from the oven, especially if you've added toppings, flatbread will firm up in the center as it cools.

Plain/Pizza Crust

STEPS

1. Prepare batter for plain farinata and bake.

2. Once baked, load up with tomato sauce and desired toppings — shown here Margherita style with Easy Tomato Sauce (page 209), Cashew Sauce (page 209), and fresh basil.

3. Bake again directly on the rack for 10 — 15 minutes for a crispy crust.

Tomato, Pesto & Red Onion

STEPS

1. Prepare batter.

2. Pour into baking dish(es) and swirl in Kale & Walnut Pesto (page 208).

3. Add sliced tomato, red onion, a pinch of fine-ground sea salt, and fresh cracked pepper.

4. Bake for 25 – 30 minutes.

Fresh Greens & Avocado

STEPS

1. Prepare batter according to all steps above and bake.

2. Top with fresh greens, avocado, fresh green apple, a drizzle of olive oil, and fresh cracked pepper.

3. Also delicious drizzled with Balsamic Reduction (page 227).

Herbes de Provence

STEPS

1. Prepare batter.

2. Pour into baking dish(es) and add 1 tablespoon of Herbes de Provence seasoning (page 203).

3. Bake for 25 – 30 minutes.

Blackberry, Balsamic & Fresh Thyme

STEPS

1. Prepare batter.

2. Pour into baking dish(es) and swirl in Cashew Sauce (page 209).

3. Add fresh or frozen blackberries, fresh thyme leaves, and drizzle with Balsamic Reduction (page 227).

4. Bake for 25 – 30 minutes.

Sweet Potato Spice

STEPS

1. Prepare batter.

2. Whisk in 1½ teaspoons cinnamon, ¼ teaspoon nutmeg, and ¼ cup toasted pecans.

3. Pour into baking dish(es) and top with 1 cup diced, steamed sweet potato.

4. Bake for 25 – 30 minutes.

psst! If only garbanzo/fava bean flour is available, that will work, just sub in equal amounts.

—

This chickpea flatbread recipe can be prepared without oil, just note that the texture may be cracked and drier (still very delicious, though).

—

You can bake the batter in individual ramekins lined with parchment. Just place all the ramekins on a baking sheet first to easily get them in and out of the oven. Ramekin-sized flatbreads make for fun individual servings, and it's helpful for easy meals throughout the week.

Popped Amaranth Bread

Amaranth can be popped like tiny, adorable popcorn (read the directions below or visit yumuniverse.com/how-to-pop-amaranth for a helpful how-to video). It makes the flavor of this hearty bread something truly special. Enjoy it with hearty Multi-Bean Chili (page 214) and save extra popped amaranth to sprinkle into soups and salads.

INGREDIENTS

Wet

1 tablespoon coconut oil

2 tablespoons honey

1 red apple, core and seeds removed (about 1 cup)

2 tablespoons lime juice

¾ cup water

2 teaspoons chia seeds

—

1½ cups popped amaranth (start with 5 – 7 tablespoons dry amaranth)

Dry

1 cup almond flour

1 cup sorghum flour

¼ cup brown rice flour

¾ teaspoon baking soda

¾ teaspoon baking powder

1 teaspoon sea salt

1 teaspoon lime zest

psst! Fill ramekins with Multi-Bean Chili (page 214) and top with Popped Amaranth Bread batter. Bake at 325°F for 20 minutes for single-serving casseroles — great for busy weeknights or entertaining.

—

Spoon batter into muffin tins lined with parchment for muffins.

STEPS

1. Preheat oven to 325°F and grease or line a 9" x 9" baking dish with parchment paper. Or grease a cast-iron skillet.

2. Place all wet ingredients in the blender and let it sit so chia can plumpen while you pop some amaranth.

3. Warm an ungreased large skillet (with a lid) to high. You want a dry pan. Add ¼ teaspoon of amaranth to the pan and give it a shake; it should pop immediately. If you burn some, don't fret, it usually takes a few tries to get the temp just right. It may seem counterintuitive, but turn the heat up. (Gas ranges usually need to be set to high, and electric to medium or medium-high). Keep shaking that pan back and forth, and once the amaranth is popped, fluffy, and white, transfer to a bowl and repeat spoonful by spoonful until you have what you need.

4. Sift together dry ingredients and fold in lime zest in a large bowl.

5. Blend the wet ingredients in the blender.

6. Add the wet ingredients to the dry, folding them together until well mixed. Then fold in adorable popped amaranth.

7. Spread into baking dish or skillet and bake for 25 – 30 minutes or until a knife comes out clean when inserted into bread.

Almond Dulse Crackers

10+ SERVINGS

These buttery-tasting crackers are easy to prepare and a great way to get beneficial sea veggies like dulse into the mix. Top them with Simple Cashew Cheese Spread (page 270) or enjoy them alongside a bowl of Sweet Potato, Kale & Lentil Stew (page 218).

INGREDIENTS

2 cups almond flour

1 tablespoon dulse flakes

1 tablespoon coconut oil

2 tablespoons water

1 teaspoon sea salt

STEPS

1. Preheat oven to 325°F and lay out two baking sheet-sized pieces of parchment paper.

2. In a large bowl, mix together all ingredients with a fork until dough forms. Use your hands to roll it into a ball, and place it on one sheet of parchment.

3. Place other sheet of parchment on top of dough, and using a rolling pin, roll out until flat, about ⅛" thick. Peel back top sheet of parchment. (Wipe it off and save it for another use.)

4. Working on that bottom sheet of parchment, use a chef's knife to carefully shape the dough into a rectangle on the paper.

5. Score cracker shapes by pressing knife down into dough to create vertical lines about 1½" apart and then horizontal lines about 1½" apart. Slide the parchment and dough directly onto your baking sheet.

6. Bake for 10 minutes, no longer. You want to remove from the oven just before crackers begin to brown. Allow to cool on the pan.

psst! Add 1–2 tablespoons of fresh herbs, spices, or seasoning mixes (page 202–203) for different flavors.

—

Feel free to create any cracker shapes you like — diamonds, flowers, fish, whatever makes your heart happy.

Banana Bread Muffins

MINIS: 16+ SERVINGS, REGULAR SIZE: 8+ SERVINGS

I brought some of these muffins for my friend Bernardine to take home after boxing training one night. After we said goodbye for the evening, I got home and saw a note on my phone from her saying, "Muffins didn't have a prayer. Gone before I hit my front door." Now that's a review!

STEPS

1. Preheat oven to 325°F and line muffin tin with parchment liners or homemade ones (page 104).

2. Place all the wet ingredients in the blender and let them sit for 5 minutes so chia seeds can plumpen.

3. In a large bowl, sift together the dry ingredients, and prepare your fold-ins.

4. Blend all wet ingredients until smooth and fold into the dry ones. Once mixed, add fold-ins and mix.

5. Fill muffin tin to the top with batter and bake for 35 minutes. Remove from oven and cool in the pan.

---

psst! If you're cutting oil, no need to substitute here — simply omit it.
—
Use mini muffin tins for adorable bite-sized banana muffins. (If you do, shave 5 – 10 minutes off baking time.)

INGREDIENTS

Wet

2 tablespoons chia seeds

1½ cups warm water

1 tablespoon lime juice

1 banana

3 tablespoons coconut oil

1½ teaspoons vanilla extract

Dry

¾ cup almond flour

1 cup sorghum flour

¼ cup arrowroot starch/flour

1½ teaspoons baking soda

1 teaspoon baking powder

¼ teaspoon sea salt

1 cup Sucanat

Fold-ins

½ cup walnuts, toasted and chopped

½ cup banana, chopped

Sides & Small Plates

Roasted Veggies

psst! Save turnip greens and beet tops for an easy sauté. Toss one bunch of tops in a skillet over medium-high heat for 3 minutes with 1 teaspoon of coconut oil, 2 cloves of minced garlic, ¼ cup veggie stock (page 122), 2 teaspoons of red wine vinegar, 2 heaping tablespoons of pumpkin seeds, and then salt and pepper to taste. Try this preparation with kale, collards, and chard, too — infinite possibilities indeed.

4+ SERVINGS (PHOTO PREVIOUS PAGE)

Roasted veggies can transform a salad, wrap, or rice bowl, and they're always delicious on their own. The combinations you can try are infinite, and I've listed a few of my favorites for inspiration here.

STEPS

1. Preheat oven to 325°F.

2. Sprinkle with seasoning and toss with ½ teaspoon coconut oil (or 2 tablespoons veggie stock, page 122) for every cup of veggies.

3. Roast for 20 – 40 minutes or until easily pierced with a fork.

TRY TURNIPS

Toss with coconut oil and season with simple sea salt and pepper.

EAT SOME BEETS

Try them with lemon juice, lemon wedges, fresh thyme, coconut oil, sea salt, and pepper.

CHOMP A FEW CARROTS

Balsamic vinegar, coconut oil, Sucanat, and sea salt — wow.

ROAST TOMATOES

Simple sea salt, pepper, and coconut oil prepares these guys for all sorts of tasty recipes like Roasted Cherry Tomato Salsa (page 272).

OH YES, SWEET POTATOES, TOO

Toss with minced garlic, thyme, sage, rosemary, coconut oil, sea salt and pepper, sunflower seeds, and pumpkin seeds for a little crunch factor.

Traditional Cole Slaw

4+ SERVINGS

This is a simple recipe that I enjoy often by the bowlful. No shame.

STEPS

1. In a blender, blend together all dressing ingredients until smooth.

2. Slice cabbage, onion, and carrot very thin with a chef's knife, or better yet, a mandoline.

3. Toss all ingredients together and season with celery seed and pepper to taste.

psst! Try adding green apple and/or radish to this recipe.

—

Toast celery seed over medium heat in a dry skillet for 1 minute for extra flavor.

—

A pinch of cumin added to this recipe is a tasty way to change it up.

INGREDIENTS

Dressing

¼ cup cashews, soaked

½ cup water

1 teaspoon apple cider vinegar

1 teaspoon sea salt

Slaw

6 cups shredded cabbage (about 1 small head)

1 cup red onion

½ cup carrot

Celery seed to taste

Black pepper to taste

Buffalo Roasted Cauliflower

4+ SERVINGS

My high-school summers were spent at the beach. I'd jam into one car with all my friends, and we'd make our way down the Maryland/Delaware coast. Back then, my piddly student savings had to stretch a ways food-wise. I remember eating nothing but lemon Italian ices and spicy-hot chicken wings for weeks because each only cost one dollar. This recipe reminds me of the wings joint in Dewey Beach that kept me fed all summer long. They kept it simple with three flavor levels, "mild," "hot," and "suicide." I'm pretty sure it's where I fine-tuned my love of spicy food.

INGREDIENTS

4 cups cauliflower florets

1 tablespoon coconut oil

Hot Sauce

¼ cup white onion, minced

3 tablespoons coconut oil*

4 cloves garlic, minced

⅓ cup hot pepper sauce

2 tablespoons apple cider vinegar

3 tablespoons Sucanat

1 teaspoon sea salt

STEPS

1. Preheat oven to 325°F.

2. Toss cauliflower with 2 teaspoons coconut oil, spread out on a pan, and roast for 30 – 40 minutes.

3. While the cauliflower is roasting, in a skillet, sauté onion with 1 teaspoon coconut oil for 5 minutes over medium heat. Add garlic and sauté for 3 minutes. Add remaining oil and all other ingredients, whisk together, and bring to a boil over medium-high heat. Once boiling, whisk, then remove from heat and set aside.

4. In a large bowl, toss together roasted cauliflower and sauce. Serve it old-school classic style with cooling ranch (page 227) and crisp celery. Or make it a fun salad with fresh mixed greens, ranch dressing, celery, and red onion.

psst! You can back off on the heat by adding 1 tablespoon of hot sauce at a time to taste.

—

Look for hot sauce like organic Sriracha hot sauce or wings sauce where you recognize all ingredients listed. I use an organic Sriracha for this recipe.

Shredded Brussels Sprouts & Kale *with* Miso Dijon Sauce

4+ SERVINGS

One of my favorite quick-and-easy meals that doesn't taste quick and easy. I often use this recipe as a base and toss in other goodies I have on hand for the week, like carrots, chickpeas, and zucchini.

STEPS

1. Wash and slice Brussels sprouts into strips with chef's knife. If you have a food processor, save time by running your sprouts through the shredder blade. Place them in large glass bowl.

2. Roll up kale leaves lengthwise and chiffonade into thin strips.

3. Slice onion and set aside.

4. In a small bowl, mix together sauce ingredients. Set aside.

5. Heat skillet to medium-high and then add oil. Place sliced onion, shredded kale, and Brussels sprouts into pan. Sear veggies for 2 – 3 minutes and then stir. Sear another 3 minutes and then stir. Repeat one more time and remove from heat.

6. Fold in sauce, top with sesame seeds and pepper. (You can add salt, but you probably won't need it thanks to the saltiness of the miso.) Serve warm.

---

psst! Add shredded carrots and/or toasted walnuts to the mix.

—

Any light, soy-free, gluten-free miso will do.

—

Serve with cooked brown rice, quinoa, or buckwheat.

INGREDIENTS

12 Brussels sprouts

3 – 4 large leaves kale, stems removed

2 green onions, sliced

Miso Dijon Sauce

1 tablespoon chickpea miso

1 teaspoon Dijon mustard

2 teaspoons pure water

¼ teaspoon wasabi powder*

¼ teaspoon dulse flakes*

—

1 teaspoon coconut oil*

2 teaspoons sesame seeds, toasted

Pinch black pepper

Sea salt to taste*

Simple Sautéed Snap Peas

4+ SERVINGS

I'm crazy for snap peas. I love their crisp sweetness with homemade Hummus (page 273), in salads (page 223), and on their own, simply sautéed in irresistible sauces like the one used for this recipe.

STEPS

1. In a medium bowl, whisk together all the sauce ingredients. Set aside.

2. Heat a skillet to medium-high and add peas and veggie stock, letting them sear for 1 minute on each side. Remove from heat; you only want to cook them for 2 – 3 minutes so they stay vibrant and crisp.

3. Toss with sauce and serve.

---

psst! Add these sautéed snap peas to mixed greens, hemp seeds, and toasted almonds for a bowl-licking-worthy salad.

—

Swap the peas for carrots or kale (or simply add 1 cup of each to the mix and double your sauce quantities) for a tasty veggie bowl that would be dynamite with cooked buckwheat, quinoa, or brown rice and fresh, chopped cilantro.

—

Whisk in 1 – 2 teaspoons of miso into the sauce for extra beneficial probiotics and umami flavor (pronounced "oo-mommy"— it's the 5th taste besides sweet, sour, salt, and bitter).

—

For the masochists out there like me that love some kick, add more heat with sriracha and/or wasabi.

INGREDIENTS

Sauce Magic

2 tablespoons veggie stock

2 teaspoons toasted sesame oil

¼ teaspoon red pepper flakes

½ teaspoon ground coriander

2 tablespoons orange juice

Pinch or two of sea salt

—

2 cups sugar snap peas, ends and strings removed

1 tablespoon veggie stock

Mini Chesapeake Veggie Cakes

8+ SERVINGS

I grew up in eastern Maryland, and there, as soon as you can eat solid food, you started eating crabcakes. Real crabcakes — not the sad, mostly breaded attempts I later found in even the fanciest Midwest restaurants but plump, creamy, flavorful crabcakes. The kind that can only be created with key ingredients like Old Bay Seasoning and a restrained hint of breadcrumbs. Here's my take on a tasty veggie version that would make a true Marylander raise an eyebrow in proud disbelief.

STEPS

1. Lay out a clean dish towel and spread zucchini and squash across entire surface. Sprinkle with sea salt and let it sit for 5 – 10 minutes. Then roll up entire towel, with veggies, and press the excess water out. Sometimes I'll roll it all up, head over to the sink, and give it a good twist a few times. Unroll and transfer zucchini and squash to a large glass bowl.

2. Place the rest of the ingredients into the bowl (minus the coconut oil). Add ⅓ cup Cashew Sauce. Fold well.

3. Heat a skillet to medium, add a dollop of the coconut oil, and spoon in little 2" cakes. Cook for about 5 minutes, then flip. Repeat a few more times if you need to, in order to reach desired browning.

4. Serve each with a tiny drop of Cashew Sauce, a pinch of lemon zest, or a slice of green onion.

INGREDIENTS

3 cups zucchini, grated

1½ cups yellow squash, grated

½ teaspoon sea salt

¾ cup carrot, grated

3 green onions, chopped
(maybe more for garnish)

1 tablespoon Old Bay Seasoning

¼ cup almond flour

1 teaspoon psyllium husk powder

1 tablespoon lemon juice
(zest for garnish)

¼ cup red bell pepper, seeds and ribs removed, finely chopped

1 batch Cashew Sauce (page 209)

Coconut oil for skillet

Lemon zest*

Green onion*

---

psst! Enjoy this recipe for lunch or dinner. Make 'em full size and serve with a fresh salad (page 223).

—

You can skip the psyllium, but be extra careful when flipping cakes since the binding action will be gone.

—

Instead of making cakes and sautéing, enjoy this as a raw Chesapeake-style veggie slaw. Simply skip the psyllium, coconut oil, and almond flour.

Toppings, Spices & Sauces

Sweet Cherry
Rose Compote

INGREDIENTS

5 cups sweet cherries, pitted

3 tablespoons honey

¾ cup water

¼ – ½ teaspoon rosewater*

4+ SERVINGS (PHOTO PREVIOUS PAGE)

Once you top Chia Pudding (page 164) or Easy Vanilla Bean Ice Cream (page 285) with this magic, dessert may never be the same. Follow the steps below to make a compote out of any fruit you like.

STEPS

1. Bring all ingredients except rosewater to a boil.

2. Reduce heat and simmer for 10 minutes and then stir in rosewater.

3. Remove from heat and serve warm or chilled.

psst! Try apricots or strawberries instead of cherries.

—

You can use frozen cherries here.

—

Compote will thicken the longer you simmer and as it cools. But for a thicker compote, simply stir 1 teaspoon arrowroot into 2 tablespoons water and add to compote while it simmers.

Spicy Almonds

8+ SERVINGS

Try these spicy, crunchy, toasty almonds on Confetti Kale Salad (page 228) or enjoy them as a snack on their own.

STEPS

1. Preheat oven to 325°F and line a baking sheet with parchment paper.

2. Mix all ingredients in a bowl until almonds are thoroughly coated.

3. Spread onto baking sheet one-almond-deep. Make sure almonds are spaced apart so they have room for heat to reach all sides.

4. Bake for no longer than 7 – 10 minutes. Remove from oven and slide parchment paper off baking sheet onto counter top so almonds can cool.

---

psst! For more lime flavor, add a pinch of lime zest to the mix before toasting.

—

Add sesame seeds to your mixture before toasting for simple flavor, color, and texture.

—

Have fun changing this recipe up by swapping almonds for other nuts and seeds, or just adding more to the mix. Play.

INGREDIENTS

1 cup almonds

1 tablespoon lime juice

1 tablespoon Sucanat

1 teaspoon chili powder

¼ teaspoon sea salt

Pinch cayenne pepper

Homemade Spice Mixes

Keep these homemade spice mixes on hand for dinners (page 233), snacks (page 255), salad toppings (page 223), and breakfast cereals (page 163). Add them to any cooked grain and sautéed veggie combo for an instant meal.

STEPS FOR ALL

Mix together in a glass bowl and store in an airtight glass container in a cool pantry or fridge for one to two months.

Ethiopian Berbere Spice

INGREDIENTS

3 tablespoons paprika

1 tablespoon + 1½ teaspoons red pepper flakes

2 teaspoons ground cumin

1 teaspoon ground cardamom

½ teaspoon allspice

1 teaspoon ground fenugreek

1 teaspoon ground coriander

1 teaspoon fresh-cracked black pepper

1 teaspoon ground ginger

1 teaspoon ground turmeric

1 teaspoon sea salt

½ teaspoon cinnamon

¼ teaspoon ground clove

HOW TO ENJOY

Sprinkle on sautéed greens (page 192 sidebar), on Roasted Veggies (page 192), or in a pot filled with lentils and kale.

Montreal Veggie Seasoning

INGREDIENTS

1 teaspoon paprika

1 teaspoon black pepper

1 teaspoon sea salt

½ teaspoon dried onion

½ teaspoon dried garlic

1½ teaspoons ground coriander

1 teaspoon dried thyme

1 teaspoon dried rosemary

1 teaspoon red pepper flakes

HOW TO ENJOY

Sprinkle on sautéed kale (try the steps in the sidebar on page 192) and Roasted Veggies (page 192), or use for Chickpea Protein Burgers (page 244).

Taco Seasoning

INGREDIENTS

2 tablespoons chili powder

1 tablespoon ground cumin

2 teaspoons sea salt

2 teaspoons ground coriander

1 teaspoon paprika

½ teaspoon fresh-cracked black pepper

Dry zest from 1 lime*

Pinch cayenne pepper*

HOW TO ENJOY

Easily dry zest in a dish on a sunny windowsill like you would fresh herbs. Sprinkle this seasoning on Roasted Veggies (page 192), or cooked legumes or pseudograins. Add some to the Almond Crunch Kale Chips (page 33), and by all means, use it for the Lentil, Kale & Quinoa Tacos (page 237).

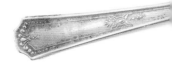

Chai Spice

INGREDIENTS

1 tablespoon cardamom pods

1 tablespoon whole
pink peppercorns

1 vanilla bean, diced

1 tablespoon shredded
coconut, lightly toasted

1 tablespoon dried
orange peel

2 teaspoons dried
allspice berries

1 cinnamon stick, cracked

1½ teaspoons dried ginger

1 teaspoon whole Tellicherry
black peppercorns

½ teaspoon whole cloves

HOW TO ENJOY

Steep 2 teaspoons of Chai
Spice with hot water and 1
tablespoon of Rooibos tea, top
with Latte Foam (page 278),
and sweeten with honey for a
rich Chai Latte. Also use this
mix to make Comforting Chai
Power Cereal (page 176).

Jamaican Jerk Seasoning

INGREDIENTS

1 tablespoon dried
onion powder

2 teaspoons dried
garlic powder

2 teaspoons dried thyme

2 teaspoons sea salt

2 teaspoons Sucanat

1 teaspoon dried ginger

1 teaspoon dried parsley

1 teaspoon ground allspice

1 teaspoon black pepper

1 teaspoon paprika

½ teaspoon dry ground
Scotch bonnet chili pepper
(can substitute cayenne)

¼ teaspoon ground cinnamon

¼ teaspoon cayenne pepper

¼ teaspoon ground cloves

¼ teaspoon ground nutmeg

HOW TO ENJOY

Season sautéed greens with
lentils, Roasted Veggies (page
192), or the tasty Jerk Lentil &
Avocado Wrap (page 248) with
this spicy seasoning mix.

Herbes de Provence

INGREDIENTS

3 tablespoons dried tarragon

1 tablespoon dried
summer savory

1 tablespoon dried sage

1 tablespoon dried thyme

1 tablespoon dried lavender

1 tablespoon dried marjoram

1 teaspoon cracked fennel seed

HOW TO ENJOY

Sprinkle on Roasted Veggies
(page 192) or add 1 tablespoon
to Almond Dulse Crackers
(page 188) or 1 tablespoon to
Chickpea Flatbread (page 184).

Chinese Spice

INGREDIENTS

1 tablespoon ground
anise seed

2 teaspoons ground
Szechuan pepper

2 teaspoons cracked
fennel seed

2 teaspoons ground cloves

2 teaspoons ground cinnamon

2 teaspoons sea salt

1 teaspoon dried ground
ginger root

1 teaspoon ground
white pepper

HOW TO ENJOY

This spice is perfect for making
flavorful toppings for salads
like Chinese Spice Pecans
(page 206).

Raspberry & Chia Jam

INGREDIENTS

1½ cups raspberries

¼ cup water

1 tablespoon raw honey*

½ teaspoon lemon juice

2 teaspoons chia seeds

6+ SERVINGS

You can make jam in about 10 minutes. No canning. No special techniques. Just some berries, some chia seeds, and a pot and — Presto! — you have jam. Spread on Chickpea Flatbread (page 184) or Toasted Super Seed Power Bread (page 182). Yum.

STEPS

1. In a saucepan over high heat, bring all ingredients except chia seeds to a rolling boil.

2. Reduce heat and simmer for 3 minutes.

3. Remove from heat and stir in chia seeds.

4. Allow to cool and enjoy. While jam cools, the chia seeds will plumpen and thicken the jam.

psst! Try strawberries, blackberries, blueberries, raspberries, huckleberries, boysenberries, and/or a mixture of all.

—

Fresh herbs like thyme or mint take the flavor to the next level.

—

For even more fiber, stir in one teaspoon of psyllium husk powder and add 2 tablespoons water.

—

This is delicious with a squeeze of fresh orange juice and ¼ teaspoon fresh orange zest, too.

—

Give your jam some kick with red pepper flakes — oh my!

—

Since there are no preservatives in this jam, store in the fridge for up to 3 weeks.

Chinese Spice Pecans

6+ SERVINGS

Use the Chinese Spice Mix recipe (page 203) to prepare these pecans or buy some from the store. These magical pecans can be enjoyed alone; mixed with various nuts, seeds, and dried fruit for an exotic trail mix; or used for salads like Baby Kale & Blueberries with Chinese Spiced Pecans (page 225).

STEPS

1. Preheat oven to 325°F and line a baking sheet with parchment paper.

2. Mix all ingredients in a bowl until pecans are thoroughly coated.

3. Spread pecans onto baking sheet one-pecan-deep. Make sure pecans are spaced apart so they have room for heat to reach all sides.

4. Bake for 7–10 minutes. Remove from oven, shuffle with a fork, and bake for another 3–5 minutes. Remove and slide parchment paper off baking sheet onto counter top so pecans can cool.

INGREDIENTS

2½ cups pecans

2 tablespoons Chinese Spice (page 203)

¼ cup Sucanat

3 tablespoons orange juice

½ teaspoon orange zest

Pinch sea salt

psst! Add sesame seeds to your mixture before toasting for added flavor, color, and texture.

—

Try a mixture of nuts and seeds for more variety.

Basil & Pepper Pine Nut Crisps

10+ SERVINGS

These guys are just fantastic — buttery, peppery, herb-y, and downright dunkable for soups like Roasted Red Pepper & Tomato Bisque (page 217). Crumble them into salads (page 223) and enjoy them plain, too.

STEPS

1. Preheat oven to 325°F.

2. Place pine nuts and cashews on a parchment-lined cookie sheet, toast in the oven for 10 minutes, then transfer to food processor.

3. Place all remaining ingredients into the food processor and mix until a "cheesy" dough forms.

4. Using a spatula, press and spread the mixture flat onto a parchment-lined cookie sheet.

5. Score by pressing knife down into dough to create vertical lines and then horizontal lines — create diamonds, irregular shapes, or whatever you like. (You can skip this step and break off irregularly-sized pieces once baked.)

6. Bake for 12 minutes, no longer. Remove from oven and allow to cool on the pan.

psst! Try different herbs like sage, thyme, or rosemary in your crisps.

INGREDIENTS

1 cup pine nuts

¼ cup cashews

1 tablespoon basil leaves, chopped

¼ cup +2 tablespoons water

2 teaspoons olive oil

½ teaspoon sea salt

2 teaspoons lemon juice

2 teaspoons nutritional yeast

1 teaspoon apple cider vinegar

1½ teaspoons black pepper

Sausome Sauces

4+ SERVINGS ON ALL

One of the secrets to easy meals is a simple, delicious sauce. Any of these creations can transform veggies, noodles, grains, and pseudograins into rich, comforting meals like Creamy Broccoli & Red Pepper Macaroni (page 236) or a flavorful farinata (page 184). While they taste indulgent, they're made simply with seeds, nuts, and veggies, so you can feel great about every bite. Try them on whatever you have in the house that can be quickly cooked, roasted, sautéed, steamed, or enjoyed raw (including salads).

Sweet Potato Sauce

Try with noodles (gluten-free or veggie), cooked grains, pseudograins, veggies, and/or kale for a macaroni & cheese kinda dish. It's also great as a cheesy spread in wraps.

INGREDIENTS

1 cup sweet potato, diced

2 tablespoons cashews, soaked

1 tablespoon nutritional yeast

1 teaspoon lemon juice

¼ cup water or veggie stock

½ teaspoon sea salt

1 teaspoon coconut oil*

STEPS

1. Steam or roast sweet potato until soft.

2. Place all ingredients in a blender and mix until smooth.

---

psst! Make this creamy sauce nacho-y by adding ¼ teaspoon red pepper flakes or a pinch of cayenne.

—

Make this sauce with butternut squash instead of sweet potato.

Kale & Walnut Pesto

Try this with noodles (gluten-free or veggie), cooked grains, pseudograins, veggies, and/or kale for rich Italian flavor. Excellent in farinata (page 184).

INGREDIENTS

2 cloves garlic

¼ cup pine nuts

3 leaves of kale

½ packed cup fresh basil

Juice from 1 lemon

1 tablespoon nutritional yeast

¼ cup walnuts, soaked

½ cup olive oil*

½ teaspoon sea salt

Black pepper to taste

STEPS

1. Preheat oven to 325°F and toast peeled garlic and pine nuts for 3 – 5 minutes.

2. Place all ingredients in the blender (or food processor) and mix until smooth (or lightly chunky depending on how you like your pesto).

---

psst! This is a great way to use leftover kale stems.

Creamy Cauliflower Sauce

Just as amazing as the Cashew Cheese Sauce (so use it to top the same foods) but made with veggies.

INGREDIENTS

3 cups cauliflower florets

2 cloves garlic

½ cup veggie stock

1 tablespoon nutritional yeast

1 tablespoon cashews, soaked*

2 teaspoons coconut oil*

½ teaspoon sea salt

Black pepper to taste

STEPS

1. Steam cauliflower and roast garlic cloves.

2. Place all ingredients in a blender and blend until ultra-smooth. If you're skipping the cashews, you can process in a food processor.

---

psst! Make it spicy with ¼ – ½ teaspoon chipotle powder or a pinch or three of cayenne.

Cashew Sauce

Thicken soups, toss with noodles, veggies, greens, and more for a non-dairy cheese sauce. Use as a base for all sorts of herb combos or add roasted garlic or roasted red pepper. Try a sweet version with honey and cinnamon or maple and chopped pecans.

INGREDIENTS

1 cup cashews, soaked

½ cup water

2 teaspoons lemon juice

½ teaspoon sea salt

STEPS

1. Place all ingredients in the blender and purée until smooth. Add more water 1 tablespoon at a time if you need to in order to reach desired consistency.

---

psst! Try equal amount of soaked sunflower seeds instead of cashews.

—

For a more cheesy flavor, add 1 tablespoon nutritional yeast and 1–2 teaspoons of apple cider vinegar.

—

For a sour cream, add more water until you reach proper consistency, and add 1–2 teaspoons of apple cider vinegar for sourness.

—

For a mayo, use India black salt for egg-y flavor.

Easy Tomato Sauce

Toss this sauce with noodles (gluten-free or veggie), homemade Skillet Crusted Sweet Potato Gnocchi (page 252), or cooked grains, pseudograins, veggies, kale, or use it as a pizza sauce for Kale Pizza (page 240).

INGREDIENTS

1 tablespoon coconut oil*

1 yellow onion, diced

3 stalks celery, diced

2 carrots, diced

2–4 cloves garlic, minced

10 large tomatoes, blanched and skins removed (page 134)

2 cups pure water

Sea salt to taste

Black pepper to taste

STEPS

1. Heat a large stockpot to medium-high, then add oil and diced onion, celery, and carrots. Sauté for 15 minutes, and add garlic. Stir veggies for 3 minutes.

2. Chop blanched tomatoes, add to the pot with water, and bring to a boil, stirring often.

3. Once boiling, reduce heat and simmer for 20 minutes. Transfer to a blender (or food processor) and purée. Add salt and pepper to taste.

---

psst! You can skip blanching, but it keeps those tiny splintery rolls of tomato skin from getting stuck in your teefs if you blanch before cooking.

—

Stir in some Beautiful Breakfast Patty (page 171) crumbles for a "meaty" sauce.

Chipotle Sauce

Mmm, this is amazing stuff right here. Try tossed with veggies, noodles, kale, or psuedograins like quinoa, or as a sauce for Lentil, Kale & Quinoa Tacos (page 237).

INGREDIENTS

1 cup cashews, soaked

½ cup water

2 teaspoons lime juice

2 tablespoons cilantro leaves

¼–½ teaspoon chipotle powder

½ teaspoon sea salt

STEPS

1. Place all ingredients in the blender and purée until smooth. Add more water 1 tablespoon at a time if you need to in order to reach desired consistency.

---

psst! Try equal amount of soaked sunflower seeds instead of cashews.

—

For a more cheesy flavor, add 1 tablespoon nutritional yeast and 1–2 teaspoons of apple cider vinegar.

—

For more kick, add ¼ teaspoon chipotle powder at a time, to taste.

—

Add a little bit more water or veggie stock and you have the tastiest salad dressing around.

Crispy Chickpeas

4+ SERVINGS

True confession time: I'm addicted to these crispy chickpeas. I put them in salads (page 223) and in soups like Roasted Butternut Squash Soup (page 221), and I'll nibble on them by the handful. They're also a great way to add nut-free crunch to recipes for peeps with nut allergies.

STEPS

1. Preheat oven to 325°F.

2. Toss all ingredients in a bowl, spread out chickpeas on parchment-lined cookie sheet, and bake 40 – 55 minutes. At the 20-minute mark, remove baking sheet and shuffle the little garbanzos around the pan with a fork to help them cook evenly. Pop 'em back in the oven to finish up.

3. Remove from oven and let them cool on the baking sheet. Try not to burn your fingers when you grab for a few samples right away.

---

psst! Play around with this recipe. Try herbs, Taco Seasoning (page 202), or make them sweet with cinnamon and Sucanat.

—

Try using cooked lentils instead of chickpeas — they're especially tasty with pepper, garlic, and lemon.

INGREDIENTS

3 cups chickpeas, cooked (¾ cup dry)

1 tablespoon coconut oil or avocado oil

1 teaspoon paprika

2 teaspoons lime juice

2 teaspoons garlic, minced

½ teaspoon sea salt

Black pepper to taste

Beet & Eggplant Crisps

20+ SERVINGS

These smoky, salty, sweet, and crispy thin strips of eggplant add great flavor and texture to sandwiches and salads of all kinds.

STEPS

1. Using a mandoline, shave paper-thin strips of eggplant, lengthwise.

2. Place all marinade ingredients in the blender and mix until smooth.

3. In a 9" x 13" baking dish, lay down a layer of eggplant strips and pour marinade over top. Repeat these steps until you fill dish with eggplant and marinade. Cover and place in the fridge overnight.

4. Preheat oven to 200°F and line two baking sheets with parchment paper (or line just one and make a few batches).

5. Lift eggplant out of marinade dish and lay onto baking sheets, filling all open space but not really overlapping pieces.

6. Bake 1½ hours, then remove from oven and flip. Bake ½ hour more and remove from oven.

7. Cool on the pan until crispy.

INGREDIENTS

1 medium eggplant

Marinade

1 cup beets, diced

¼ cup olive oil

2 tablespoons raw honey

¼ cup ume plum vinegar

½ teaspoon sea salt

½ cup water

¼ teaspoon liquid smoke

psst! Instead of liquid smoke, replace regular sea salt with smoked sea salt.

—

Use a dehydrator for this recipe if you have one.

—

No mandoline? Use a veggie peeler. You won't end up with wide crisps, but they will still work and taste yummy.

—

If you can't find ume plum vinegar, substitute apple cider vinegar.

MULTI-BEAN CHILI

Soups, Stew & Chili

Also see: Homemade Veggie Stock on page 122.

Multi-Bean Chili

8+ SERVINGS (PHOTO PREVIOUS PAGE)

Sometimes the best way to spend a Sunday is making an incredible pot of homemade chili to serve with fresh Popped Amaranth Bread (page 187). And with each day that goes by throughout the week, the flavors meld and become better and better. This recipe requires a bit more effort, but it's really worth it.

INGREDIENTS

1½ teaspoons coconut oil

½ yellow bell pepper, seeds and ribs removed, diced

½ orange bell pepper, seeds and ribs removed, diced

½ jalapeño pepper, seeds and ribs removed, diced

1 large yellow onion, diced

5 cloves garlic, minced

2 tablespoons cocoa powder (or cacao powder)

1 tablespoon + 2 teaspoons ground cumin

1 tablespoon + 2 teaspoons chili powder

1½ teaspoons paprika

½ teaspoon ground coriander

¼ – ½ teaspoon ground chipotle powder

2 cups black beans, cooked (¾ cup dry)

1½ cups red kidney beans, cooked (½ cup dry)

1 cup chickpeas, cooked (¼ cup dry)

½ cup green lentils, cooked (¼ cup dry)

8 medium tomatoes, blanched and chopped

1 tablespoon apple cider vinegar

1 tablespoon lime juice

1½ teaspoons of sea salt (or more to taste)

¼ teaspoon black pepper

2 tablespoons cilantro leaves, chopped

STEPS

1. Heat a large stockpot to medium, add coconut oil, peppers (yellow, orange, and jalapeño), and onion, and sauté for 5 minutes. Then add garlic and sauté for 3 minutes. Add spices (cocoa powder, cumin, chili powder, paprika, coriander, and chipotle powder) and stir into veggies for about 2 minutes.

2. Add all remaining ingredients to pot except cilantro and salt and pepper and bring to a boil. Reduce heat and simmer for 20 – 30 minutes. Now season with salt and pepper.

3. If your chili is too thick, add some optional veggie stock (page 122) or water until you reach a desired consistency. Often, thanks to the juicy tomatoes, it doesn't need extra liquid. It's up to you.

4. Top the chili with cilantro, or stir it in before serving.

psst! Use this recipe with the batter from Popped Amaranth Bread (page 187) to make a chili casserole.

—

Change up the types of beans you use as long as the quantity totals around 5 cups of cooked beans and/or legumes before you start.

—

Try adding ½ teaspoon of liquid smoke for a smoky depth of flavor.

—

Freeze spoonfuls of chili in ice-cube trays for quick seasoning of veggies and/or cooked pseudograins to eat in a bowl, as a wrap or as tacos or burritos.

Comforting Veggie Noodle Soup

4+ SERVINGS

Just as flavorful and comforting as Mama's chicken noodle soup, with all the health-boosting ingredients we need to fight colds and flu naturally. It's like a big hug in a bowl.

STEPS

1. Heat a large stockpot to medium, add oil, celery, carrots, and onion and sauté for 7 minutes.

2. Add veggie stock, parsley, bay leaf, and chickpeas to pot and bring to a boil over high heat. Once boiling, reduce heat to a simmer and cover pot for 30 minutes until chickpeas soften.

3. While chickpeas cook, boil some water in a medium saucepot and prepare pasta spirals according to the instructions on the box.

4. Once chickpeas are firm, but soft (not mushy), add mushrooms, kale, salt and pasta to the soup. Season with extra salt if you like, and pepper to taste.

5. If you like, blend one cup of prepared soup until smooth and add back into the stockpot for more body.

6. Serve nice and warm with fresh lemon juice and cuddle up with a quilt and a good book.

psst! Use cannellini beans or black-eyed peas instead of chickpeas.
—
Toast some Super Seed Power Bread (page 182) and spread with coconut oil and a pinch of sea salt — so lovely with this warm and comforting soup.

INGREDIENTS

2 teaspoons coconut oil*

2 celery stalks, diced

1 large carrot, peeled, sliced into rounds

1 yellow onion, diced

6 cups veggie stock

2 tablespoons parsley, chopped

1 bay leaf

½ cup chickpeas, soaked (3 tablespoons dry)

2 cups gluten-free pasta spirals

1 cup white mushrooms, sliced

1 cup kale, stems removed and chopped

2 teaspoons sea salt + more to taste

Black pepper to taste

1 tablespoon lemon juice

Roasted Red Pepper & Tomato Bisque

2–4 SERVINGS

In high school, my bestie, Lisa, and I would go to her house after the bell rang (okay, maybe before) and eat a whole mess of homemade ground beef piroshkis that her Baba made from scratch. We'd dress it up with a slice of American cheese, pop it in the microwave, and wash it down with a pint of Ben & Jerry's Heath Bar Crunch. When we wanted to change it up, we'd end up at our favorite restaurant eating gallons of creamy crab bisque. We've both come a long way since those days, but the memories don't fade. Each bite of this veggified bisque reminds me of laughs, love, and getting into all sorts of character-building trouble with her. Detention forever, Lis.

INGREDIENTS

2 red bell peppers, seeds and ribs removed, quartered

2 large tomatoes, quartered

½ cup yellow onion, quartered

1 – 1½ teaspoons sea salt or more to taste

Pinch of black pepper, plus more to taste

2 teaspoons rosemary leaves, chopped

4 cloves garlic, sliced in half

1¼ cups veggie stock

⅓ cup cashews, soaked

STEPS

1. Preheat oven to 325°F and grease a large baking dish with oil, or line with parchment paper. Place red bell peppers and tomatoes face down in baking dish with onion, sprinkle with a pinch of salt and pepper, and roast for 25 minutes.

2. Remove baking dish and add rosemary and garlic and roast another 7 minutes.

3. Transfer all ingredients to the blender and purée until smooth. Season with additional salt and pepper to taste. Serve warm, so heat up on the range if you need to.

psst! This also makes a nice cold soup.

—

Serve with Cashew Sauce (page 209) and Basil & Pepper Pine Nut Crisps (page 207) to take it all to the next level of tastiness.

—

Add cooked quinoa, buckwheat, lentils, or brown or Forbidden rice for more texture.

Sweet Potato, Kale & Lentil Stew

4+ SERVINGS

My sweetie loves a stew. And while I make so many that he can't really keep track, whether he realizes it or not, this recipe is one of his favorites. I know because every time I drop a bowl off in front of him, it gets plenty of nom nom sounds and the most emphatic "that's a good stew" as feedback.

STEPS

1. Heat a large stockpot to medium, add coconut oil, sweet potato, yellow bell pepper, and onion, and sauté for 15 minutes, stirring occasionally. Add garlic and cumin and stir occasionally for 3 minutes.

2. Now add lime juice, veggie stock, buckwheat, lentils, and bay leaf. Bring to a boil.

3. Reduce heat to simmer and cook, covered, another 15 minutes. Stir in kale and cook for 1 – 2 minutes. Season with salt and fresh ground pepper to taste.

---

psst! Try butternut squash instead of sweet potato, or use both.

—

Try any hearty greens in this soup, like mustard greens or collards.

—

For extra texture, generously top with Almond Crunch Kale Chips (page 33).

—

Try a red or orange bell pepper if you can't find yellow.

INGREDIENTS

1 tablespoon coconut oil*

2 cups sweet potato, diced

½ yellow bell pepper, seeds and ribs removed, diced

1 yellow onion, diced

4 cloves garlic, minced

1½ teaspoons ground cumin

1 tablespoon lime juice

6 cups veggie stock

½ cup hulled buckwheat groats, soaked

1 cup French green lentils, soaked

1 bay leaf

3 large kale leaves, stems removed, chopped

2 teaspoons sea salt, or more to taste

Black pepper to taste

Black Bean Soup

4+ SERVINGS

*This is a recipe that I receive the most email love about —
YU will love this black bean soup!*

STEPS

1. Heat a large stockpot to medium, add coconut oil,
red bell pepper, and onion, and sauté for 10 minutes,
stirring occasionally. Add garlic, lime juice, spices
(cumin, smoked sea salt, coriander, and chipotle
pepper), and cilantro leaves and stir together for
3 minutes.

2. Now add water and cooked beans and bring to a boil.
Reduce heat and simmer together for about 20 minutes.

3. Take half of your soup and purée it in the blender.
Fold back into remaining soup mixture.

4. Season with smoked sea salt and pepper to taste.

psst! Serve topped with additional cilantro leaves and Cashew Sauce
(page 209).

—

Try making this soup with lentils, chickpeas, or different beans.

—

Freeze into ice cube-trays for quick seasoning of veggies and/or
cooked pseudograins to eat in a bowl, or as a wrap, as tacos
or burritos.

—

You can easily blend all of the soup if you want a purée.

—

You can use regular sea salt instead of applewood smoked salt.

INGREDIENTS

1 tablespoon coconut oil*

2 red bell peppers, seeds and
ribs removed, diced

1 yellow onion, diced

6 cloves garlic, minced

3 tablespoons lime juice

2 tablespoons ground cumin

2 teaspoons applewood
smoked sea salt + more to taste

2 teaspoons ground coriander

½ teaspoon ground
chipotle pepper

¼ cup cilantro leaves

4 cups water

6 cups black beans, cooked
(2 cups dry)

Black pepper to taste

Roasted Butternut Squash Soup

INGREDIENTS

1 butternut squash about 8" long

1 teaspoon sea salt + a pinch

Pinch of black pepper

¼ cup cashews, soaked

6 sage leaves

3 cups veggie stock

1 tablespoon coconut oil*

1 shallot, diced

1 Granny Smith apple, cored and diced

---

psst! Top with hemp oil, Cashew Sauce (page 209) and/or Balsamic Reduction (page 227).

—

Add chopped kale, cooked quinoa, brown rice, or buckwheat for texture.

—

You can also roast your squash diced in cubes, or steam it (saves about 20 minutes but you won't get the roasted flavor).

—

Try equal amounts of sweet potato, Hubbard squash, or acorn squash instead of butternut squash.

—

Use this soup as a decadent sauce over gluten-free noodles, veggie noodles, cooked quinoa, brown rice, or buckwheat.

4+ SERVINGS

Nothing says, "Fall is here!" like a creamy bowl of Butternut Squash Soup with Granny Smith apple. Try topping with Almond Crunch Kale Chips (page 33) and/or Crispy Chickpeas (page 210).

STEPS

1. Preheat oven to 325°F.

2. Slice squash in half lengthwise, scoop out the seeds and discard. Brush open faces of butternut squash with coconut oil and sprinkle with a pinch of salt and pepper. Place squash face down in a baking dish and roast for 45 – 60 minutes or until soft.

3. In the blender, blend together cashews, sage, and stock until smooth. Leave in the blender and set aside.

4. Heat a large stockpot to medium, add oil, shallot, and Granny Smith apple, and sauté for 5 – 7 minutes. Then add to the blender mixture.

5. Once squash is cooked, scoop out the flesh. Add it to the blender and purée until smooth and creamy.

6. Pour blender contents into stockpot, heat to medium, and season with remaining salt and additional pepper to taste. Serve warm.

SNAP PEA & RADISH SALAD WITH GINGER MISO DRESSING

Salads & Dressings

Also see: Mixed Berry Fruit Salad *with* Tangerine Juice & Fresh Mint on page 36, Creamy Quinoa & Kale Salad on page 39, and On-the-Go Salad on page 90.

Snap Pea & Radish Salad *with* Ginger Miso Dressing

INGREDIENTS

1 large head Boston lettuce, torn into bite-sized pieces

1 cup snap peas, ends and strings removed, sliced

¼ cup red onion, sliced thinly

2 green onions, sliced thinly

¼ cup radish, sliced thinly

Handful sprouts (optional, try mung bean, sweet pea, and/or sunflower; see page 142)

2 teaspoons black or gold sesame seeds, toasted

Beet & Eggplant Crisps (page 211)*

Ginger Miso Dressing (page 227)

4+ SERVINGS (PHOTO PREVIOUS PAGE)

The buttery soft leaves of Boston lettuce pairs so nicely with the crunchy snap of peas, fresh radish, and creamy, toasty, gingery dressing. I also love the pink and green color combination of this one.

STEPS

1. In a large bowl, toss salad fixins together.

2. Top with the dressing amount you like (start with less and add more), toss together again, and serve.

---

psst! For more color and sweetness, add some shaved carrot, cucumber, and/or green apple.

—

If you can't find Boston lettuce, substitute any mild-flavored greens for this salad.

Baby Kale Salad & Blueberries *with* Chinese Spiced Pecans

4+ SERVINGS

Years ago on a girls' trip in Michigan, my gals and I sat at a large table in the woods and threw together this salad out of separate ingredients we all brought for the weekend. It was a combination I'll never forget — the flavors, the stories shared, and the collaboration. How every meal should be. Baby kale is less bitter than full-grown kale, so no need to massage, but if you like, feel free.

STEPS

1. In a large bowl, toss all ingredients, minus the Balsamic Reduction, together.

2. Top with a drizzle of the Balsamic Reduction or go right ahead and toss it in with the other ingredients in step 1.

---

psst! Sub dried blueberries, cherries, or cranberries for the fresh blueberries.

—

Try making your Balsamic Reduction with blueberries for an infused dressing. Either puree them into the reduction, serve as-is, or strain them out.

—

Substitute mixed baby greens or full-grown kale for baby kale.

INGREDIENTS

5 cups baby kale leaves

Chinese Spiced Pecans (page 206)

½ – 1 cup fresh blueberries

2 – 3 tablespoons hemp seeds

Balsamic Reduction (page 227)

Dressings &
Vinaigrettes Galore

8+ SERVINGS FOR ALL

Salad dressings can do so much for a salad, and they can also do so much for non-salad dishes, too, if we think outside of the box. Sauté or roast veggies and drizzle with any of these recipes. Add some cooked buckwheat, quinoa, beans, and/or rice for even more tastiness.

Turn any of these vinaigrettes into a creamier version simply by blending in ½ avocado or ¼ cup soaked cashews or soaked sunflower seeds. Substitute equal amounts of vegetable stock or water for oil if you like. And try out any of these sweeteners: maple syrup, Sucanat, or raw, wild-harvested honey.

I like to sauté garlic for 3 – 5 minutes before adding to any dressing — this is a personal choice and an extra step that you can skip. Raw garlic has a peppery spiciness that can dominate a dressing, and a little bit of time in a skillet rounds out that sharp flavor.

STEPS FOR ALL

Blend or whisk together all ingredients unless specified otherwise.

Pomegranate Vinaigrette

INGREDIENTS

¼ cup + 2 tablespoons pomegranate juice

3 tablespoons red wine vinegar

2 tablespoons olive oil*

1 tablespoon raw honey

2 teaspoons lime juice

Pinch sea salt

Pinch black pepper

Ginger Miso Dressing

INGREDIENTS

¼ cup mellow soy-free, gluten-free miso (try brown rice or chickpea miso)

¼ cup rice wine vinegar

1 tablespoon + 1 teaspoon ginger, peeled and finely minced

2 cloves garlic, finely minced and sautéed

1 tablespoon raw honey

2 tablespoons veggie stock (page 122)

1 tablespoon toasted sesame oil

Pinch sea salt

Honey Mustard Dressing

INGREDIENTS

¼ cup apple cider vinegar

¼ cup + 1 tablespoon olive oil

1 tablespoon + 1 teaspoon stone-ground mustard (any mustard you like will do)

1 tablespoon shallot, minced

1 tablespoon raw honey

Pinch sea salt

Black pepper to taste

Goddess Dressing

INGREDIENTS

¼ cup tahini

1 tablespoon coconut aminos

2 tablespoons lemon juice

2 teaspoons apple cider vinegar

2 tablespoons toasted sesame oil

2 cloves garlic, minced and sautéed

¼ teaspoon sea salt

1 teaspoon raw honey

¼ cup veggie stock (page 122)

2 tablespoons chives, chopped

2 teaspoons parsley, chopped

psst! If blending, stir in chives and parsley afterward so you get pretty green speckles.

Balsamic Reduction

INGREDIENTS

2 cups balsamic vinegar

STEPS

1. Pour vinegar into a small saucepan.

2. Grab a skewer, toothpick, or popsicle stick and dip it vertically into the vinegar, touch the bottom, then remove. This will help you gauge how much your vinegar has reduced — you want it to be 60 – 70 percent lower than this mark when done.

3. Bring balsamic vinegar to a boil over medium-high heat in a small saucepan, whisking often. Once boiling, reduce heat to a low simmer until liquid reduces about 60 percent.

4. Remove from heat. The liquid will thicken as it cools.

---

psst! If you reduced the liquid too much, simply add more vinegar 1 tablespoon at a time and whisk together until desired consistency is achieved.

—

Add fresh herbs and/or lemon while reducing for extra flavor.

—

Start with a naturally flavored balsamic vinegar like fig or blueberry. Or simmer your reduction down with fresh berries to infuse flavor.

—

Try this reduction on Easy Vanilla Bean Ice Cream (yes, really! See page 285) or on the farinatas on page 184.

Orange & Turmeric Dressing

INGREDIENTS

¼ cup veggie stock (page 122)

¼ cup orange juice

1 teaspoon orange zest

2 teaspoons apple cider vinegar

1 teaspoon ground turmeric

1 tablespoon olive oil

1 clove garlic, minced and sautéed

2 teaspoons raw honey

¼ teaspoon sea salt

Blueberry Vinaigrette

INGREDIENTS

¼ cup veggie stock (page 122)

¼ cup fresh or frozen blueberries (or 2 tablespoons dried blueberries)

2 tablespoons red wine vinegar

1 tablespoon balsamic vinegar

¼ teaspoon sea salt

1 teaspoon raw honey

---

psst! If whisking, make sure to really mash up your berries well with some elbow grease.

Ranch Dressing

INGREDIENTS

1 cup coconut milk (homemade — page 276, canned, or carton)

1 tablespoon + 1 teaspoon apple cider vinegar

2 teaspoons lemon juice

¾ cup cashews, soaked

¼ cup onion, minced and sautéed

2 – 3 cloves garlic, minced and sautéed

¼ teaspoon coconut oil

½ teaspoon sea salt, or more to taste

1 tablespoon parsley, chopped

½ teaspoon dill, chopped

1 teaspoon chives, chopped

STEPS

1. Make a "buttermilk" by stirring together coconut milk, apple cider vinegar, and lemon juice in a bowl. Set aside to "curdle" for 10 – 30 minutes.

2. In a blender, blend together all ingredients except parsley, dill, and chives until creamy. Add parsley, dill, and chives and pulse a few times to break them up, but not enough to blend them into the dressing completely — you want specks.

Roasted Garlic & Lime Dressing

INGREDIENTS

½ cup olive oil

¼ cup red wine vinegar

3 cloves garlic, sautéed and finely minced

2 tablespoons raw honey

1 tablespoon lime juice

½ teaspoon sea salt

Confetti Kale Salad

4+ SERVINGS

Folks new to plant-inspired foods are often a bit scared of kale (whether they admit it or not), but this salad will turn them into believers. The trick: massaging kale reduces the mild bitterness and toughness that are inherent in the raw leaves. And tossed with the sweetness of pomegranate and the crunch of Spicy Almonds, this just may become their new favorite.

STEPS

1. Tear the kale leaves into bite-sized pieces and knead the leaves for about 3 – 5 minutes until softened and dark. Add a pinch of fine-ground sea salt; it'll help speed up the softening process and add flavor and trace minerals.

2. In a bowl, toss kale, onion, red bell pepper, dried cranberries, cilantro, and Pomegranate Vinaigrette together until well mixed.

3. Top with sesame seeds, Spicy Almonds, and tortilla chips, if using, and serve.

---

psst! For extra color, use a medley of yellow, orange, and red bell pepper.

—

Since kale is so hardy, you can store this salad (even dressed!) in the fridge for 2 – 3 days.

INGREDIENTS

7 – 10 large leaves kale, stems removed

Pinch sea salt

½ cup of red onion, diced or sliced thinly

½ cup of red bell pepper, seeds and ribs removed, diced

Unsweetened (or naturally sweetened) dried cranberries

¼ cup cilantro leaves

Pomegranate Vinaigrette (page 226)

1 – 2 tablespoons sesame seeds, toasted

½ cup Spicy Almonds (page 201)

Handful of non-GMO certified tortilla chips, crushed*

Nectarine & Fresh Lemon Salad

4+ SERVINGS

Sometimes, we don't need a dressing at all to enjoy an incredible salad. My friend Sage always dresses greens simply with fresh lemon juice, olive oil, and cracked pepper so she can "taste the greens." She served a version of this salad at one of the photo shoots for this book and I had to include it for YU — I ate it for a few weeks straight I was so in love.

STEPS

1. In a large bowl, toss all goodies (minus lemon juice, salt, and pepper) together.

2. Dress with fresh lemon juice, salt, and pepper to taste.

---

psst! Try this salad with apricots or peaches instead of nectarines.
—
Use mixed greens or massaged kale instead of romaine.

INGREDIENTS

5 cups romaine hearts, chopped

2 ripe nectarines, pitted and sliced

1 cup mung bean sprouts
(see page 142)

2 – 3 radishes, thinly sliced

¼ cup sunflower seeds, toasted

¼ cup hemp seeds

1 lemon, juiced

Pinch or two of sea salt

Generous black pepper to taste

Asian Cabbage Salad

This is a highly addictive salad thanks to the kick, the crunch factor, the freshness, and the lovely colors. It's easy to prepare and holds up in the fridge for a few days if you have leftovers.

STEPS

1. In a small bowl, whisk together dressing ingredients.

2. In a large bowl, toss all salad ingredients together. Drizzle the dressing over all the goodness and serve.

---

psst! Use a mandoline for extra-thin shreds.

—

Top Buckwheat Noodle Pad Thai (page 243) with some of this colorful "slaw" or toss it with a big bowl of salad greens for an incredible raw salad.

—

Add julienned yellow, orange, and red bell peppers for even more vibrant color.

—

Also delicious topped with fresh cilantro leaves.

INGREDIENTS

Dressing

1½ teaspoons lime juice

1 tablespoon rice wine vinegar

1 tablespoon toasted sesame oil

1½ teaspoons Sriracha sauce (or your favorite hot sauce)

Pinch sea salt

Salad

4 cups Savoy or green cabbage, shredded

1 Granny Smith apple, grated

1 cup carrots, grated

4 radishes, thinly sliced

4 scallions, thinly sliced

2 tablespoons black or gold sesame seeds, toasted

Lunch & Dinner

Sammiches!

Almond Butter, Honey & Strawberry

Almond Butter
(try homemade, page 269)

Strawberries

Raw honey

Pinch sea salt

STEPS

Spread Almond Butter on bread and top with sliced strawberries. Drizzle with honey and a pinch of sea salt.

Grape & Greens

Simple Cashew Cheese Spread (page 270)

Dijon mustard

Mixed greens

Red grapes

STEPS

Layer Simple Cashew Cheese Spread and Dijon onto bread. Top with mixed greens and sliced grapes.

Artichoke & Black Pepper

2 tablespoons Artichoke Cashew Cheese Spread (page 271)

Marinated artichoke hearts

Black pepper

STEPS

Spread cheese onto bread. Top with halved artichoke hearts and fresh pepper.

Chipotle Avocado

Avocado

Chipotle Sauce (page 209)

Granny Smith apple

Cilantro

STEPS

Toss sliced or diced avocado with Chipotle Sauce and place on bread. Top with a few thin slices of apple and fresh cilantro.

Smoky Lentil & Dill

Cooked lentils

Fresh dill

Pinch of sea salt

Pinch of black pepper

Sliceable Cashew Cheese (page 266)

STEPS

Smash cooked lentils. Add a pinch of salt and black pepper to taste. Lay a slice of Cashew Cheese onto bread and top with lentils and fresh dill.

Cucumber & Cayenne

Cashew Sauce (page 209)

Fresh lemon juice

Cucumber

Cayenne*

STEPS

Stir together ¼ cup of Cashew Sauce with 1–2 teaspoons of fresh lemon juice to taste. Spread onto bread and top with thinly sliced cucumber. Add a pinch of cayenne.

I love to throw a proper tea party with a beautiful variety of tea and mini treats — cookies, tarts, and of course, darling little tea sandwiches. I've come up with some tasty combinations that you can use for your next get-together, a simple lunch at home or the office. Use the Chickpea Flatbread (page 184) or Toasted Super Seed Power Bread (page 182) to make these beauties.

Carrot & Almond Pâté

Onion Cashew Cheese Spread (page 270)

Carrot & Almond Pâté (page 267)

Handful of slivered almonds, toasted

STEPS

Layer Onion Cashew Cheese Spread onto bread and top with pâté and toasted almonds.

Pear & Thyme

Sour & Stinky Cashew Cheese Spread with Toasted Walnuts (page 271)

Anjou or your favorite type of pear

Fresh thyme

STEPS

Spread cheese onto bread and layer with thinly sliced pear. Top with fresh thyme.

Hummus & Radish

Simple Hummus (page 273)

Radish

Cucumber

Sweet sprouts like sunflower or sweet pea*

STEPS

Spread hummus onto bread and top with thinly sliced radish, cucumber, and sprouts.

Crispy Eggplant, Sprouts & Tomato

Cashew Sauce (page 209)

Fresh tomato (cherry, grape, or heirloom)

Beet & Eggplant Crisps (page 211)

Sweet sprouts like sunflower or sweet pea

STEPS

Spread bread with Cashew Sauce and layer on sliced tomato, Beet & Eggplant Crisps, and sprouts.

Asparagus & Turmeric Mayo

Asparagus spears (blanched, grilled, or sautéed)

Cashew Sauce (page 209)

Ground turmeric

STEPS

Slice prepared asparagus spears in half lengthwise. Fold together ¼ cup of cashew sauce with 1 teaspoon of turmeric and spread onto bread. Top with asparagus.

Sundried Tomato & Zucchini

Sundried Tomato Cashew Cheese Spread (page 270)

Zucchini

Black pepper

Chives

STEPS

Spread Sundried Tomato Cashew Cheese Spread onto bread and top with thinly sliced zucchini. Sprinkle on black pepper and sliced chives.

Creamy Broccoli & Red Pepper Macaroni

4+ SERVINGS

This is one of the recipes that I love to try out on the biggest skeptics because they all end up loving it — simultaneously proclaiming their disbelief that it's dairy-free and asking for more.

STEPS

1. Bring a large pot of water to a boil. Add noodles and cook according to manufacturer's instructions.

2. Blend together all sauce ingredients until smooth and set aside.

3. While noodles cook, place coconut oil in a skillet heated to medium and add diced red bell pepper. Stir often for 5 – 7 minutes.

4. Add broccoli and water to skillet, stir, cover, and steam for 3 – 5 minutes. Remove from heat.

5. Return to the noodles. If they've finished cooking, drain and rinse and return them to the pot. Mix together cooked and rinsed noodles, veggies, and sauce over medium heat. Season with more salt and black pepper to taste if necessary.

INGREDIENTS

2 cups gluten-free macaroni noodles

Sauce

1 tablespoon lemon juice

¾ cup water

1 tablespoon coconut oil*

1 tablespoon nutritional yeast

1 cup cashews, soaked

1 clove garlic

¾ teaspoon sea salt

2 – 3 drops liquid smoke*

—

1 teaspoon coconut oil*

1 red bell pepper, seeds and ribs removed, diced

1 cup broccoli florets

1 – 2 tablespoons water

Sea salt to taste

Black pepper to taste

psst! Swap mushrooms for broccoli, or add mushrooms to the mix.
—
You can use applewood-smoked sea salt for the sea salt called for in this recipe if you aren't using liquid smoke.
—
Top this recipe with Almond Crunch Kale Chips (page 33) for a healthy non-breading texture that's outta this world.
—
Just as tasty with or without the red bell pepper.

Lentil, Kale & Quinoa Tacos

8+ SERVINGS

This is an updated version of one of the most popular recipes from YumUniverse.com. I've received countless comments over the years, especially from the herbivore mamas out there, claiming that when they make these tacos for the family, their kiddos and husbands happily mumble, with mouths full of seconds, "If all vegan food tastes this good, I'll never eat meat again!"

STEPS

1. In a large pot heated to medium, fold together cooked quinoa, lentils, Taco Seasoning, coconut oil, and kale. Stir well for 3 – 5 minutes until heat wilts the leaves.

2. Toast taco shells on a parchment-lined baking sheet according to manufacturer's instructions.

3. Load shells with filling, then top with avocado, cilantro, and a squeeze of lime. Serve warm.

---

psst! Easily turn this goodness into a burrito with a collard green or brown rice tortilla.

—

Try gluten-free non-GMO soft tortillas instead of hard or roll it all up in lightly steamed collard greens for burritos.

—

This recipe also makes a tasty taco salad. Just toss with loads of greens and a squeeze of lime. Top it with Chipotle Sauce (page 209). Or try it as a Mason jar salad to take on the go (see page 90).

INGREDIENTS

Filling

3 cups quinoa, cooked
(1 cup dry)

1 cup lentils, cooked
(½ cup dry)

One batch of Taco Seasoning
(page 202 or store bought)

1 tablespoon coconut oil*

2 – 3 large leaves kale, stems
removed, chopped

—

Non-GMO blue-corn
taco shells

Toppings

1 – 2 avocados, pitted,
peeled, and sliced

Fresh cilantro leaves

Fresh lime wedges

Fig & Caramelized Onion Tart

INGREDIENTS

Crust

1 cup almond flour

1 cup all-purpose
gluten-free flour

1 teaspoon sea salt

3 tablespoons coconut oil*

3 tablespoons cold water

Lemon Cashew Cheese

1 cup cashews, soaked

½ cup + 2 tablespoons water

2 teaspoons lemon juice

1 teaspoon apple
cider vinegar

1 teaspoon lemon zest

¼ teaspoon sea salt

Filling

2 teaspoons coconut oil*

1 packed cup red onion,
sliced thinly

1 tablespoon Sucanat

3 – 5 ripe figs (any kind),
sliced thinly

1 tablespoon thyme leaves

Pinch sea salt

psst! Before serving, drizzle
Balsamic Reduction (page 227)
over a slice or two — yum.

6+ SERVINGS

The sweet, honey taste of fresh figs is magic when paired with caramelized onions and lemon cashew cheese. When it's not fig season, try using apples or pears instead.

STEPS

1. Preheat oven to 325°F and lay out two baking sheet-sized pieces of parchment paper on the counter.

2. With a fork, mix together crust ingredients until it crumbles and dough begins to stick together. Use your hands to form a ball and place it on one sheet of parchment paper. Place the other sheet of parchment on top and roll out until ¼" thickness. Peel back top parchment and use a knife, more rolling, and hands to sculpt a nice rectangle (or whatever shape you'd like) directly on the bottom sheet of parchment. Slide the parchment paper and crust onto a baking sheet.

3. Prebake crust for 10 minutes.

4. While the crust is baking, add all Lemon Cashew Cheese ingredients into the blender. Blend together until smooth. Set aside.

5. In a pan heated to medium-high, add coconut oil, onion, and Sucanat and stir often for 7 minutes, or until onion caramelizes and browns.

6. Once crust is removed from the oven, spread with Lemon Cashew Cheese and layer on onions and figs. Sprinkle with thyme and a pinch of sea salt.

7. Pop back in the oven and bake for 25 minutes.

8. Let tart cool on the baking sheet for about 7 minutes, slice, and serve warm or at room temperature.

Quick & Easy Kale Pizza

1+ SERVINGS

On the busiest of nights, this recipe comes to the rescue. Definitely play around with this one. Sprinkle on Breakfast Patty (page 171) crumbles, cooked lentils, or sliced, sautéed mushrooms for a meaty topping, or try the variety of sauces from pages 208–209.

STEPS

1. Preheat oven to 325°F.

2. In a large bowl, toss kale with almond flour and a pinch of salt.

3. Spoon sauces onto tortilla and top with kale.

4. Bake directly on the oven rack for 20 minutes, until crispy. Place your pizza on the top rack and a cookie sheet below it to catch any potential but rare spillage.

---

psst! You can easily use store-bought tomato sauce on this pizza instead of homemade.

—

Make it BBQ! Top with cooked chickpeas, vegan BBQ sauce, and caramelized onions. Yes!

—

Try using a Chickpea Flatbread Pizza Crust from page 185 instead of the tortilla.

—

Crumble some spicy Beautiful Breakfast Patties (page 171) onto this pizza for a sausage-like taste and texture.

INGREDIENTS

1 cup chopped kale, stems removed, chopped

3 tablespoons almond flour

Pinch sea salt

¼ cup Easy Tomato Sauce (page 209)

2 tablespoons Sweet Potato Cheese Sauce (page 208)*

1 large gluten-free, dairy-free tortilla

Mung Bean &
Eggplant Curry

4+ SERVINGS

When I got this book deal, I had to thank YU by offering up the chance to be published with me. So we held a recipe contest, and this winner is courtesy of Stefanie Ramsden Dougherty (GreenSageBlog.com).

STEPS

1. In a saucepan bring 2 cups of salted water and drained mung beans to a boil. Reduce heat to low and partially cover the pot; simmer for 20 minutes or until the beans are soft. If beans soften to "al dente" before the water evaporates, drain excess water. Replace the lid firmly on the pot to keep them warm.

2. In a separate saucepan, bring 2 cups of salted water to a boil. Add the soaked, drained basmati rice, return to a boil, reduce heat to simmer, and cover. Leave it simmering until all the water evaporates and the rice is cooked, roughly 12 – 15 minutes. Again, if the rice cooks before the water evaporates, pour the rest out.

3. Heat a large saucepan to medium-high and add coconut oil. Sauté onions for 3 minutes, then add the garlic and sauté for 3 minutes. Add broccolini and stir occasionally for a minute or two. Next, add mushrooms and eggplant, and stir until the veggies begin to soften.

4. In a small bowl, stir together paprika, coriander, cumin, curry powder, black pepper cayenne pepper, and 1½ teaspoons of sea salt. Sprinkle over the veggies and stir until they evenly coated.

5. Add mung beans, spinach, and the remaining sea salt. Stir until the spinach begins to wilt.

6. Stir in the dried cranberries. Turn off the heat and add the coconut milk and stir together. Serve the vegetable curry over the cooked basmati rice.

psst! Zucchini is a delicious alternative to eggplant.

Photo ©Stefanie Ramsden Dougherty

INGREDIENTS

1 cup dry split mung beans, soaked

1 cup basmati rice, rinsed and soaked for 15 minutes

2 tablespoons coconut oil*

2 cups yellow onion, diced

3 cloves garlic, sliced

2 cups broccolini, chopped

2 cups cremini mushrooms, chopped

1 cup eggplant, chopped

2 teaspoons sea salt

½ teaspoon paprika

1 teaspoon ground coriander

1 teaspoon ground cumin

1 tablespoon curry powder

½ teaspoon black pepper

¼ teaspoon cayenne pepper or more, to taste

4 cups packed baby spinach, chopped ½ cup sweetened dried cranberries

¾ cup coconut milk

Buckwheat Noodle Pad Thai

INGREDIENTS

1 8-oz. package
buckwheat noodles

Sauce

2 tablespoons
coconut aminos

3 tablespoons lime juice

2 tablespoons raw
almond butter

1 teaspoon Sriracha

3 tablespoons Sucanat*

2 tablespoons toasted
sesame oil

2 green onions, sliced thinly

—

1 – 2 teaspoons coconut oil*

1 red onion, diced

4 cloves garlic, minced

1 teaspoon ginger, minced

1 zucchini, diced

1 yellow squash, diced

Cilantro leaves,
roughly chopped

2 tablespoons sesame
seeds, toasted*

4+ SERVINGS

This is a veggie-powered, peanut-free version of the popular stir-fried Thai noodle dish. Experiment and prepare it with black bean noodles, mung bean noodles, rice noodles, or veggie noodles (page 251) and a variety of veggies because it's all about the sauce here.

STEPS

1. Bring a large pot of water to a boil and prepare noodles according to the manufacturer's instructions.

2. In a small bowl, whisk together sauce ingredients.

3. Heat a skillet (or a wok) to medium-high heat and add coconut oil and onion. Sauté for 5 minutes, then add garlic and ginger and stir for 3 minutes.

4. Toss cooked, rinsed, and drained noodles, zucchini, squash, and the sauce into skillet. Fold together, but allow the noodles to sear a bit, about 1 – 2 minutes on each side. Remove from heat after 3 – 5 minutes and serve warm topped with cilantro, extra green onion, and toasted sesame seeds if you like.

---

psst! If buying buckwheat noodles, make sure the ingredients don't include wheat. While buckwheat is gluten-free, many buckwheat noodles contain a combination of buckwheat and wheat flour.

—

Prepare this sauce and use it to season rice, kale, and sautéed vegetables for a tasty veggie bowl. Top with toasted almonds.

—

Use this sauce as a dressing for salads. (No judgments from me if you lick the bowl.)

—

Sometimes I'll add a red bell pepper or mushrooms to this recipe. Skip the yellow squash and just use zucchini or vice versa. Make raw noodles out of veggies instead. Play.

—

Make a raw version of this Pad Thai by using zucchini noodles (page 251) and all raw veggies.

Chickpea Protein Burgers

4+ SERVINGS

When my friend Matt Frazier's book "No Meat Athlete" released, I used his genius "veggie burger formula" from it to create this Chickpea Protein Burger. It was fun to plug in and play with ingredients that ultimately resulted in a new favorite for the menu rotation. Thanks, Matt!

STEPS

1. Place chickpeas, sweet potato, mustard, liquid smoke, Worcestershire, Montreal Veggie Seasoning, oats, quinoa, and coconut aminos into the food processor.

2. Heat a large pan over medium heat and add 1 teaspoon of coconut oil. Sauté the onion, garlic, celery, and red bell pepper until softened, about 5 minutes.

3. Transfer veggies to the food processor. Pulse together about 10 times until combined, but still chunky. Season to taste with salt and pepper.

4. Form into golf-ball-sized balls and flatten into patties for sliders (or bigger patties for larger burgers).

5. In a large pan over medium-high heat, warm remaining coconut oil. Sauté the patties in batches for 5–7 minutes per side until golden browned and heated through.

6. Serve solo or inside your favorite gluten-free bun.

INGREDIENTS

1½ cups chickpeas, cooked (½ cup dry)

1 cup sweet potato, diced and steamed until soft

1 tablespoon Dijon mustard

1 teaspoon liquid smoke

1 tablespoon +2 teaspoons vegan Worcestershire

1 tablespoon Montreal Veggie Seasoning (page 202)

1 cup rolled oats

½ cup quinoa, cooked

1 tablespoon coconut aminos

1 tablespoon coconut oil*

½ cup yellow onion, diced

1 clove garlic, minced

½ cup celery, diced

½ cup red bell pepper, seeds and ribs removed, diced

Sea salt to taste

Black pepper to taste

psst! Crumble one burger into a big bowl of greens with hemp oil, sliced radish, fresh-squeezed lemon, and fresh black pepper. Delish.
—
For extra egg-like binding power, stir 1 teaspoon psyllium husk powder into the mix before cooking.
—
Try black beans instead of chickpeas and Taco Seasoning (page 202) instead of Montreal Veggie Seasoning.

Spicy Chioggia Beet Maki Roll *with* Brown Sushi Rice

2+ SERVINGS

When roasted or steamed, Chioggia beets ("key-oh-gee-ah"— also known as candy cane beets) look an awful lot like tuna from a spicy tuna roll—yay! Quinoa also works instead of brown rice.

STEPS

1. Slice beet into long ½"-thick strips. Steam or roast for 40–50 minutes until firm but easily pierced with a fork.

2. Place rice in a large bowl and cover with water. Swish rice by moving your hands back and forth 10 to 15 times. Repeat and rinse rice until the water runs almost clear. Transfer rice to a pot. Add water and kombu. Bring rice to a boil, cover with a lid, and reduce heat for a low simmer for 30 minutes.

3. Stir together vinegar, Sucanat, and salt until dissolved.

4. Remove rice from heat, keep lid on, and let sit in the pot for 10 minutes.

5. Spoon cooked rice into a large mixing bowl and pour vinegar mixture over the top. Cut through rice with a wooden spoon until vinegar mixture is evenly distributed and rice cools to room temp.

6. Place all Spicy Sauce ingredients in the blender and blend until smooth. Set aside.

7. Lay a 12"-long piece of parchment paper on the counter and place a sheet of nori on top. Using hands or a spoon, spread nori with rice so there are no empty spots and the rice fills the entire sheet. Along the entire edge closest to you, lay Chioggia, avocado, cucumber, sesame seeds, and a drizzle of Spicy Sauce in a 1"-wide line. Use thumbs to lift parchment paper and sushi, and fingers to hold the ingredients in place while you start to roll over. Use parchment paper to tighten that first roll-over, release it, and use it to continue to roll the maki away from you.

8. Place maki roll seam-side down on a cutting board. With a sharp chef's knife, slice into pieces and enjoy.

INGREDIENTS

One 4–5" Chioggia beet

Brown Sushi Rice
¾ cup short grain brown rice
1¾ cups water
Piece of kombu
2 tablespoons rice wine vinegar
1 tablespoon Sucanat
¼ teaspoon sea salt

Spicy Sauce
½ cup cashews, soaked
½ cup water
1 teaspoon coconut aminos
¼ teaspoon toasted sesame oil
1 tablespoon hot sauce/Sriracha
1–2 drops liquid smoke*
—
2 sheets nori (toasted or raw)
1 ripe avocado*
1 cucumber, sliced
Sesame seeds, toasted

Individual Super-Veggie Pot Pies

INGREDIENTS

Vegetable Pie Filling

1 teaspoon coconut oil*

1 yellow onion, diced

3 stalks celery, diced

2 large carrots, diced

1 cup sweet potato, diced

¼ cup dry white wine*

3 cloves garlic, minced

2 – 4 leaves kale, stems removed, chopped well

1 cup fresh green peas

1 cup chickpeas, cooked (⅓ cup dry)*

1½ teaspoons thyme leaves

¾ teaspoon sea salt

¼ teaspoon black pepper

Sauce

2 tablespoons chickpea miso

2 cups veggie stock (page 122 or store bought)

1 cup water

2 teaspoons arrowroot starch/flour

¼ cup cashews, soaked

Crust

1½ cups sorghum flour

1½ cups almond flour

¾ teaspoon sea salt

¼ cup + 1 teaspoon coconut oil*

½ cup cold water

2 teaspoons lemon juice

6+ SERVINGS

Tender veggies in creamy gravy. Buttery crust. Heaven. I have a love affair with things in mini, but if you'd like to prepare a large pot pie, please do! Just fill a 9" glass pie pan and serve in bowls. Otherwise, you'll need twelve 3" ramekins, or six to eight 4" ramekins.

STEPS

1. Preheat oven to 325°F.

2. Warm a skillet to medium-high, add coconut oil, onion, celery, carrots, sweet potato, and wine. Sauté for 7 minutes. Add garlic and sauté for 3 minutes.

3. While veggies cook, add all sauce ingredients to a blender. Purée until smooth. Set aside.

4. In a large mixing bowl, use a fork to combine all crust ingredients until crumbly and starting to stick together.

5. Add kale, green peas, chickpeas, thyme, and sauce to your skillet, and stir for 5 minutes. Season with salt and pepper to taste. Remove from heat and fill ramekins almost to the top with the filling.

6. If you're rolling out a crust, roll dough into a ball with your hands, place on a sheet of parchment paper, and top with another piece of parchment. Roll, then peel back top layer. Cut pieces of dough to cover the entire top of the ramekin. If you're doing a crumble crust, break up dough with fork and sprinkle over top of filling — cover the entire top.

7. Bake ramekins for 25 – 30 minutes. Serve warm.

---

psst! The heat will compromise the probiotic benefits of the miso a bit — it's used in this recipe mainly as a tasty seasoning.

—

Roll out dough onto parchment, cut, then slide onto a cookie sheet and freeze for 5 minutes. Use an offset spatula to easily lift up crust "disks" to lay on top of ramekins.

Jerk Lentil & Avocado Wrap

4+ SERVINGS

There's a comfort-food vegan restaurant in Chicago that was a big help for me as I transitioned to plant-based foods. I used to order their spicy Jerk Tofu Wrap a few times a week. It was incredible — fiery-hot spice dancing around with the perfect amount of creamy, cooling ranch dressing. As time went by and I discovered how much better I felt without gluten or soy, the day came when I had to own up to the fact that my beloved wrap was really vegan junk food. So I said goodbye to my training wheels wrap and filled that comfort food void with this cleaner, whole-food replacement.

INGREDIENTS

2 cups green or brown lentils, cooked (1 cup dry)

2 – 3 leaves of kale, stems removed, chopped

Jamaican Jerk Seasoning to taste (page 203)

Sea salt and black pepper to taste

Gluten-free tortillas or collard greens (chef's choice)

Ranch Dressing (page 227)

One avocado, pitted and sliced

Sprouts*

Mixed greens*

STEPS

1. In a pot or skillet heated to medium, stir together lentils, kale, and Jamaican Jerk Seasoning for 3 – 5 minutes until warm and kale wilts a tad. Season with salt and pepper to taste.

2. If using collard greens for wraps or gluten-free tortillas, refer to page 146 for some helpful tips. Either way, prepare your wraps by scoring or by steaming for a few minutes to soften. Lay out on a large plate, cutting board, or counter space.

3. Fill wraps with lentils and kale and top with Ranch Dressing, avocado, and maybe sprouts and greens, leaving about 3" on all sides of wrap — the more space you leave, the tighter the wrap you can get, so don't overfill. Fold two sides in tightly, tuck the third side in tightly, and roll, roll, roll.

psst! You can easily use a store-bought dry rub or a jar of jerk seasoning rub for this recipe. Just season to taste, starting with ¼ teaspoon, because this stuff has kick. Remember when seasoning that the Ranch Dressing and creamy avocado will cool the heat.

—

Substitute chickpeas for lentils in this recipe.

—

Add some diced, roasted sweet potato, carrots, or butternut squash — a great combo with the kick of the Jerk Seasoning.

Beet, Apple & Onion Gratin

6+ SERVINGS

I love to try this recipe out on the "I don't like beets" crew because they almost always change their minds after the first bite. I recommend this dish for entertaining and dinner parties because it sure is a purty one and it's rich and full of flavor like a lasagna.

STEPS

1. Preheat oven to 325°F.

2. In a skillet heated to medium-high, add 1 teaspoon coconut oil, onion, and Sucanat. Stir occasionally for 7 – 10 minutes until onion caramelizes and browns.

3. Now, use a mandoline to cut all beets and apple into thin rounds. When you reach the apple core, just cut out with a knife and remove seeds.

4. Set up a workstation by loading up a plate with beet and apple slices, a bowl full of Cashew Sauce, a small dish of sea salt, and a pepper mill. Place a 7" x 9" or 9" x 9" baking dish in front of you on the counter.

5. Grease dish and lay 4 – 6 red beet rounds into it. They can overlap a bit. Spoon and spread some sauce onto rounds. Lay 7 – 10 caramelized onions on top. Season layer with a pinch of salt and a few grinds of pepper.

6. Repeat step 5 until you use up all red beet rounds. Salt and pepper each layer, too; it won't be oversalted if you use a pinch. Now, with each new layer, before you add sauce, press down firmly on the rounds. Sauce will rise up through the cracks. Use this sauce to spread. "Pressing" makes the gratin nice and tight once baked.

7. After all red beet rounds are used, continue layering with Chioggia rounds until used up. Move on to gold beet rounds and repeat layering steps. Finish up with the Granny Smith following the same onion, sauce, salt, and pepper steps for each layer. Finish the top off with sauce, salt and pepper, and a few onions.

8. Bake for 60 – 70 minutes. Serve warm, not hot.

INGREDIENTS

2 teaspoons coconut oil*

1 large yellow onion, sliced

1 tablespoon Sucanat

1 4 – 5" red beet

1 4 – 5" Chioggia beet

1 4 – 5" gold beet

1 large Granny Smith apple

1 batch Cashew Sauce (page 209)

Sea salt to taste

Black pepper to taste

psst! This recipe can be prepared a few days in advance, which makes it an even better dinner party choice.

—

Use ramekins to make individual gratins. Repeat all layering steps, just fill a 3½" or 4" ramekin instead.

Rainbow Veggie Ribbon Alfredo

INGREDIENTS

Alfredo Sauce

½ cup sunflower seeds, soaked

½ cup cashews, soaked

2 tablespoons lemon juice

1 teaspoon tahini*

3 cloves garlic, roasted

1½ cups water

1 tablespoon coconut oil*

1 tablespoon nutritional yeast

Sea salt to taste

Black pepper to taste

Veggies

1 zucchini

1 carrot

2 – 3 leaves of kale (purple, green curly or Tuscan)

1 broccoli stalk

1 yellow squash

¼ red bell pepper

¼ yellow bell pepper

4+ SERVINGS

I want to show you how many options you have for making noodles out of veggies simply with a mandoline, veggie peeler, and/or chef's knife. Try combining your favorites from this dish with different sauces (pages 208 – 209) for a variety of tasty options. Play and make it your own.

STEPS

1. In a blender, blend together all Alfredo Sauce ingredients and set aside.

2. Using a mandoline or veggie peeler, peel all of your veggies top to bottom in order to get long strips. At this point, some may be the desired noodle size, while others may be too wide for you. Stack those wide ones on top of each other, and using a chef's knife, slice them into the right size.

3. If you like, steam your veggies for 1 – 3 minutes to soften them and bring out bold color.

4. Warm Alfredo Sauce in a pot over medium heat. Toss sauce with veggie noodles and serve.

---

psst! Lacinato (aka Tuscan kale) has a leaf that isn't curly, so it's easier to slice into strips. Try that if it's available to you.

—

This recipe should be your gateway to noodle-izing all sorts of veggies.

—

Save your broccoli stalks from the Broccoli & Red Pepper Macaroni (page 236) for noodles.

INGREDIENTS

Gnocchi

4 cups sweet potatoes, diced

1½ cups oat or sorghum flour, plus more for dusting

¼ cup brown rice flour

2 tablespoons nutritional yeast

2 tablespoons water

2 tablespoons arrowroot starch/flour

1 tablespoon + 1 teaspoon psyllium husk powder

2 cloves garlic, sautéed

2 teaspoons sea salt

—

Easy Tomato Sauce (page 209)

2 teaspoons coconut oil

Handful of basil leaves, chiffonade

½ cup grape tomatoes, sliced in half and roasted*

Skillet Crusted Sweet Potato Gnocchi

2–4+ SERVINGS (MAKES 120 1" GNOCCHI)

I have worked on this recipe for years and finally have something that my sweetie says "tastes as incredible as the first bowl of gnocchi I ever had." And from a man who loves pasta, I'll take that as a double thumbs-up.

STEPS

1. Using a double boiler or a steaming basket, steam sweet potatoes until soft, about 20 – 30 minutes.

2. Place all Gnocchi ingredients into the food processor and pulse until a dough forms. Transfer to a large bowl.

3. Dust a flat work surface (counter top) with extra oat or sorghum flour. Pinch off some dough and roll out a 1"-wide, long strip. Using a chef's knife, cut the strip into 1" pieces. If you want, lightly press the top of each gnocchi with the back of a fork. Reshape if you need to. Repeat these steps until all gnocchi are formed.

4. In a pot heated to medium-low, warm Easy Tomato Sauce. Stir occasionally.

5. Fill a large pot with water and bring it to a boil. Once boiling, drop gnocchi into the water and stir. Cook for 2 minutes, remove, and rinse.

6. Heat a skillet to medium-high and add oil and gnocchi. Let them sear for 1 minute, flip, and sear on other sides so the outside gets crispy.

7. Transfer to a bowl and toss with sauce, fresh basil, and roasted tomatoes. Serve warm.

psst! If you go oil-free on this one, you won't be able to get that brown, crispy sear on the gnocchi, so skip step 6.

—

Freeze these gnocchi for speedy meals on busy nights.

—

Try adding fresh herbs and spices to the gnocchi dough like rosemary, basil, thyme, sage, or even cinnamon.

Chickpea, Tarragon & Cranberry Salad

4+ SERVINGS

This is an alternative to chicken salad that's loaded with protein, fiber, color, and flavor. Scoop it onto salads like mixed greens with Honey Mustard Dressing (page 226) or toast some Toasted Super Seed Power Bread (page 182) and enjoy an open-faced sandwich.

STEPS

1. Place all ingredients except cranberries into the food processor and pulse together about 3 – 5 times, just to break everything up a bit.

2. Transfer to a bowl, fold together with cranberries, and enjoy.

---

psst! Try adding diced Granny Smith apple to this salad.

—

Load up a collard green or a gluten-free wrap with this salad, add sprouts, greens, and extra Cashew Sauce.

—

If you don't have a food processor, simply mash your chickpeas with a fork and some elbow grease. Also, chop up your almonds with a chef's knife.

INGREDIENTS

2 tablespoons or more of Cashew Sauce (page 209)

1½ cups chickpeas, cooked (½ cup dry)

3 tablespoons almonds, toasted

2 green onions, sliced

2 tablespoons celery, diced

1 – 2 teaspoons of fresh tarragon to taste

½ – 1 teaspoon salt or more to taste

Black pepper to taste

¼ cup dried cranberries

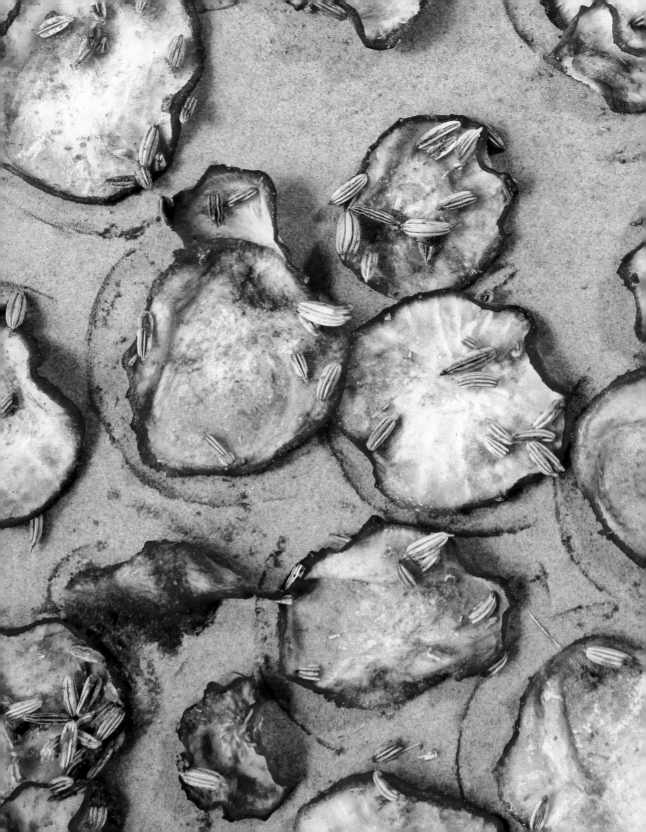

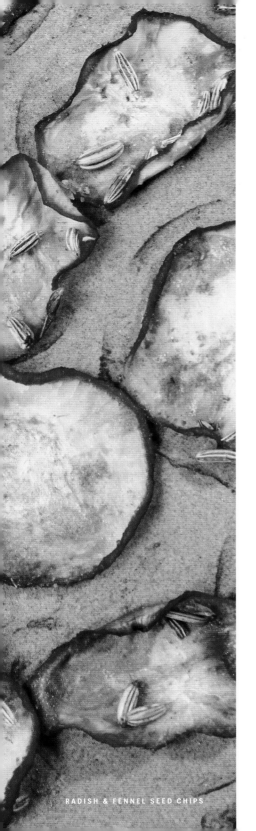

Snacks

RADISH & FENNEL SEED CHIPS

Radish & Fennel Seed Chips

INGREDIENTS

6 large radishes

Pinch of sea salt

2 teaspoons fennel seed, roughly chopped

1½ teaspoons ground cumin

2 teaspoons avocado or coconut oil

2+ SERVINGS (PHOTO PREVIOUS PAGE)

Skip the bag of deep-fried potato chips and make these crispy, pretty, and flavorful radish chips at home instead. Add them to salads and soups for texture and crunch, too.

STEPS

1. Preheat oven to 325°F and line two baking sheets with parchment paper.

2. Using a mandoline, shave thin rounds out of all radishes.

3. Lay out a clean towel on the counter and cover with radish rounds. Add a pinch of salt and let them sit for 10 minutes. Lay another clean towel on top of them and press out the excess water. Transfer rounds to a bowl.

4. Add another teeny, tiny pinch of salt, fennel seeds, cumin, and oil, and massage with hands until all rounds are coated.

5. Line entire pan with rounds. They can overlap a tiny bit but not too much; you want even cooking.

6. Bake for 15 minutes, remove pan, flip chips, bake another 10 – 15 minutes, and remove from oven. Chips will crisp up as they cool on baking sheet.

psst! Make 'em raw in a dehydrator if you have one.

—

It's very important that these slices are paper thin, so if you don't have a mandoline, slice radishes with a veggie peeler and use those. They won't be round, but you'll be able to enjoy this snack.

—

Add these radish chips to Almond Crunch Kale Chips (page 33) for extra flavor and color, especially if you're having a party.

—

Follow these same steps, but use zucchini instead of radish.

Chocolate & Cherry Hemp Bars

10+ SERVINGS

Pack up these guys for a hike, or enjoy them as a simple treat. They're an amped-up, gelatin-free, antioxidant- and protein-rich version of a rice crispy treat.

STEPS

1. Grease a 9" x 13" glass baking dish with coconut oil. Set aside.

2. Place sunflower seeds, coconut, oats, cherries, rice crisps, and chocolate chips into a large glass bowl.

3. In a medium saucepot, bring brown rice syrup, vanilla extract, almond butter, coconut oil, and sea salt to a boil over medium-high heat. Whisk often.

4. Once boiling, pour over dry ingredients in the bowl. Use a silicone spatula to fold everything together until well integrated; chocolate will melt. Fold in hemp seeds.

5. Transfer to the greased baking dish and use a spatula to really press mixture into the dish so it reaches all corners evenly. Or try laying a sheet of unbleached parchment paper on top of treat mixture and pressing down with your hands — easy peasy and less mess.

6. Allow to cool, then slice.

---

psst! You can use a chopped gluten-free, vegan chocolate bar instead of chips if that's easier to find.

—

Try dried blueberries, goji berries, raisins, or cranberries instead of, or in addition to, cherries.

—

Make them poppers! This preparation is a bit sticky to work with, but it's worth it for fun bite-sized treats. Toast ½ cup of almonds and throw them in food processor and pulse them into fine bits. Keep the bar mixture on the stove top over low heat while you work. Using your hands, pinch off a bit, drop it into a bowl of almonds. Sprinkle entire dollop with almonds to cover as much as possible. Pick it up and roll it into a ball. Cover with more almonds until outside isn't sticky anymore. Repeat until bar mixture is all used up.

INGREDIENTS

1 teaspoon coconut oil, plus more to grease the dish

¾ cup sunflower seeds, toasted

1 cup flaked coconut, toasted

½ cup rolled oats, toasted

1 cup dry cherries, chopped

2½ cups brown rice crisps cereal (not puffs)

¾ cup gluten-free, vegan chocolate chips

1 cup brown rice syrup

½ teaspoon vanilla extract

2 tablespoons almond butter

½ teaspoon sea salt

¼ cup hemp seeds

Almond & Coconut Antioxidant Trail Mix

INGREDIENTS

1 cup almonds

½ cup pumpkin seeds

½ cup sunflower seeds

Pinch sea salt

1 cup flaked coconut

½ cup dry goji berries

4+ SERVINGS

Pre-packaged trail mixes usually contain sugars, sulphered dried fruits, GMO-fried fruits, and snack sticks, and the prices per package are borderline astronomical. You can make your own clean trail mix in about 5 minutes instead. It's a super filling, nutrient-dense snack to keep in your on-the-go bag.

STEPS

1. Preheat oven to 325°F and line a baking sheet with a sheet of parchment paper.

2. Place almonds, pumpkin seeds and sunflower seeds on lined baking sheet with a pinch of salt and toast for 7 minutes. Remove and toss into a large bowl.

3. Using the same parchment-lined baking sheet, toast coconut for 3 minutes. Add to bowl of almonds and seeds. Fold in dry goji berries.

psst! Add some dry blueberries, cherries, or raisins to the mix, or use them to sub for gojis.

—

Sprinkle in some ground cinnamon and cardamom.

—

For optimal assimilation of nutrients, soak and dehydrate (or dry at a low temp in the oven) nuts and seeds before mixing all ingredients.

Strawberry-Banana Crunch Snack Wraps

2+ SERVINGS

If you're a fan of PB&J, try this simple, healthier version that can be made in 5 minutes flat. You'll be surprised how tasty a lettuce wrap can be.

STEPS

1. Lay out your Boston lettuce leaves.

2. Spread a little bit of almond butter on half of a leaf. Top with toasted almonds, sunflower seeds, hemp seeds, and layer strawberries and banana on top. Add a teeny pinch of sea salt and roll 'er up. Repeat these steps with more leaves until you make as many as you need.

---

psst! You can use romaine instead of Boston lettuce, just know that Boston is the softest and easiest to roll.

—

Try different berries and nut butters in your wrap.

INGREDIENTS

4 large leaves of Boston butter lettuce

Raw almond butter

2 tablespoons almonds, chopped and toasted

2 tablespoons sunflower seeds, chopped and toasted

1 – 2 teaspoons hemp seeds*

4 – 5 strawberries, sliced

½ – 1 banana, sliced

Pinch of sea salt

Raspberry & Peach Fuit Leather

8+ SERVINGS

*Fruit leather is colorful, chewy food that you can play with —
what's not to love? Well, the majority of fruit leathers that line
grocery-store shelves are loaded with dyes, sugars, preservatives,
and other health diminishers, but you can easily make your own
with a few simple ingredients and a silpat (silicone baking mat).*

STEPS

1. Preheat oven to 170°F and line a baking sheet with
a silpat.

2. In a blender, add all ingredients and blend together
until smooth.

3. Using a silicone spatula, spread mixture evenly into
a rectangular shape onto your silpat. You want about
⅛" thickness and no weak spots where you could see
through the puréed fruit to the silpat.

4. Bake for 2 – 3 hours until dry.

5. Let it cool completely. Peel from silpat and transfer
to a sheet of parchment paper. Cut into strips (through
both leather and parchment) and roll up.

INGREDIENTS

1 cup peaches, fresh or frozen,
pits removed

1 cup raspberries, fresh or frozen

1 – 2 teaspoons raw honey to taste

---

psst! I made a swirl here by combining two different flavors, but
you can keep it simple if you like. Just follow the recipe as is with
one flavor.

—

Use cookie cutters to cut the fruit leather into shapes once dry. Then
cut strips of parchment, transfer shapes to those strips, and roll them
on up.

—

Add fresh in herbs and/or spices to the blender. Try blueberry and
thyme or peach and coriander.

—

Make it raw in a dehydrator if you have one.

Toasted Sesame & Wasabi Seaweed Snacks

INGREDIENTS

Untoasted nori sheets

Toasted sesame oil

Handful of sesame seeds

Sea salt

Wasabi powder*

PREPARE AS MANY AS YOU LIKE

I brought these on a plane with my girlfriends once. They looked at me like I was crazy. "Seaweed snacks?!" By the end of the flight, they had "helped me" eat them all and soon were smiling wide to each other, asking, "Do I have any in my teeth?"

STEPS

1. Preheat oven to 300°F and line a baking sheet with a sheet of parchment paper.

2. Lay nori on baking sheet and pour some sesame oil in a small dish. Using a basting brush or your fingers, paint a little bit of sesame oil over the surface. Keep the oil to a minimum; you want just enough so your salt and seeds will stick.

3. Sprinkle with a pinch of sea salt and sesame seeds.

4. Toast for 5 minutes max and remove from oven. Raw nori goes in the oven purple and comes out green. Sprinkle on as much wasabi powder as you like. (Don't add wasabi before baking because it will burn and taste like burned popcorn.)

5. Once cooled, with kitchen scissors, cut your snacks into rectangles, triangles, hearts, little fish, or any shape you'd like.

---

psst! Make this raw in a dehydrator if you have one.

—

You can use toasted nori sheets if that's all you can find. Adjust toasting time to 1–2 minutes.

Spreads, Dips & Condiments

Sliceable Cashew Cheese

4+ SERVINGS (PHOTO PREVIOUS PAGE)

This is a fun recipe that can be customized to make a variety of flavors. Skip the liquid smoke if you like and enjoy it plain. Or try adding Herbes de Provence (page 203) for herbed cheese; roasted red bell pepper for a rich, orange cheese; or chopped jalapeño peppers for a pepper jack.

INGREDIENTS

Coconut or avocado oil, to grease the mold

1 cup water

1 tablespoon + 1 teaspoon agar flakes (1¾ teaspoons agar powder)

¼ cup cashews, soaked

2 teaspoons nutritional yeast

1¼ teaspoons lemon juice

1 teaspoon sea salt

¼ teaspoon liquid smoke*

STEPS

1. Find a mold that you can pour cheese into. A small bowl works well; so do muffin tins. Grease them lightly with oil.

2. In a pot, bring water and agar flakes to a boil over medium heat, whisking often. Reduce heat to low, simmer for 4 minutes, and then remove from heat.

3. Place all ingredients, including agar mixture, into the blender and blend until ultra-creamy and smooth.

4. Pour into molds and transfer to the fridge to chill for at least 4 hours.

5. Flip mold and release cheese. Slice away and enjoy.

---

psst! You can replace the cashews with soaked sunflower seeds or macadamia nuts if you like. Try Brazil nuts, hazelnuts, walnuts (makes it purple, which is pretty neato), or pecans in equal amounts, too.

—

You can grate this cheese! Try it on Lentil, Kale & Quinoa Tacos (page 237).

—

If serving to guests, before you pour cheese into mold, sprinkle the bottom of the mold with toasted sesame seeds or paprika, then pour. When you flip firm cheese out of molds, the tops will have extra texture and color. Fancy.

—

Make it stinkier, like a tasty aged cheese, and add 1 – 2 teaspoons apple cider vinegar to the blended mixture.

Carrot &
Almond Pâté

2+ SERVINGS

*Enjoy this fresh pâté on Super Seed Power Bread (page 182),
Chickpea Flatbread (page 184), in a wrap, or as a dip for fresh
cut veggies.*

STEPS

1. Place everything in a food processor and pulse 5 – 7
times until well mixed, but maintain some texture.

2. Press into a greased small bowl or container and
flip onto a plate or shape with your hands into a dome
or square.

3. Serve room temp or chilled.

psst! You can try brown rice or azuki bean miso if you like. Just
look for gluten- and soy-free.

—

Try adding some green or red apple to this pâté.

—

Try sautéing onion for 5 minutes, toasting almonds and sunflower
seeds, or using roasted carrots for deeper flavor.

—

Here's an entertaining idea: in the food processor, process pâté with
a few tablespoons of Cashew Cheese Spread (page 270) until a paste
forms. Fill a fancy piping bag and pipe onto Almond Dulse Crackers
and top with a dollop of Cashew Cheese Spread and/or a fresh
parsley leaf. Pretty.

INGREDIENTS

¼ cup almonds, soaked

½ cup sunflower seeds, soaked

2 tablespoons sesame
seeds, toasted

½ teaspoon chickpea miso

1 large carrot

1 small handful parsley leaves

1 tablespoon red onion, chopped

¼ teaspoon coconut aminos

1 teaspoon lemon juice

Sea salt to taste

Black pepper to taste

Homemade Roasted Almond Butter

INGREDIENTS

1 cup almonds

---

psst! Try making a butter from pumpkin seeds, heirloom jungle peanuts (no dangerous aflatoxins in this kind), pecans, hemp seeds, hazelnuts, Brazil nuts, sunflower seeds, or walnuts.

—

Remember, if you can soak and dry (or dehydrate) nuts and seeds first, that prepares them for digestion best.

—

Flavor butters with cinnamon, cocoa, vanilla bean, maple syrup, and/or ground cardamom to taste. Infinite possibilities here. Just try not to add water-based flavorings as they will diminish shelf life.

—

If you'd like to add some hemp, sunflower, or flax oil to your butter, please do. Just store it in a dark glass container in the fridge, or wrap your jar in some dark cloth to protect fragile EFAs like hemp and flax from light. Adding oil creates a silkier texture, too. After nuts/seeds have ground to butter, start with 1 tablespoon of extra oil at a time until you reach desired consistency.

4+ SERVINGS

Making nut and seed butters at home is absolutely possible if you have a food processor. It saves you money, not to mention, a homemade almond butter and Raspberry & Chia Jam (page 205) sammie on Super Seed Power Bread (page 182) just tastes more like love.

STEPS

1. If you'd like to have a roasted nut butter, preheat oven to 325°F. Lay almonds out on a parchment-lined baking sheet about one almond deep and roast for 7 – 10 minutes. Totally optional.

2. Place nuts in the food processor and process constantly. Stop the action every 2 minutes or so to scrape down the sides. You want to let it run for about a total of 10 – 15 minutes until almonds go from dust to clumpy to butter. It will get creamy; it just takes a little time.

3. Once creamy, store in an airtight glass container in the fridge.

Simple Cashew Cheese Spreads

8+ SERVINGS FOR ALL

This easy spread is a creamy, rich, cheesy base for all sorts of flavor combinations and experimentation. Spread some on Toasted Super Seed Power Bread (page 182), Chickpea Flatbread (page 184), Almond Dulse Crackers (page 188), or fresh-cut veggies like celery, carrots, and cucumber. Super for party platters, sandwiches, salads, and wraps.

STEPS FOR ALL

1. In a blender or food processor, purée together all ingredients until super-smooth. This is the plain base (tasty as-is) that can be used for many other combinations like...

INGREDIENTS

1½ cups cashews, soaked

⅓ cup pure water

2 tablespoons lemon juice

½ teaspoon sea salt

Herbes de Provence

STEPS

Use 1–2 tablespoons of Herbes de Provence mix (page 203) for an excellent spread for Almond Dulse Crackers (page 188). Add 2 teaspoons fresh lemon zest and maybe 1 clove of minced, roasted garlic for even more flavor.

Sundried Tomato

STEPS

Simply fold in ½ cup of chopped sundried tomatoes (or use the food processor to pulse it in). Add some fresh basil and fresh black pepper for more flavor.

Onion

STEPS

Sauté ¼ cup white onion. Simply fold onion into the cheese (or use the food processor to pulse it in).

Artichoke

STEPS

Fold ¾ cup of chopped, marinated artichoke hearts into cheese. Add some fresh pepper to taste.

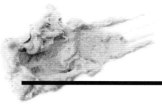

Sour & Stinky with Toasted Walnuts

STEPS

Toast ½ cup of chopped walnuts and fold into cheese with 2 teaspoons apple cider vinegar and an extra 2 teaspoons of lemon juice.

Pink Peppercorn

STEPS

Fold 1 tablespoon ground pink peppercorn into cheese.

Baked: Roasted Red Pepper & Almond

STEPS

1. Preheat the oven to 325°F.

2. Use the food processor to pulverize ½ – 1 cup of almonds into crumbles. Transfer them to a medium bowl.

3. Use the food processor again to blend ½ cup of roasted red bell pepper into the cheese spread. Scoop the red pepper cheese mixture out and drop into the bowl of almond crumbles. Roll into a large ball, coating evenly with crumbles. Place on a parchment-lined baking sheet and bake in the oven for 10 – 15 minutes. Serve warm.

psst! If you make or have access to rejuvelac (a non-alcoholic fermented drink that improves the digestion of food), use it instead of water for more authentic "cheesy" flavor. (Gain access to Book Owner Central at **yumuniverse.com/yu-book-owners** for info on rejuvelac.)

—

Add 1 – 2 teaspoons of apple cider vinegar for a more cheesy taste.

—

Try making this spread with soaked walnuts, almonds, sunflower seeds, or pecans. The flavors and textures will be different, but it's a great way to acquaint yourself with the unique properties of each.

Lemon & Garlic

STEPS

Roast 1 – 2 cloves of garlic. Use the food processor to combine the garlic with the cheese spread, 1 tablespoon of additional lemon juice, and 1 – 2 teaspoons lemon zest. Fresh cracked pepper is nice, too.

Crumbles

STEPS

1. Preheat the oven to 325°F. Spread the cheese base onto a parchment-lined baking sheet and bake in the oven for 10 – 15 minutes. Allow to cool.

2. Using a fork, break apart cheese. If it's still too sticky, turn off the oven and leave the cheese to dry out in it until you're able to break it into crumbles. It's excellent as a salad topping or on top of Lentil, Kale & Quinoa Tacos (page 237).

Roasted Cherry Tomato Salsa

2+ SERVINGS

While I love fresh, raw salsa, there's something magical that happens with the combination of roasted tomatoes and fresh ingredients. Plus, the body absorbs more of the beneficial nutrients in tomatoes when they're cooked first.

STEPS

1. Preheat oven to 325°F. Line a baking sheet with parchment paper. Toss cherry tomatoes with coconut oil and a sprinkle of sea salt. Roast for 15 minutes.

2. While cherry tomatoes roast, mix together onion, cilantro, garlic, jalapeño, lime juice, and sea salt in a medium bowl.

3. Once tomatoes have cooled, pull off the tomato skins (save for veggie stock, page 122), chop the tomatoes and fold into the fresh ingredients. Taste and add more salt or lime juice if necessary.

---

psst! Change it up: use tomatillos to replace tomatoes for a tasty roasted green version of this salsa.

—

Use 2 large tomatoes if you can't find cherry tomatoes.

—

Skip the roasting for a raw salsa.

INGREDIENTS

1 pint cherry tomatoes, sliced in half

2 teaspoons coconut oil, warmed gently to liquid*

¼ teaspoon sea salt, plus more for tomatoes

½ cup white onion, minced

1 tablespoon cilantro leaves, chopped

1 clove garlic, minced

1 teaspoon jalapeño pepper, seeds and ribs removed, minced

2 teaspoons lime juice

Simple Hummus

6+ SERVINGS

Not only will you save money making your own hummus, but there's a tremendous taste difference. Store-bought hummus just cannot compare. Plus, with homemade hummus you can soak and prepare the chickpeas in a way that boosts their nutrients (page 138).

STEPS

1. Place all ingredients in a food processor and purée until smooth. Serve room temp or store in the fridge.

---

psst! Add roasted red bell pepper to this hummus for a new flavor.
—
Try adding extra roasted garlic, too.

INGREDIENTS

2 cups chickpeas, cooked (¾ cup dry)

3 tablespoons lemon juice

2 tablespoons tahini

1 – 2 cloves garlic, roasted

¼ cup water

Pinch cayenne pepper*

2 tablespoons olive oil*

½ teaspoon sea salt or more to taste

Black pepper to taste*

Beverages

Also see: The "Training Wheels" Green Smoothie on page 27.

Non-Dairy Milks

There truly are infinite possibilities when it comes to a plant-inspired diet, and milk alternatives are no exception. While there are more and more pre-packaged non-dairy milk options hitting grocery store shelves every day, nothing tastes as delicious, offers as much variety, or packs the preservative-free, nutritional punch that homemade does. Use the following as inspiration to experiment and discover. And try some with Orange & Pepita Granola (page 168).

Homemade Almond Milk

The most alkalizing nut around.

STEPS

1. In a blender, mix ½ cup soaked almonds with 2 cups of water at high speed until smooth.

2. Over a large glass bowl or pitcher, strain mixture through a cheesecloth, twisting and squeezing from the top down. Set pulp aside. If you like, sweeten with honey, maple syrup, or Sucanat.

Hemp Seed Milk

Loaded with beneficial essential fatty acids and protein.

STEPS

1. In a blender, mix ½ cup hemp seeds with 2 cups of water at high speed until smooth. No need to strain.

2. If you like, sweeten with honey, maple syrup, or Sucanat. Or toss 1–2 dates into the blender in step 1.

Poppy Seed Milk

Listen up, insomniacs: Drink this at bedtime. It helps you have a restful sleep. It soothes achy joints and inflammation, too.

STEPS

1. In a blender, mix ½ cup soaked poppy seeds with 2 cups of water at high speed until smooth.

2. Over a large glass bowl or pitcher, strain mixture through a cheesecloth, twisting and squeezing from the top down. Set pulp aside and if you like, sweeten with honey, maple syrup, or Sucanat.

"I'm Too Busy" Almond Milk

When you need almond milk in 2 minutes instead of 10. Ha!

STEPS

1. In a blender, mix 1 tablespoon of almond butter (page 269) and ¼ teaspoon vanilla extract (optional) with 2 cups of water at high speed until smooth. No need to strain.

2. If you like, sweeten with honey, maple syrup, or Sucanat to taste. Or toss 1–2 dates into the blender in step 1.

psst! You can use any grain, nut, or seed to make your own milk. Just follow the basic soak-blend-strain steps, sweeten to taste if you like, and enjoy. Try oats, Brazil nuts, sunflower seeds, and more.

—

For extra iron, stir 1–2 teaspoons of blackstrap molasses into your milk.

—

Blend or stir in fresh berries or cacao powder for a fruity or chocolate-y milk.

—

Add fresh vanilla bean or extract, ground cinnamon, or ground cardamom for extra flavo

—

For more deliciousness, try toasting nuts and seeds before blending.

Decadent Hazelnut (aka Filbert) Milk

A great source of magnesium, which is a powerful mood and anxiety regulator.

STEPS

1. In a blender, mix ½ cup soaked hazelnuts with 2 cups of water at high speed until smooth.

2. Over a large glass bowl or pitcher, strain mixture through a cheesecloth, twisting and squeezing from the top down. Set pulp aside. If you like, sweeten the milk with honey, maple syrup, or Sucanat.

Toasted Sesame Milk

Super for bones and teeth since it's a great source of calcium and magnesium.

STEPS

1. In a blender, mix ½ cup toasted sesame seeds with 2 cups of water at high speed until smooth.

2. Over a large glass bowl or pitcher, strain mixture through a cheesecloth, twisting and squeezing from the top down. Set pulp aside. If you like, sweeten milk with honey, maple syrup, or Sucanat.

Coconut Milk

Alkalizing and loaded with vitamins, minerals, and beneficial fatty acids.

STEPS

1. In a blender, mix ¾ cup shredded coconut (or Thai coconut meat with its water) with 2 cups of water at high speed until smooth. Or you can simply blend together the meat and water from one Thai coconut, adding more plain water if you need to. No need to strain, but you can if you like.

2. Sweeten with honey, maple syrup, or Sucanat to taste if you like.

Pumpkin Seed Milk

Excellent healer for digestive ailments of all kinds, and high levels of tryptophan make is helpful for anxiety issues, too.

STEPS

1. In a blender, mix ½ cup soaked pumpkin seeds with 2 cups of water at high speed until smooth.

2. Over a large glass bowl or pitcher, strain mixture through a cheesecloth, twisting and squeezing from the top down. Set pulp aside. If you like, sweeten the milk with honey, maple syrup, or Sucanat.

Save the Pulp!

Don't toss the leftover pulp from straining milk. Use it to make crackers and even a chocolate mousse treat.

Pulp Crackers

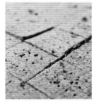

STEPS

For every ½ cup pulp add ½ cup almond or hazelnut flour, 2 rounded tablespoons coconut oil and a pinch of sea salt. Follow the steps from Almond Dulse Crackers on page 188.

Chocolate Mousse

STEPS

In a food processor, pulse ½ cup of leftover pulp with 1–2 tablespoons cacao powder, 2–3 tasty tablespoons of maple syrup, ¼ teaspoon of vanilla extract and a pinch of sea salt. Chill and serve.

Maca & Chicory Root Latte

2+ SERVINGS

Chicory Root is one of my favorite caffeine-free, health-boosting alternatives to coffee. It supports digestion and detoxification, it's full of antioxidants, it reduces inflammation, and it has a dark, rich taste that Europeans and folks from southern states like Louisiana have been enjoying in place of (or in addition to) coffee for many generations. Maca naturally boosts energy without caffeine, it helps to balance hormones, and its nutty flavor combines with chicory for a truly satisfying morning or evening beverage. And you don't need a fancy machine or dairy milk to make a decent latte foam for teas. Just use a high-powered blender and a few natural ingredients.

INGREDIENTS

2 – 3 teaspoons organic roasted chicory root (granules)

2 teaspoons ground maca root (powder)

2 cups water

Latte Foam

1 cup water

1 tablespoon almond butter

1 Medjool date, pitted (or 2 – 3 Deglet Noor)

¼ teaspoon vanilla extract

Pinch sea salt

Pinch cardamom*

1 – 2 teaspoons raw honey*

STEPS

1. Tie up a bundle of chicory root with maca root using a cheesecloth.

2. In a pot, bring water to a boil. Remove from heat and steep tea for 10 minutes.

3. Add all latte foam ingredients to the blender and blend on high for 1 – 2 minutes until smooth and frothy.

4. Transfer tea to a favorite mug or teacup and stir in some honey if you like.

5. Use a spoon to scoop out foam and top your tea. Pour in some of the almond milk you just made, too.

---

psst! You can also steep the chicory root and maca loose (stir in maca well) in the pot of hot water, then strain through a cheesecloth and serve.

Lavender-Chia Lemonade

2+ SERVINGS

I enjoy this drink for its nostalgic taste without all the dyes and processed sugars in the store-bought stuff. It's hydrating (chia) and boosts energy (honey), which makes it a powerful endurance drink for sustained fitness. The main reason I love this recipe though is because it reminds me of my friend Paul, who once said to me when he saw it on my desk at work, "Whatcha got there, Crosby, some seahorse eggs?" I can't deny it. Lavender-Chia Lemonade is a showstopper with a lovely taste to match.

STEPS

1. In a pot filled with 8 cups of water, add zest, juice, and lavender buds. Bring to a boil.

2. Turn off heat and allow to steep, like tea, until cool. Refrigerate for about 4 hours (or overnight).

3. Strain into a pitcher. Stir in chia seeds after you strain out the lavender and lemon.

4. Sweeten with honey if you like. Serve chilled or room temperature.

INGREDIENTS

8 cups water

¼ cup lemon zest

1 cup lemon juice

2 tablespoons culinary lavender buds

2 tablespoons chia seeds

½ cup raw honey*

psst! Feel free to enjoy this lemonade without the chia.

—

You'll need about 5 – 6 large lemons to make this recipe.

Green Smoothies

2+ SERVINGS FOR ALL

If there's one health-boosting addition to your daily routine that will make an incredible difference in how you feel, sleep, look, recover from exercise, and so much more, it's drinking a green smoothie. Each glass is packed with healing phytonutrients, antioxidants, vitamins, minerals, and fiber. They're a breeze to make, too. Here are a few of my faves and some tips for getting started.

I recommend trying these smoothies with a combination of greens, so swap out my call for "mixed greens" with a variety of options: Mixed greens, romaine, and baby kale are a smidge sweet, the most neutral in flavor, and taste lovely with almost everything from protein powders to fresh berries. They're great "starter greens" to begin a smoothie routine. Arugula is a peppery and tasty base in a savory smoothie. If collards, dandelion, kale, or mustard greens taste too "assertive" for you, know that eventually your taste buds will change and you may start craving them.

In the meantime, though, quickly blanch and chill or lightly steam the greens to reduce any strong flavor (leaves will wilt, but that's okay) and blend away. Add ice for a "frosty" smoothie and use coconut water for a naturally sweet, electrolyte-packed liquid base if you like. Add sprouts like sunflower or sweet pea to smoothies, too. Try milks from page 276 for more creaminess and use coconut water as a base for more electrolytes and natural sweetness. Oh my, have fun with it.

STEPS FOR ALL

In a blender, blend until smooth. Easy.

Pear & Cilantro

1 ripe pear of your choice

1 large handful of cilantro leaves

2 large handfuls of mixed greens

1 – 2 teaspoons raw honey*

2 cups water

2 teaspoons hemp seeds

1 – 2 teaspoons fresh lemon or lime juice

Savory
(also makes a nice cold soup)

2 – 3 leaves kale

½ red bell pepper, seeds and ribs removed

½ avocado, pitted

1 – 2 teaspoons jalapeño pepper, chopped and seeded

Handful of cilantro

½ cucumber

1 stalk celery

Juice from ½ lemon or lime

Sea salt to taste*

Peaches & Cream

1–2 ripe peaches, pitted
(try mango instead)

1 tablespoon almond butter

2 large handfuls of
mixed greens

1–2 teaspoons raw honey*

2 cups coconut water
(or pure water)

2 teaspoons hemp seeds

¼ teaspoon ground cinnamon

Pinch ground cardamom*

1–2 drops vanilla extract*

Ginger & Vanilla Protein

1 scoop of your favorite
plant-based, gluten-free vanilla
protein powder

2 large handfuls of mixed
greens or baby kale

1–2 teaspoons raw honey*

1 teaspoon maca powder*

2 cups water

2 teaspoons hemp seeds

1½ teaspoons ground dry
ginger (½ teaspoon fresh)

Chocolate-Covered Cherry

2 cups coconut water
(or pure water)

1 cup ice

1 handful mixed greens

1 cup cherries, pitted
(fresh or frozen)

2 tablespoons cacao powder

1 large leaf kale

1 tablespoon hemp seed*

2 Medjool dates, pitted

2 teaspoons maca powder*

¼ teaspoon vanilla extract

Creamy & Fresh Avocado

1 green apple

½ avocado, pitted

2 teaspoons raw honey*

Juice from 1 lime

2 handfuls mixed greens

2 cups water

2 teaspoons hemp seeds

Handful of fresh cilantro*

Desserts & Treats

Toasted Pecan Florentines

INGREDIENTS

1 tablespoon almond flour

2 tablespoons brown rice flour

¼ cup pecans, chopped and toasted

2 tablespoons maple syrup

3 tablespoons Sucanat

1 tablespoon coconut oil, gently warmed to liquid on the stove top

¼ teaspoon sea salt

12+ SERVINGS (PHOTO PREVIOUS PAGE)

When I'm invited to a last-minute party or dinner and I need to bring a treat, I make a version of these versatile Florentines. They require very few ingredients and even less time to make, but they taste like a fancy French cookie that took all day to prepare. They are also a nice gift, especially at holiday time.

STEPS

1. Preheat oven to 325°F and line a baking sheet with parchment paper.

2. In a medium bowl, stir together all ingredients until well mixed.

3. Pinch off some dough, enough to make a 1" ball. Place on cookie sheet and repeat so balls are 3 – 4" apart (they will spread and flatten).

4. Bake for 7 – 10 minutes, no longer. Slide parchment onto the counter to cool. Cookies will crisp up as they cool off.

---

psst! Drizzle or sandwich with a melted gluten-free, vegan chocolate bar for extra decadence.

—

Use toasted pumpkin seeds, sesame seeds, almonds, or walnuts instead of pecans.

Easy Vanilla Bean Ice Cream

8+ SERVINGS

At this point in the book, I hope you're looking at this recipe with confidence and creativity, thinking about all the goodies you can add to it or all the things you can add it to. Before freezing, fold in Sweet Cherry Rose Compote (page 200), or even the Granny Smith Apple Cobblers (page 297) for an "Apple Pie Ice Cream." Warm a Dark Chocolate, Sweet Potato & Black Bean Brownie (page 292) and make it à la mode with a scoop of this ice cream and some Hot Fudge Sauce (page 289). Or serve a scoop alongside some Chocolate & Salted Caramel Layer Cake (page 290). Want to try something unexpectedly delish? Top a bowl of this ice cream with fresh blueberries and/or strawberries and some Balsamic Reduction (page 227).

STEPS

1. Lay vanilla pod on a cutting board and press it flat with your fingers. Place your pointer finger at the top to hold in place, and using a sharp chef's knife, slice lengthwise from top to bottom, but only through the top layer of the pod if you can. Peel open and using the back of a butter knife, start at the top of the pod and scrape downward to collect the tiny, fragrant, tasty seeds. If you cut the pod all the way through, no problem, you just have to scrape twice. Tap seeds into a medium pot.

2. In a small bowl, take ¼ cup of coconut milk and whisk it together with arrowroot until well mixed. Transfer to the pot and add all remaining ingredients.

3. Cook over medium-high heat, stirring constantly until mixture comes to a boil. You may notice things are thickening. That's a great sign. Remove from heat and stir together for another 1 – 2 minutes.

4. Transfer to an airtight container and chill in the fridge overnight.

5. Pour chilled ice-cream base into the frozen bowl of your ice-cream maker and prepare according to manufacturer's instructions. No ice-cream maker? Pour into an airtight glass container. Freeze and enjoy.

INGREDIENTS

1 vanilla bean pod

2 14-oz. cans coconut milk (not reduced fat)

1 tablespoon arrowroot powder (optional)

3 tablespoons raw honey

1 tablespoon coconut oil

¼ teaspoon sea salt

psst! Easily use 2 teaspoons vanilla extract instead of vanilla bean.

—

Arrowroot powder is optional, but it's recommended because it helps create a nice, scoopable texture and minimizes ice crystals. Without it, ice cream is a little harder, but still delicious.

—

Either way, always thaw ice cream 10 – 15 minutes before serving.

Maple Spice Sandwich Cream Cookies

INGREDIENTS

Spiced Cream

1 cup cashews, soaked

½ teaspoon
ground cinnamon

1 teaspoon lemon juice

Pinch sea salt

Pinch ground clove

Pinch ground nutmeg

Pinch ground cardamom*

Wet

¼ cup + 2 tablespoons
maple syrup

¼ cup + 1 tablespoon
coconut oil

2 teaspoons vanilla extract

2 tablespoons hot water

Dry

1½ cups almond flour

⅔ cup brown rice flour

3 tablespoons Sucanat

1 teaspoon baking powder

¾ teaspoon sea salt

Fold-ins

½ cup rolled oats

½ cup raw pecans, toasted
and chopped

10+ SERVINGS

Oatmeal cookies times two with spiced cream filling. Now, that's a smart cookie.

STEPS

1. Preheat oven to 325°F and line a baking sheet with parchment paper.

2. Blend together all Spiced Cream ingredients until smooth and pop in the fridge to chill for 2 – 4 hours.

3. In a medium-sized bowl, whisk or blend together all wet ingredients and set aside.

4. In a large bowl, sift together dry ingredients. Fold wet ingredients into dry, and then add fold-ins.

5. Spoon dough into 2" rounds onto baking sheet. Press them down a touch with your hand or a silicone spatula. (They don't collapse when baking, so the height they go in is the height they come out.)

6. Bake 10 – 12 minutes. Remove from oven and cool on baking sheet. Transfer to fridge to chill.

7. Remove Spiced Cream from fridge and spread some on one cooled cookie. Top with another. Repeat until all cookies are made into magical sandwiches.

psst! You can skip the Spiced Cream and just make oatmeal cookies here. Try adding the spice from the cream into the batter first or adding ¼ cup raisins if you do.

Pretty Pretty Pie Crust

6+ SERVINGS

Here is my tried-and-true pie crust recipe, the one I use for sweet and savory dishes. (Skip the Sucanat if you're going savory.) It makes one pie crust, so double the batch if you need a top as well.

STEPS

1. Place all ingredients, minus the water, in a large bowl. With a fork, cut together all ingredients until crumbly.

2. Add water tablespoon by tablespoon until you can form the dough into a ball with your hands.

Using right away...

1. Preheat oven to 325°F. Grease bottom and sides of a 9" glass pie plate with a dollop of coconut oil.

2. No need to roll out this dough. Use your hands and press dough into pie dish and form around the dish until it uniformly covers all sides.

3. With a fork, press lines into the crust top and poke holes into the bottom of the crust.

4. Prebake for 20 minutes. Remove, add filling, and bake according to the pie recipe's instructions.

Using later...

1. Freeze or refrigerate pie crust for later use. Prebake before filling and thaw first if frozen.

INGREDIENTS

1 cup almond flour

1 cup sorghum flour

1 teaspoon sea salt

3 tablespoons solid coconut oil, chilled a bit

¼ cup Sucanat

¼ cup + 1 tablespoon cold water

psst! Fill a prebaked pie crust with 3 cups of berries and ¼ cup raw honey and top with a second pie crust (rolled or crumbled). Bake for 35 minutes. If you skip the coconut oil, I recommend making a crumble top. Oil helps bind, so set your expectations if you skip it — pie crust will be more crumbly but still yummy.

—

Make pie crust cookies! Try adding 1–2 tablespoons of natural dyes like turmeric (yellow: will add turmeric flavor), beet root powder or juice (pink/red: adds a touch of sweetness), liquid chlorophyll (green: careful it stains more than dough) or cocoa powder (brown: adds cocoa flavor). Mix, roll out, cut, and bake for 10–15 minutes at 325°F.

Hot Fudge Sauce

8+ SERVINGS

If this stuff was slathered on a tire, you may find me nibbling on that tire. It's decadent, rich hot fudge sauce that when chilled, doubles as a frosting for Chocolate & Salted Caramel Layer Cake (page 290). And when it's heated, it makes for all-out-indulgent ice-cream sundaes with Easy Vanilla Bean Ice Cream (page 285) and Salted Caramel Sauce (page 296). Knock it out of the park by adding a warm Dark Chocolate, Sweet Potato & Black Bean Brownie (page 292) and toasted nuts.

STEPS

1. Melt chocolate in a double boiler heated to medium-high.

2. While chocolate melts, in a small bowl, whisk together coconut milk and arrowroot until thoroughly dissolved.

3. Whisk cacao powder, coconut oil, Sucanat, and salt into melted chocolate.

4. Slowly pour arrowroot and coconut milk slurry into chocolate, whisking constantly until smooth. Continue for 5 minutes.

5. Remove from heat and whisk for one more minute. Serve hot or chill for frosting.

6. To enjoy as hot fudge sauce again, simply reheat on the stove top in a pot heated to medium-low. Stir constantly until melted. You don't want it to burn.

INGREDIENTS

1 3.5-oz. gluten-free, vegan chocolate bar, chopped

1 cup coconut milk

1 teaspoon arrowroot starch/flour

¼ cup cacao powder

3 tablespoons coconut oil

¾ cup Sucanat

Pinch sea salt

psst! Over medium-high heat, whisk together non-dairy milk (page 276) and Hot Fudge Sauce to taste for a rich and delicious hot chocolate. Add a pinch of cayenne and cinnamon to make it Mexican style.

Chocolate & Salted Caramel Layer Cake *with* Chocolate Frosting

8+ SERVINGS

This is truly a special occasion cake that makes everyone involved with its creation and consumption feel the love. You'll need four 9" cake pans. Or use two, but you'll split the batch and prepare that twice.

STEPS

1. Prepare Hot Fudge Sauce (page 289) and whisk in an extra ½ teaspoon of arrowroot. Chill in the fridge 4 – 8 hours until firm.

2. Prepare Salted Caramel Sauce (page 296) and whisk in an extra 2 teaspoons of arrowroot. Chill in the fridge 4 – 8 hours until firm.

3. Preheat oven to 325°F. Use kitchen scissors to cut four pieces of parchment paper into rounds that will fit the bottom of cake pans. Place them in and set aside.

4. Place all wet ingredients in the blender and set aside for 5 minutes so chia seeds plumpen.

5. In a large bowl, sift together all dry ingredients.

6. Once the chia has soaked long enough, blend together wet ingredients.

7. Fold together wet and dry until mixed. Transfer batter to pans and bake for 20 – 25 minutes. Insert a knife into the center of the cake; if it comes out clean, remove from oven; if not, bake longer until it does.

8. Remove and allow to cool in the pan. Then, transfer to the fridge to chill for at least 6 hours. The parchment makes it easy to stack cakes on one plate without them sticking together.

9. When ready to layer, create a workstation with a cake plate, two spoons, frosting, caramel, and cakes.

INGREDIENTS

Chocolate Frosting

1 batch of Hot Fudge Sauce (page 289)

½ teaspoon arrowroot starch/flour

Salted Caramel Filling

Salted Caramel Sauce (page 296)

2 teaspoons arrowroot starch/flour

INGREDIENTS CONTINUED

Wet

¼ cup chia seeds

2 cups warm water

1 tablespoon + 1 teaspoon
apple cider vinegar

1½ cups red apple,
cored and diced

¼ cup + 2 tablespoons
coconut oil

3 teaspoons vanilla extract

3 tablespoons
chocolate extract*

Dry

1½ cups almond flour

1½ cups sorghum flour

½ cup arrowroot
starch/flour

½ cup cacao powder

2 teaspoons baking soda

2 teaspoons baking powder

½ teaspoon sea salt

2 cups Sucanat

10. Place one cake on the plate and generously spread caramel on top, leaving about ½" from the edge. (The weight of the other cakes will push caramel out.) Repeat with the next two cakes. Place the fourth cake on top and spread frosting on top. Cover and chill in the fridge until ready to serve.

psst! That isn't an official cake stand in the photo — I made it out of a bowl, a plate, and some grippy kitchen drawer liner. Just set a bowl face down, place the grippy liner on top and then set your plate on top. Remove the plate before cutting the cake so there's no heart-breaking disaster, but definitely display this beauty on a stand.

—

Instead of salted caramel between the layers, make a triple batch of Raspberry & Chia Jam (page 205) and use that for a Chocolate Raspberry creation to knock everyone's socks off. That's right. Socks. Off.

—

Want something less time consuming? Split the batch and bake cupcakes. Use a piping bag to squeeze some caramel into the center of each and top with frosting. Want even simpler than that? Skip the caramel sauce altogether. Top with a fresh raspberry, toasted coconut, and/or a lovely edible flower for a pop of color and festivity.

—

Make individual mini layer cakes (minis are fun) by pouring batter ½" – ¼" deep into greased muffin tins. Split the batch if you have two muffin tins and quarter the batch if you only have one. Reduce baking time to 10 – 15 minutes. These little cakes are fun to layer with jam, frosting, caramel, and/or Sweet Cherry Rose Compote (page 200). Use different fillings. Play. And send me pics of your creations, please!

Dark Chocolate, Sweet Potato & Black Bean Brownies

12+ SERVINGS

I do love to sneak unexpected, nutrient-rich ingredients into treats, and this gluten-free recipe is a perfect example. Black beans, sweet potato, and dark chocolate combine into bona fide fudge-like decadence. You can use canned beans for this recipe, but I recommend starting with dry beans (soaked and then cooked by you) to reduce aluminum intake, boost flavor, and optimize digestion and nutritional benefits.

STEPS

1. Preheat oven to 325°F and grease a 9" x 13" or 9" x 9" baking dish or line it with parchment paper.

2. Sift or whisk together all dry ingredients in a large glass bowl. Set aside.

3. Place all wet ingredients into the food processor and pulse until super-smooth.

4. Fold together wet and dry ingredients and transfer to the parchment-lined baking dish.

5. Bake for 60 – 70 minutes. Remove from oven and allow to cool in baking pan before serving.

---

psst! For a triple dark chocolate brownie, top brownies with shaved chocolate after baking.

—

Fold some toasted almonds, pecans, and/or walnuts into your batter.

—

Fold ¼ cup cherries and ¼ cup toasted coconut into your batter before baking.

—

Make 'em Mexican style. Fold 1 teaspoon cinnamon, ½ teaspoon cayenne pepper, and ¼ teaspoon ground nutmeg to the batter before baking.

INGREDIENTS

Dry

1½ cups almond flour

⅓ cup Sucanat

½ cup cacao powder

1 teaspoon baking powder

½ teaspoon sea salt

Wet

⅔ cup sweet potato, diced and steamed

2¼ cups black beans, cooked (1 cup dry)

2 teaspoons vanilla extract

One 3 – oz. gluten-free, vegan chocolate bar

⅓ cup maple syrup

2 tablespoons coconut oil*

¾ cup water

Mexican Unfried Ice Cream

4+ SERVINGS

This recipe is just plain fun, plus it's that salty-sweet combo that everyone loves. I recommend it for dinner parties because guests get a real kick out of the creativity with this one.

STEPS

1. In a food processor, add chips, cacao, and Sucanat. Pulse until chips break up into a dust with some texture but not quite a powder. You want to maintain the crunch factor.

2. Create a workstation. Pour chip dust into a bowl and put it near you. Grab a large cereal spoon, a glass container with a lid (ideally frozen overnight to keep things cool as you work), some parchment paper, and possibly some kitchen scissors.

3. Scoop some ice cream and drop it into your chip dust. Push 1 – 2 pieces of strawberry into the center and use spoon or finger to cover with ice cream. Sprinkle dust all around, and pick up your dollop. Roll in hands, adding dust as needed to form a ball. Set into chilled storage container and continue until you fill the entire container. Freeze until serving.

4. Since you're working with meltable ingredients, time is of the essence. If your little ice creams aren't perfect spheres, that's okay. Freeze them anyway, save some dust, and once frozen solid, re-roll in dust before serving.

5. Thaw for 5 – 10 minutes before serving.

INGREDIENTS

3 cups non-GMO certified blue corn tortilla chips

1 tablespoon cacao powder

2 tablespoons Sucanat

2 cups Easy Vanilla Bean Ice Cream (page 285)

2 – 3 strawberries, diced

psst! You can always use a pint or two of store-bought dairy-free, soy-free, gluten-free vanilla ice cream with this recipe, which I recommend for those unexpected dinner parties where you need a fun dessert, fast.

—

Drizzle them in Hot Fudge (page 289) before serving.

Cantaloupe & Fresh Black Pepper Granita

INGREDIENTS

3 cups ripe cantaloupe, seeded and diced

2 teaspoons lemon juice

3 tablespoons raw honey

Fresh black pepper

6+ SERVINGS

I know I mentioned earlier that my grandfather introduced me to the ingenious flavor combination that is juicy, ripe cantaloupe and fresh black pepper. This simple recipe is for him. And YU. Enjoy it as a quick treat on a hot summer day.

STEPS

1. In a blender, blend together all ingredients except pepper until smooth.

2. Pour into a loaf pan, cover, and freeze.

3. Once frozen take a fork and grate the granita until it's a lovely shaved ice. Serve in a lovely bowl and sprinkle with a pinch or two of fresh black pepper.

psst! Try this recipe with ripe honeydew melon or watermelon instead of cantaloupe. If you go watermelon, blend in some fresh basil instead of pepper.

—

Of course, if you must, you can skip the pepper (wink).

—

Use these steps and quantities to make a granita out of any fruit you like. Blueberry and thyme is a favorite of mine, and so is fresh Meyer lemon and thyme or Meyer lemon and lavender buds (add more sweetener here).

Salted Caramel Sauce

8+ SERVINGS

A salty-sweet sauce that you can pour over Easy Vanilla Bean Ice Cream (page 285), or Chocolate Cake (page 290).

STEPS

1. Make an arrowroot slurry by mixing arrowroot and water in a small bowl or cup until arrowroot is thoroughly dissolved.

2. In a large saucepan, whisk together all caramel ingredients constantly over medium-high heat.

3. Once the mixture boils, whisk in the arrowroot slurry until it's completely incorporated. Then, remove from heat but continue to whisk vigorously. As it cools, the caramel will thicken nicely. Store in an airtight container in the fridge and reheat in a pot over medium for warm caramel.

INGREDIENTS

1½ teaspoons arrowroot starch/flour

¼ cup water

Caramel

1½ cups coconut milk

1 cup Sucanat

⅓ cup brown rice syrup

2 tablespoons coconut oil

1 teaspoon vanilla extract

1 teaspoon sea salt

Granny Smith Apple Cobblers

6 SERVINGS

This is another crunch-time dessert that will wow dinner guests without a ton of effort. Take it to the next level by serving à la mode with Easy Vanilla Bean Ice Cream (page 285).

STEPS

1. Preheat oven to 325°F.

2. Fill six 4" ramekins with sliced apples and set aside. They can exceed the top by quite a bit because everything will bake down significantly in the oven.

3. In a medium bowl, add all the crumble ingredients. Use a fork to mix together and set aside.

4. In a small saucepan heated to medium, whisk together all caramel ingredients until mixed.

5. Spoon caramel over apples and top with crumble. Feel free to pack that crumble down on top of your apples. (Go ahead and use hands.)

6. To make getting in and out of the oven easier, place all ramekins on a baking sheet. Bake for 25 minutes. Remove from oven and serve warm.

---

psst! Use red or golden apples in this recipe. Or try pears or peaches.
—
Add raisins and a squeeze of orange juice in the caramel if you like.
—
For fun flavor, try adding some fresh thyme or chamomile buds ground in the coffee grinder.

INGREDIENTS

2 Granny Smith apples, cored, peeled, and sliced

Crumble

2 cups almond flour

¼ teaspoon sea salt

½ teaspoon Sucanat

1 tablespoon coconut oil

Pinch sea salt

Caramel

½ teaspoon ground cinnamon

1 teaspoon vanilla extract

Pinch sea salt

¼ cup Sucanat

1 tablespoon coconut oil

Appendix

Measurements & Conversions

Cheat Sheet:

1 tablespoon = 3 teaspoons

4 tablespoons = ¼ cup

⅓ cup = 5 tablespoons + 1 teaspoon

½ cup = 8 tablespoons

⅔ cup = 10 tablespoons = 2 teaspoons

¾ cup = 12 tablespoons

1 cup = 16 tablespoons = 48 teaspoons

8 fluid ounces (fl. oz.) = 1 cup

1 pint (pt.) = 2 cups

1 quart (qt.) = 2 pints

4 cups = 1 quart

4 quarts = 1 gallon (gal)

16 ounces (oz.) = 1 pound (lb.)

Temperature:

For everything from dehydrating to broiling.

°F	°C
90°F	32°C
95°F	35°C
115°F	46°C
170°F	77°C
200°F	93°C
250°F	121°C
275°F	135°C
300°F	149°C
325°F	163°C
350°F	177°C
375°F	191°C
400°F	204°C
425°F	218°C
450°F	232°C
475°F	246°C

Volume Conversions (liquids):

In cases where you don't have to be as precise, you may want to round up as follows:

1 cup = 250 ml

1 pint = 500 ml

1 quart = 1 L

1 gallon = 4 L

4 quarts = 1 gallon (gal)

16 ounces (oz.) = 1 pound (lb.)

Otherwise:

1 teaspoon = 5 ml

1 tablespoon = ½ fl. oz. = 15 ml

1 fl. oz. = ⅛ cup = 30 ml

¼ cup = 2 fl. oz. = 60 ml

⅓ cup = 80 ml

½ cup = 4 fl. oz. = 120 ml

⅔ cup = 160 ml

¾ cup = 6 fl. oz = 180 ml

1 cup = 8 fl. oz. = ½ pint = 240 ml

1½ cups = 12 fl. oz. = 350 ml

2 cups = 1 pint = 16 fl. oz. = 475 ml

3 cups = 1½ pints = 700 ml

4 cups = 2 pints = 1 quart = 950 ml

4 quarts = 1 gal = 3.8 L

Resources

BONUS GOODIES FOR BOOK OWNERS: yumuniverse.com/yu-book-owners

There are certain helpful goodies I wanted to give you that simply wouldn't fit into this book. So I've developed a bunch of bonus materials for book owners to learn more, find support, and stay inspired:

Bonus cooking classes and videos

Links to important articles

Printables and charts to keep in your wallet or purse — master meal planning and shopping, identify dangerous ingredients, and uncover sneaky labeling

Terms and ingredient glossaries

Easy shopping links for recommended tools, appliances, and more

Gain access to your bonus materials by visiting the link above.

MORE FROM YUMUNIVERSE

If you want to simply "test drive" a plant-based diet, or get some planning help with a meal plan subscription, or you're ready to venture even further with lifetime support, there are loads of eBooks, packages, and programs available on YumUniverse.com to suit a variety of needs.

I'm always adding new goodness, so be sure to stop by and see if any of the resources I've developed inspire YU:

yumuniverse.com/store

Recommended Books

Food & Nutrition

The China Study
T. Colin Campbell

**The Complete
Idiot's Guide to
Plant-Based Nutrition**
Julieanna Hever

**Dr. Neal Barnard's
Program for
Reversing Diabetes**
Neal Barnard

**Eating on the Wild Side:
The Missing Link to
Optimum Health**
Jo Robinson

Eat to Live
Joel Fuhrman

Food Over Medicine
Pamela Popper
Glen Merzer

The Food Revolution
John Robbins

**Food Rules:
An Eater's Manual**
Michael Pollan

**GRUB: Ideas for an
Urban Organic Kitchen**
Anna Lappé
Bryant Terry

**In Defense of Food:
An Eater's Manifesto**
Michael Pollan

Organic Manifesto
Maria Rodale

The Pleasure Trap
Douglas Lisle

Thrive
Brendan Brazier

Wheat Belly
William Davis

**Whole: Rethinking the
Science of Nutrition**
T. Colin Campbell

Wild Fermentation
Sandor Ellix Katz

Cookbooks

Blissful Bites
Christy Morgan

**The China Study
All-Star Collection**
LeAnne Campbell
Features YU recipes

The China Study Cookbook
LeAnne Campbell,
Steven Campbell Disla
T. Colin Campbell

Choosing Raw
Gena Hamshaw

**Forks Over Knives:
The Cookbook**
Del Sroufe

Happy Herbivore
Lindsay S. Nixon

Let Them Eat Vegan!
Dreena Burton

**The Oh She
Glows Cookbook**
Angela Liddon

Rawsome Vegan Baking
Emily von Euw

**SuperFood Kitchen:
Cooking with Nature's
Most Amazing Foods**
Julie Morris

Thrive Energy Cookbook
Brendan Brazier

Thrive Foods
Brendan Brazier

UnDiet
Meghan Telpner

Veganomicon
Isa Chandra Moskowitz
Terry Hope Romero

Fitness & Inspiration

Finding Ultra
Rich Roll

No Meat Athlete
Matt Frazier

The Power of Habit
Charles Duhigg

Power Vegan
Rea Frey

Thrive Fitness
Brendan Brazier

Digging Deeper

Eating Animals
Jonathan Safran Foer

**Salt, Sugar, Fat:
How the Food
Giants Hooked Us**
Michael Moss

Seeds of Deception
Jeffrey M. Smith

**Selling Sickness:
How the World's
Biggest Pharmaceutical
Companies Are Turning
Us All into Patients**
Ray Moynihan

Documentary Films

Earthlings

Food, Inc.

Food Matters

Forks Over Knives

The Future of Food

Hungry for Change

King Corn

Vegucated

Recommended Magazines, Websites & Blogs

Plant-Inspired

Choosing Raw
choosingraw.com

One Part Plant
onepartplant.com

The Little Foxes
thelilfoxes.com

Meghan Telpner
meghantelpner.com

No Meat Athlete
nomeatathlete.com

Oh She Glows
ohsheglows.com

Post Punk Kitchen
theppk.com

Thrive Forward
thriveforward.com

VegNews
vegnews.com

YumUniverse
yumuniverse.com

Shopping & Eating Resources

The Environmental Working Group
ewg.org

EWG's Skin Deep® Cosmetics Database
ewg.org/skindeep

Happy Cow
happycow.net

Local Harvest
localharvest.org

Non-GMO Project
nongmoproject.org

A handful of photos are from istock.com: pages 12, 13, 42, 43, 68, 74–75, 83, 126, 128–129

Photographers/Stylists

The following peeps shared time, talent, and support while I created this book. Please go say "hi" to them and see more of their work, they're pretty wonderful.

Marta Sasinsowska
martasasinowska.com

Photography/styling: spine, 4–5, 8 (top), 9 (middle, bottom), 20 (top), 33, 53, 63 (background), 79, 108 (left, middle), 133 (top, bottom), 135, 154 (top middle, middle left), 155 (top right), 218, 242, 248, 279, 298, 307, 310, 312, 314, 320 (top left, top middle top, top right)

Photography on pages: cover, 31, 58 (left), 132 (bottom), 131, 132 (bottom), 133 (middle), 154 (bottom right), 162–163, 316

Julia Stotz
juliastotz.com

Photography: 22–23, 45, 76–77, 156–157

Sage Reed
sagereed.com

Styling: 22–23, 45, 58 (left), 76–77, 131, 132 (bottom), 133 (middle), 154 (bottom right), 156–157, 162–163, 316

Mele Ortiz

Styling: 22–23, 45, 76–77, 156–157

Bob Coscarelli
coscarelli.com

Photography: 14

Acknowledgments

The book-writing process has reinforced the notion that more often than not, the most challenging experiences are ultimately the most rewarding. It takes passion, a smidge of vulnerability, and a whole lot of tireless effort to create something that connects with others and has the potential to make a real difference. And without a doubt, something that special cannot be done alone.

Thank you to Glenn Yeffeth and the team at BenBella Books for allowing me to create the book that I wanted to share. Thank you to my editor, Maria Hart, for your incredible guidance and support. Thank you to my agent, Linda Konner, for believing in me and helping me make it happen. Brendan Brazier, thank you for supporting my baby from the very, very beginning. You didn't hesitate to help support my launch party, and you haven't stopped since. Thank you to leaders like Dr. T. Colin Campbell, Dr. Neal Barnard, Dr. Joel Fuhrman, Dr. Douglas Lisle, Dr. Caldwell Esselstyn, Dr. Dean Ornish, and other groundbreakers for your brave, revealing work.

Thank you to the YumUniverse community and my beloved YU members for your inspiration and support — we're in this together. Maya Henderson, you're forever the original YU cheerleader, and I can't thank you enough for being enthusiastic from day one. Kathy Beymer, my dear old pal, thank you for inspiring me to start a blog (whether you realize you did or not) and for your unconditional support of whatever I've gotten myself into over the years. And Marta Sasinowska, my soul sister, the yin to my yang, my Skoo ("little darling"), thank you for making me laugh every second of the day, for sending the "Happy" song my way when I needed it most, and for sharing your incredible photography gift with me and YU. I couldn't be luckier that you bought a hoop from me so many years ago.

Dear, dear, beautiful Sage Reed, Mele Ortiz, Julia Stotz, and Kathleen Hajduk, my heart fills up when I think about how grateful I am to you for sharing your time, talent, and creative gifts for this project. Paul Mougey, you are a true gem and I'm lucky to know you. Thank you for your kindness, humor, time, generosity, genius, and eagle eye. Thank you to my West Virginia pals for always dropping off homegrown goodness, for taste-testing creations, and for illustrating how camping is done for this book. And my sweet home Chicago pals, you'll always be my family. Thank you for helping me show how brunching and entertaining is done for YU. Rea Frey, I don't know if I'd have written *YumUniverse* if it weren't for your encouragement to write a book and your generous gift of the tools I needed to get started — thank you, sister. I have to also thank the loving healers that have helped me find my way on this wellness adventure: Diane Miller and Deborah Arneson, you are beautiful, kind, generous women and your maternal guidance is priceless.

Thank you to Bob Coscarelli for making time at Art Camp Wandawega to take a lovely bio photo of me for the book. And thank you to my friends, family, and colleagues for believing in what I have to share. I'm a lucky lady. And finally, my M. These letters I type into words just don't do justice to the gratitude that I need to send your way. Thank you for your infinite patience, nature walks, encouragement, being Captain Dishwasher, the jokes, the zigzag dance, your friendship, and simply keeping it all together (even me) while I wrote and turned every room in our home into a photo set for *YumUniverse*. **Love.**

Notes

Why Plant-Powerful?

1. National Center for Health Statistics. Health, United States, 2012: With Special Feature on Emergency Care. Hyattsville, MD, 2013. Table 63. <http://www.cdc.gov/nchs/data/hus/hus12.pdf#063>

2. Prieidt, Robert. 01/06/10. "Hazards of Obesity Now Rival Smoking in U.S." *USA Today*, 6 Jan. 2010. <http://usatoday30. usatoday.com/news/health/weightloss/2010-01-06-obesity-smoking_N.htm>

3. Hellmich, Nancy. "Rising Obesity Will Cost U.S. Health Care $344 Billion a Year." *USA Today*, 17 Nov. 2009. <http:// usatoday30.usatoday.com/news/health/weightloss/2009-11-17-future-obesity-costs_N.htm>

4. Pollack, Andrew. "Health Care Costs Climb Moderately, Survey Says." *The New York Times*, 20 Aug. 2013. <http://www. nytimes.com/2013/08/21/business/survey-finds-modest-rise-in-health-insurance-premiums.html>

5. Glass, Ira. Transcript: "More Is Less." This American Life, 9 Oct. 2009. <http://www.thisamericanlife.org/radio-archives/ episode/391/transcript>

6. Kane, Jason. "Health Costs: How the U.S. Compares with Other Countries." PBS NewsHour, 22 Oct. 2012. <http://www.pbs. org/newshour/rundown/2012/10/health-costs-how-the-us-compares-with-other-countries.html>

7. Van Dusen, Allison and Ana Patricia Ferrey. "World's Healthiest Countries." *Forbes*, 8 Apr. 2008. <http://www.forbes. com/2008/04/07/health-world-countries-forbeslife-cx_avd_0408health.html>

8. Fuhrman, Joel, MD. "The Cure for the American Diet: Nutrient Density." *The Huffington Post: Healthy Living*, 9 Sept. 2010. <http://www.huffingtonpost.com/joel-fuhrman-md/the-cure-for-the-american_b_695474.html>

Plant-Powerful Benefits

1. Hever, Julieanna. 2011. *The Complete Idiot's Guide to Plant-Based Nutrition.* New York: Penguin, 5 – 6.

2. "Phytochemicals." The American Cancer Society, 2013. <http://www.cancer.org/treatment/treatmentsandsideeffects/ complementaryandalternativemedicine/herbsvitaminsandminerals/phytochemicals>

3. Cross, A.J. and R. Sinha. "Meat-related Mutagens/Carcinogens in the Etiology of Colorectal Cancer." *Environmental and Molecular Mutagenesis* 44:1 (2004): 44 – 56.

4. Cassidy, E. S., P. C. West, J. S. Gerber, and J. A. Foley. "Redefining Agricultural Yields: From Tonnes to People Nourished per Hectare." *Environmental Research Letters* 8: 3 (2013). <http://doi:10.1088/1748-9326/8/3/034015>

5. UN News Centre. "Rearing Cattle Produces More Greenhouse Gases Than Driving Cars, UN Report Warns." 29 Nov. 2006. <http://www.un.org/apps/news/story.asp?newsID=20772&CR1=warning#.UqUTpGRDsg0>

6. Monastra, G. and L. Rossi. "Transgenic Foods as a Tool for Malnutrition Elimination and Their Impact on Agricultural Systems." *Rivista di Biologia* 96:3 (2003): 363 – 84. <http://www.ncbi.nlm.nih.gov/pubmed/15055878>

7. Gurian-Sherman, Doug. "Failure to Yield: Evaluating the Performance of Genetically Engineered Crops." Cambridge, MA: Union of Concerned Scientists, 2009. <http://ucsusa.org/food_and_agriculture/science_and_impacts/science/failure-to-yield. html>

8. Strom, Stephanie. "Food Companies Claim Victory against Labeling Initiative in Washington State." *The New York Times*, 6 Nov. 2013. <http://www.nytimes.com/2013/11/07/us/politics/food-companies-claim-victory-against-labeling-initiative-in-washington-state.html>

9. Schiffman, Richard. "Unsafe to Eat: A New Report Highlights the Dangers of Genetically Modified Foods." *The Huffington Post: Green*, 6 July 2012. <http://www.huffingtonpost.com/richard-schiffman/gm-foods_b_1650576.html>

10. Gammon, Crystal. "Weed-Whacking Herbicide Proves Deadly to Human Cells." *Scientific American*, 29 June 2009. <http:// www.scientificamerican.com/article.cfm?id=weed-whacking-herbicide-p>

11. Mercola, Joseph, MD. "Study Found Toxin from GM Crops Is Showing up in Human Blood." Organic Consumers Association, 31 May 2011. <http://organicconsumers.org/articles/article_23308.cfm>

12. Vendomois, J.S., D. Cellier, C. Velot, E. Clair, R. Mesnage, and G. E. Seralini G.E. "Debate on GMOs Health Risks After Statistical Fndings in Regulatory Tests." *International Journal of Biological Sciences* 6:6 (2010): 590 – 598. <http://biolsci.org/ v06p0590.htm>

13. Davis, William, MD. *Wheat Belly: Lose the Wheat, Lose the Weight, and Find Your Path Back to Health.* New York: Rodale, 2011, 6.

14. "Celiac Disease Facts & Figures." National Foundation for Celiac Awareness, accessed 30 Dec. 2013. <http://www. celiaccentral.org/celiac-disease/facts-and-figures>

15. Ibid.

Turning Down the Noise

1. Kolata, Gina. "Side Effects? These Drugs Have a Few." *The New York Times*, 4 June 2011. <http://nytimes.com/2011/06/05/ weekinreview/05drugs.html>

2. "Nearly 7 in 10 Americans Take Prescription Drugs, Mayo Clinic, Olmsted Medical Center Find." Mayo Clinic News Network, 19 June 2013. <http://newsnetwork.mayoclinic.org/discussion/nearly-7-in-10-americans-take-prescription-drugs-mayo-clin-ic-olmsted-medical-center-find>.

3. Britt, Russ. "Top 11 Drug Firms Made $711 Billion in Last Decade, Report Points Out." *The Wall Street Journal: Market Watch*, 8 Apr. 2013. <http://blogs.marketwatch.com/health-exchange/2013/04/08/top-11-drug-firms-made-711-billion-in-last-decade-report-points-out>

4. Chen, Pauline W., MD. "Teaching Doctors about Nutrition and Diet." *The New York Times*, 16 Sept. 2010. <http://www. nytimes.com/2010/09/16/health/16chen.html>

5. Adams, Kellt M., MPH, RD; Martin Kohlmeier, MD; and Steven H. Zeisel, MD, PhD. "Nutrition Education in U.S. Medical Schools: Latest Update of a National Survey." *Academic Medicine* 85:9 (2010): 1537 – 1542. <http://journals.lww.com/ academicmedicine/Abstract/2010/09000/Nutrition_Education_in_U_S__Medical_Schools_.30.aspx>

6. Soyk, Cody, BS; Branden Pfefferkorn, MD, MPH; Patrick McBride, MD, MPH; and Richard Rieselback, MD. "Medical Student Exposure to and Attitudes about Pharmaceutical Companies." *Wisconsin Medical Journal* 109:3 (2010). <http://www.wisconsinmedicalsociety.org/_WMS/publications/wmj/pdf/109/3/142.pdf>

7. Gagnon, M.A. and J. Lexchin. "The Cost of Pushing Pills: A New Estimate of Pharmaceutical Promotion Expenditures in the United States." *PLOS Medicine* 5:1 (2008). < http://www.plosmedicine.org/article/info%3Adoi%2F10.1371%2Fjournal.pmed.0050001>

8. Greger, Michael, MD. "Dietary Guidelines: Advisory Committee Conflicts of Interest." NutritionFacts.org, 3 Nov. 2011. <http://nutritionfacts.org/video/dietary-guidelines-advisory-committee-conflicts-of-interest>

9. "PCRM Sues USDA Over Deceptive Dietary Guidelines." Physicians Committee for Responsible Medicine, accessed 30 Dec. 2013. <http://pcrm.org/good-medicine/2011/springsummer/pcrm-sues-usda-over-deceptive-dietary-guidelines>

10. Parker-Pope, Tara. "How the Food Makers Captured Our Brains." *The New York Times,* 22 June 2009. <http://nytimes.com/2009/06/23/health/23well.html?>

The YU Approach

1. Donaldson James, Susan. "Orange Juice's 'Secret' Flavor Packet Surprises Some Moms." ABC News, 16 Dec. 2011. <http://abcnews.go.com/Health/orange-juice-moms-secret-ingredient-worries/story?id=15154617#.TutfSiNWp8t>

2. Watzl, Bernhard. "Anti-Inflammatory Effects of Plant-Based Foods and of Their Constituents." *International Journal for Vitamin and Nutrition Research* 78: 6 (2008): 293 – 298. < http://www.ncbi.nlm.nih.gov/pubmed/19685439>

3. Carr, Kris. "A Little pH Refresher Course." KrisCarr.com, 29 Apr. 2009. <http://kriscarr.com/blog/a-little-ph-refresher-course>

What YU Need

1. "The Protein Myth." Physicians Committee for Responsible Medicine, accessed 30 Dec. 2013. <http://pcrm.org/health/diets/vegdiets/how-can-i-get-enough-protein-the-protein-myth>

2. "Calcium: Fact Sheet for Consumers." National Institutes of Health: Office of Dietary Supplements, accessed 30 Dec. 2013. <http://ods.od.nih.gov/factsheets/Calcium-QuickFacts/>

3. Ross, Catharine A., Christine L. Taylor, Ann L. Yaktine, and Heather B. De Valle. "Dietary Reference Intakes for Adequacy: Calcium and Vitamin D." In *Dietary Reference Intakes for Calcium and Vitamin D by the Committee to Review Dietary Reference Intakes for Vitamin D and Calcium.* Washington, DC: The National Academies Press, 2011. <http://www.ncbi.nlm.nih.gov/books/NBK56056>

4. Abelow, B.J., T.R. Holford, and K.L. Insogna. "Cross-Cultural Association between Dietary Animal Protein and Hip Fracture: A Hypothesis." *Calcified Tissue International* 50:1 (1992): 14 – 18. <http://www.ncbi.nlm.nih.gov/pubmed/1739864>

5. USDA National Nutrient Database for Standard Reference, accessed 30 Dec. 2013. <http://ndb.nal.usda.gov/>

6. Hazum, E., J.J. Sabatka, K.H. Chang, D.A. Brent, J.W. Findlay, and P. Cuatrecasas. "Morphine in Cow and Human Milk: Could Dietary Morphine Constitute a Ligand for Specific Morphine (mu) Receptors?" *Science,* 28 Aug. 1981. <http://www.ncbi.nlm.nih.gov/pubmed/6267691>

7. Kurek, M., B. Przybilla, K. Hermann, and J. Ring. "A Naturally Occurring Opioid Peptide from Cow's Milk, Beta-Casomorphine-7, Is a Direct Histamine Releaser in Man." *International Archives of Allergy and Immunology* 97:2 (1992): 115 – 120. <http://www.ncbi.nlm.nih.gov/pubmed/1374738>

8. Hever, Julieanna. *The Complete Idiot's Guide to Plant-Based Nutrition.* New York: Penguin, 2011, 28.

9. Hever, Julieanna. *The Complete Idiot's Guide to Plant-Based Nutrition.* New York: Penguin, 2011, 10 – 11.

10. Ibid.

11. Ibid.

12. Ibid., 19 – 24.

13. Ibid.

14. Simopoulos, A.P. "The Importance of the Ratio of Omega-6/Omega-3 Essential Fatty Acids." *Biomedicine & Pharmacotherapy* 56:8 (2002): 365 – 379. <http://www.ncbi.nlm.nih.gov/pubmed/12442909>

15. St-Onge, M.P., Bosarge A., Goree, L.L., Darnell B. "Medium Chain Triglyceride Oil Consumption as Part of Weight Loss Diet Does Not Lead to an Adverse Metabolic Profile When Compared to Olive Oil." *Journal of the American College of Nutrition* (2008): 547-52 <http://www.ncbi.nlm.nih.gov/pubmed/18845704>

16. NYU Langone Medical Center "Medium Chain Triglycerides." Accessed April 20, 2014. <http://www.med.nyu.edu/content?ChunkIID=21809>

17. Reiser, R., J.L. Probstfield, A. Silvers, L.W. Scott, M.L. Shorney, R.D. Wood, B.C. O'Brien, A.M. Gotto Jr., and W. Insull Jr. "Plasma Lipid and Lipoprotein Response of Humans to Beef Fat, Coconut Oil and Safflower Oil." *American Journal of Clinical Nutrition* 42:2 (1985): 190 – 197. <http://www.ncbi.nlm.nih.gov/pubmed/4025191>

18. Müller, H., A.S. Lindman, A.L. Brantsaeter, and J.I. Pedersen. "The Serum LDL/HDL Cholesterol Ratio Is Influenced More Favorably by Exchanging Saturated with Unsaturated Fat Than by Reducing Saturated Fat in the Diet of Women." *Journal of Nutrition* 133:1 (2003): 78 – 83. <http://www.ncbi.nlm.nih.gov/pubmed/12514271>

19. Nevin, K.G. and T. Rajamohan. "Beneficial Effects of Virgin Coconut Oil on Lipid Parameters and in Vitro LDL Oxidation." *Clinical Biochemistry* 37:9 (2004): 830 – 835. <http://www.ncbi.nlm.nih.gov/pubmed/15329324>

20. "Mental Stress May Be Another Culprit in Raising Cholesterol Levels in Healthy Adults, According to Study." American Psychological Association, 22 Nov. 2005. <http://apa.org/news/press/releases/2005/11/marital-stress.aspx>

21. Irwin, M., J. McClintick, C. Costlow, M. Fortner, J. White, and JC Gillin. "Partial Night Sleep Deprivation Reduces Natural Killer and Cellular Immune Responses in Humans." *FASEB Journal* 10:5 (1996): 643 – 653. <http://www.ncbi.nlm.nih.gov/pubmed/8621064>

22. Schwartz, J., M.A. Allison, S. Ancoli-Israel, M.F. Hovell, R.E. Patterson, L. Natarajan, S.J. Marshall, and I. Grant. "Sleep, Type 2 Diabetes, Dyslipidemia, and Hypertension in Elderly Alzheimer's Caregivers." *Archives of Gerontology and Geriatrics* 57:1 (2013): 70 – 77. <http://www.ncbi.nlm.nih.gov/pubmed/23522093>

23. AlDabal, Laila and Ahmed S. BaHammam. "Metabolic, Endocrine, and Immune Consequences of Sleep Deprivation." *The Open Respiratory Medical Journal* 5 (2011): 31 – 43. <http://www.ncbi.nlm.nih.gov/pubmed/21754974>

24. "Chronic Stress Puts Your Health at Risk." Mayo Clinic, accessed 30 Dec. 2013. <http://www.mayoclinic.com/health/stress/SR00001>

25. Reiter, R.J. "The Pineal Gland and Melatonin in Relation to Aging: A Summary of the Theories and of the Data." *Experimental Gerontology* 30:3 – 4 (1995): 199 – 212. <http://www.ncbi.nlm.nih.gov/pubmed/7556503>

26. Watanabe, Fumio. "Vitamin B$_{12}$ Sources and Bioavailability." *Experimental Biology and Medicine* 232:10 (2007): 1266 – 1274. <http://ama-marketing.at/home/groups/24/Vitamin_B12_Verfuegbarkeit.pdf>

27. Ibid.

28. Herbert, Victor MD, JD. "Vitamin B-12: Plant Sources, requirements, and Assay." *American Journal of Clinical Nutrition* 48:3 (1988): 852 – 858. <http://ajcn.nutrition.org/content/48/3/852.full.pdf+html>

29. Ibid.

30. Centers for Disease Control and Prevention. "Organic Solvents." NIOSH: Workplace Safety and Health Topics, accessed 30 Dec. 2013. <http://www.cdc.gov/niosh/topics/organsolv>

31. United States Environmental Protection Agency. "About Air Toxics." Technology Transfer Network: Air Toxics, accessed 30 Dec. 2013. <http://epa.gov/ttn/atw/allabout.html>

32. United States Environmental Protection Agency. "hexane Summary." Technology Transfer Network: Air Toxics, accessed 30 Dec. 2013. <http://epa.gov/ttn/atw/hlthef/hexane.html>

33. Martinez, J. and J.E. Lewi. "An Unusual Case of Gynescomastia Associated with Soy Product Consumption." *Endocrine Practice* 14:4 (2008): 415 – 418. <http://www.ncbi.nlm.nih.gov/pubmed/18558591>

34. Nebesio, T.D. and O.H. Pescovitz. *When Puberty Is Precocious: Scientific and Clinical Aspects.* New Jersey: Humana Press, 2007, 425 – 442.

35. Roy, J.R., S. Chakraborty, and T.R. Chakraborty. "Estrogen-Like Endocrine Disrupting Chemicals Affecting Puberty in Humans — A Review." *Medical Science Monitor* 15:6 (2009): 137 – 145. <http://www.ncbi.nlm.nih.gov/pubmed/19478717>

36. Massart, F., R. Parrino, P. Seppia, G. Federico, and G. Saggese. "How Do Environmental Estrogen Disruptors Induce Precocious Puberty?" *Minerva Pediatrica* 58:3 (2006): 247 – 254. <http://www.ncbi.nlm.nih.gov/pubmed/16832329>

Plant-Powering Your Kitchen

1. "Teflon Toxicosis: EWG Finds Heated Teflon Pans Can Turn Toxic Faster Than DuPont Claims." Environmental Working Group, 15 May 2003. <http://www.ewg.org/research/canaries-kitchen>

2. Rodale, Maria. "How Safe Is Your Cookware?" *The Huffington Post: Healthy Living,* 17 Apr. 2012. <http://www.huffingtonpost.com/maria-rodale/how-safe-is-your-cookware_b_1430891.html>

3. "Teflon Toxicosis: EWG Finds Heated Teflon Pans Can Turn Toxic Faster Than DuPont Claims." Environmental Working Group, 15 May 2003. <http://www.ewg.org/research/canaries-kitchen>

4. "Healthy Home Tips: Tip 6 — Skip the Non-Stick to Avoid the Dangers of Teflon." Environmental Working Group, accessed 30 Dec. 2013. <http://www.ewg.org/research/healthy-home-tips/tip-6-skip-non-stick-avoid-dangers-teflon>

5. "Teflon Toxicosis: EWG Finds Heated Teflon Pans Can Turn Toxic Faster Than DuPont Claims." Environmental Working Group, 15 May 2003. <http://www.ewg.org/research/canaries-kitchen>

6. Kumar, V. and K.D. Gill. "Aluminum Neurotoxicity: Neurobehavioural and Oxidative Aspects." *Archives of Toxicology* 83:11 (2009): 965 – 978. <http://www.ncbi.nlm.nih.gov/pubmed/19568732>

7. Jansson, E.T. "Aluminum Exposure and Alzheimer's Disease." *Journal of Alzheimer's Disease* 3:6 (2001): 541 – 549. <http://www.ncbi.nlm.nih.gov/pubmed/12214020>

Shopping & Storage

1. Wagner, M. and J. Oehlmann. "Endocrine Disruptors in Bottled Mineral Water: Total Estrogenic Burden and Migration from Plastic Bottles." *Environmental Science and Polllution Research International* 16:3 (2009): 278 – 86. <http://www.ncbi.nlm.nih.gov/pubmed/19274472>

2. Yang, Chun Z., Stuart I. Yaniger, Craig V. Jordan, Daniel J. Klein, and George D. Bittner. "Most Plastic Products Release Estrogenic Chemicals: A Potential Health Problem That Can Be Solved." *Environmental Health Perspectives* 119:7 (2011): 989 – 996. <http://www.ncbi.nlm.nih.gov/pmc/articles/PMC3222987>

3. Lee, W.J., K. Teschke, T. Kauppinen, A. Andersen, P. Jäppinen, I. Szadkowska-Stanczyk, N. Pearce, B. Persson, A. Bergeret, L.A. Facchini, R. Kishi, D. Kielkowski, B.A. Rix, P. Henneberger, J. Sunyer, D. Colin, M. Kogevinas, and P. Boffetta. "Mortality from Lung Cancer in Workers Exposed to Sulfur Dioxide in the Pulp and Paper Industry." *Environmental Health Perspectives* 110:10 (2002): 991 – 995. <http://researchonline.lshtm.ac.uk/1459/>

Prep, Cooking & Baking

1. Nagel, Ramiel. "Living with Phytic Acid." The Weston A. Price Foundation, 26 Mar. 2010. <http://www.westonaprice.org/food-features/living-with-phytic-acid>

2. Rodhouse, J.C., C.A. Haugh, D. Roberts, and R.J. Gilbert. "Red Kidney Bean Poisoning in the UK: An Analysis of 50 Suspected Incidents Between 1976 and 1989." *Epidemiology and Infection* 105:3 (1990): 485 – 491. <http://www.ncbi.nlm.nih.gov/pmc/articles/PMC2271815>

Heather Crosby is a T. Colin Campbell Foundation-certified wellness coach who has developed an inspired and well-loved collection of over 500 gluten-free, plant-powerful recipes on her popular website YumUniverse.com. In an effort to kick medication and heal naturally from disease, she's been living a plant-inspired lifestyle for almost a decade and sharing what she's learned with thousands of folks all over the world — *because she knows a journey is always better shared with pals.*

Index

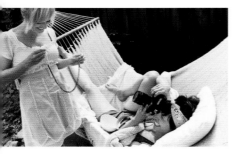

Recipe Index

Inspired by the healthy, delicious recipes in YumUniverse?

Download a **FREE** digital copy of *BenBella's Best of Plant-Based Eating* and sign up for more exclusive offers and info at

BENBELLAVEGAN.COM

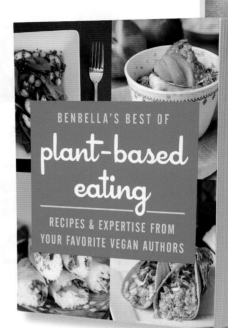

CHERRY QUINOA SALAD

TRICOLORED VEGETABLE PASTA WITH SUN-DRIED MARINARA AND CASHEW CHEESE

CAULIFLOWER HOT WINGS

BUDDHA LENTIL BURGER

BLUEBERRY BUNDT CAKE

MEDITERRANEAN CHARD

WITH NEARLY 50 RECIPES FROM

The China Study Cookbook | *The Happy Herbivore series*
Better Than Vegan | *Blissful Bites*
The Best Green Smoothies on the Planet
The HappyCow Cookbook | *Jazzy Vegetarian Classics*
The PlantPure Nation Cookbook | *YumUniverse*

AND SELECTIONS FROM

Whole | *The Low-Carb Fraud*
Food Over Medicine | *Healthy Eating, Healthy World*

GET COOKING. HAVE FUN. SHARE.